Irregular Mi

Irregular Migration

The Dilemmas of Transnational Mobility

Bill Jordan

Professor of Social Policy, University of Exeter, Professor of Social Policy, University of Huddersfield and Reader in Social Policy, University of North London, UK

Franck Düvell

Research Fellow, University of Exeter, UK and Lecturer, University of Bremen, Germany

Edward Elgar
Cheltenham, UK • Northampton, MA, USA

Published by
Edward Elgar Publishing Limited
Glensanda House
Montpellier Parade
Cheltenham
Glos GL50 1UA
UK

Edward Elgar Publishing, Inc.
136 West Street
Suite 202
Northampton
Massachusetts 01060
USA

A catalogue record for this book
is available from the British Library

Library of Congress Cataloguing in Publication Data
Jordan, Bill, 1941–
    Irregular migration : the dilemmas of transnational mobility / Bill Jordan,
Franck Düvell.
        p. cm.
    Includes index.
        1. Emigration and immigration. 2. Great Britain–Emigration and immigration.
    3. Europe–Emigration and immigration. 4. Illegal aliens. I. Düvell, Franck,
    1961– II. Title.

JV6035 .J67 2003
325–dc21
                                                                          2002072151
ISBN 1 84376 027 4

Typeset by Manton Typesetters, Louth, Lincolnshire, UK.
Printed and bound in Great Britain by MPG Books Ltd, Bodmin, Cornwall.

Contents

Tables

Acknowledgements

We would like to thank the ESRC (Grant Number R000236838) for funding the main research project reported in this book and the Nuffield Foundation for its support for the study of Brazilian migrants on which we additionally drew. We also acknowledge with thanks the funding provided by the European Commission for our part in the comparative project on immigration control practices and migrant strategies in the UK, Germany, Italy and Greece.

We are very grateful to the representatives of all the refugee and immigrant support groups, and the staff of public services, who gave us interviews about their work. We thank the then Immigration Service Enforcement Directorate for giving us access to, and interviews about, its operations, and the managers and staff of Work Permits (UK) for their time and trouble, not only in taking part in our research on their organisation, but also for helping us recruit work permit holders to be interviewed.

The research could not have been carried out without the skill and commitment of our interviewers, Kylza Estrella, Emilia Breza, Thomas Stapke and Akgül Baylav, who traced and enlisted the interviewees from Brazil, Poland and Turkey. We very much appreciate their contribution to the work.

We are also very grateful to the interviewees for their participation, trust and openness. Their accounts form the main body of the book.

During the fieldwork, we had encouragement, support and helpful criticism from a wide range of colleagues, social workers and community activists. Among the many we would like to thank are Norman Ginsburg, Philip Pinto, Liz Fekete, Pierre Makhlouf, David Hudson and Tekin Kartal.

We have also benefited from the assistance and critical comments of many colleagues in several countries during the writing of the book. These include Bridget Anderson, Alice Bloch, Michael Breuer, Mita Castle-Kanerova, Norbert Cyrus, Iordanis Psimmenos, Anna Triandafyllidou and Dita Vogel. They share no responsibility for the final product, or the views expressed about this controversial topic.

Finally, we are very grateful to Gill Watson and Di Cooper for all their excellent work on preparing and revising the text, in the long process of its production.

Introduction: theoretical framework and plan of the book

This book is about a group of topics – irregular migration, migration control and the effects of migration – that has gained great prominence among the policy concerns in First World countries. But it is also one over which much confusion prevails. Concepts such as 'illegal immigrant', 'economic migration', 'bogus asylum seeker' and even 'global terrorist' have entered debates, often without clear definition, research evidence or careful analysis. Nowhere is this more obviously the case than in the UK, where a series of 'moral panics' about asylum seeking peaked in the early days of September 2001, with media stories about people from Afghanistan, Iraq and Somalia 'storming the Channel Tunnel'. When these, in turn, were driven off the front pages by the attacks on the World Trade Centre and the Pentagon in the USA, the Home Secretary immediately announced a plan to improve internal security through identity cards, and an overhaul of the asylum system.

The events of 11 September 2001 prompted a reappraisal of an emerging consensus in Europe around migration control. Institutions that had evolved in response to the worldwide rise in asylum seeking in the 1990s were being reconciled with the need for new recruitment, in response to skills shortages, bottlenecks in the supply of unskilled labour, and demographic imbalances. The crisis over terrorism and security added a dimension to the task of designing a multipurpose system.

So there are certain fundamental tensions at the heart of all attempts to manage the movement of population in today's world. Business is transnational, and so increasingly are the lives of those who strike its deals, transact its processes, market its products and research its outcomes. But politics is still national, despite the emergence of supranational institutions and international organisations of many kinds. Hence, international business demands unimpeded movement of people across borders, but nation states, which give priority to the security and protection of their citizens, and to competition with other states, need border controls. Taking account of wars, internal conflict, persecution of minorities and now global terrorism, the dilemmas are self-evident.

This book aims to provide a theoretical framework for the analysis of transnational migration, and the policy issues at stake for the UK and other

European Union (EU) member states. It draws on our research, conducted between 1996 and 2001, on people working in the UK without proper immigration status, on the organisations that support refugees and immigrants, and on immigration control agencies and the public services. It also draws on parallel studies of immigrant workers and control agencies in Germany and other EU countries. Since the mid-1980s (Ardill and Cross, 1987) ours has been, as far as we are aware, the first study to be carried out in the UK on this group of related topics.

Both economic migration and asylum seeking have been important parts of a long history of population movements into, through and out of Europe. By no means have all of these involved migrations by poor people, or from poorer countries to richer ones. At many times, those who moved were skilled workers, responding to demand for their services in expanding cities or regions (Sassen, 1996, pp. 23–5). During forced migrations, as a result of wars or persecution, it was usually better-educated and better-off people who managed to move. The mass migration of refugees after the Second World War made a significant contribution to Europe's postwar growth (Kindleberger, 1967). The relationship between economic migration and asylum seeking has changed over time, but both have been perceived as positive for receiving countries in certain periods.

Accelerated movement of people between countries is intrinsic to a period of world economic development in which transnational exchanges of all kinds are growing more rapidly than production itself (Grimwade, 1989, ch. 2); indeed this is what is meant by 'globalisation' (Held and McGrew, 1994). Most of such movements take place within the immigration categories of tourism, study or business visits, and the policies of European governments promote and facilitate them. Neither these, nor longer-term transfers of staff between branches of transnational companies or international organisations, are seen by governments as problematic. Indeed they are perceived as responses to a reduction in the barriers to transnational exchanges, from which all benefit.

THE SIGNIFICANCE OF MOBILITY

The model of the world economy that underpins all these developments asserts that openness increases efficiency, promotes growth and allows poorer regions to catch up with richer ones. It is based on a simplified version of economic life, focused on production and exchange, in which movements of people, like movements of capital, overcome local surpluses and scarcities in the supply of productive resources. 'In a world with no national borders and no limits to the internationally free movement of labour, migration is welfare improving for the world as a whole' (Straubhaar, 2000, p. 17).

Since this is the model that has driven most of the changes in the world's economic institutions in the past 20 years, we might expect the barriers to migration, like those to trade and capital movements, to be coming down, leading to a new international regime of free mobility for all people. In fact, there has been a growth in border crossings, but there has also been – especially in Europe – a tightening of the rules restricting residence of people from outside one country (or group of countries, such as the EU). By definition, this means that there has been an increase in irregular migration. More mobility plus more restrictions equals more breaches of migration law.

The reasons why states limit migration can be traced to factors not taken into account by the simplified model of the world economy. In the real world, some people own capital and others do not, some have many skills and others few. In addition, there are collective goods, shared between populations of a locality or a state. Gains from mobility are not equally spread between individuals and groups – there are losers as well as winners. Just as individuals choose to move only when it is to their advantage, so states try to reserve the benefits of mobility for their citizens, and to avoid the costs. In a globalised economic environment, inequalities have increased, because some individuals have been able to make enormous gains from greater mobility, and some states have followed successful strategies over attracting productive resources and skills, and protecting public infrastructures.

Migration rules reflect political struggles, both between those individuals and groups who have gained advantages from greater mobility and those who have lost out, and between states over how to maximise gains and minimise losses for their citizens. People who break migration rules must therefore be seen as acting, both individually and collectively, to deal with the consequences of these struggles on their lives.

These responses form part of a wider social phenomenon, now closely studied by geographers, sociologists and anthropologists, and referred to as 'transnationalism', 'transnational communities' and 'globalisation from below' (Portes, 1998; Smith and Guarnizo, 1998). This research acknowledges that the present unrestrained form of capitalism – 'turbo-capitalism' (Luttwak, 1999) – erodes all social formations, but draws attention to the new economic activities and social networks that now straddle political boundaries. These follow the logic of capitalism itself, but allow their participants alternative ways to adapt to its destructive consequences. 'Transnationalism' is a concept that embraces an enormous diversity of relationships (Vertovec and Cohen, 1999; Vertovec, 2001) and 'social spaces' (Faist, 1999), including entrepreneurial initiatives, informal exchanges and resistance movements. Common themes are sustained ties across borders, and adaptation to global economic conditions.

Our aim in this book is to relate this rich and detailed literature – to which our study of irregular migrants in London in Parts II and III makes a contribution – to economic theory of mobility and to policy studies and political theory on migration. Irregular migration is a part of the emergence of transnational communities, but transnationalism itself must be understood within a broader analysis of how individuals and groups respond to globalisation (Kennedy and Roudometof, 2001) – moving between communities, forming and joining associations, clubs and networks. More generally, it raises the question of whether such movements across jurisdictions and among groups represents an alternative to collective action and political participation within them. In particular, when millions of individuals from countries that are poor and oppressive arrive in countries that are relatively rich and free, does this constitute a kind of claim for justice? And what does it tell us about the relative payoffs for democratic activity and for 'voting with the feet' under the new world order that has prevailed since the end of the Cold War in 1989?

Asylum seeking is the most visible and politically sensitive aspect of transnationalism. As globalisation proceeds, opportunities for migration grow. Improved transport, communication links and commercial exchanges provide the pathways for movements of people. Most migrants travel in disguise, as the very business people, tourists and students who make capitalism's routine journeys. Saskia Sassen pointed out that migration flows follow the reverse path of foreign direct investment; migration to the USA in the 1970s and 1980s was from exactly those countries in which the USA invested most, in both export-processing zones and export-orientated agriculture (Sassen, 1988). Irregular migration uses the covert 'weapons of the weak' (Scott, 1985) to evade states' barriers against those who (because of the colour of the skin or the poverty of their countries of origin) have not been selected for recruitment. 'In a world of winners and losers, the losers do not simply disappear, they seek somewhere else to go' (Stalker, 2000, p. 2).

MOBILITY AND MEMBERSHIP

Our analysis starts from the idea that *mobility* is fundamental to the microeconomics of production and exchange on which the world's economic system is based, but this is in tension with ideas of *membership* on which the economics of welfare and distributive justice is founded. This tension was disguised in the postwar period, when the notions that societies corresponded to economic systems, and that members were linked together in reciprocal relationships within such systems, could be credibly sustained. In an integrated world economy, the nation state is notoriously less able to implement redistributive policies for the sake of justice, because of the threat that citizens will move their savings out of the country, and firms will choose not to invest in it. Politicians who favour markets, and those who espouse 'Third Way' versions of social democracy, are keen to remind their electorates of these constraints, in order to discourage them from making claims through collective action.

If free trade and unrestricted mobility are potentially welfare-enhancing for the world as a whole, it should, in principle, be possible to establish global regimes to distribute these benefits fairly. These might be seen as the counterparts to the institutions under which trade and capital movements have been liberalised now – the World Trade Organisation (WTO) – and to the agreements struck, such as the recent General Agreement on Trade in Services (GATS). The main objectives would be to set up systems through which the 'externalities' from increased mobility (positive or negative effects of actions on other people, for which the actors themselves do not have to pay) were adjusted, losers were compensated, and – above all – polarisation of welfare, through cumulative gains or losses of advantage, was prevented (Straubhaar, 2000).

In the real world, however, no such international institutions yet exist, and the tendency is for greater mobility to undermine national systems of solidarity among citizens, making groups such as unskilled workers more vulnerable to competition from their counterparts in lower-wage economies, through the penetration of cheaper imports from abroad. So there are strong incentives for states to try to capture the gains from mobility, by attracting not only international capital to complement their labour forces, but also mobile, high-skilled migrant workers, who can boost the productivity of their most advanced sectors. This can lead to a 'brain drain' from developing countries (Bhagwati and Wilson, 1989), which would far rather promote the migration of their surpluses of less-skilled workers. Hence, instead of promoting greater equality within the world economy, the policies of states can produce polarisation and a cycle of disadvantage for the weaker economies.

Furthermore, this polarisation process operates also within states, through competition between local authorities and regions. From the perspective of individuals and households, each jurisdiction represents a system of membership, in which the price of collective infrastructural goods (everything from local leisure amenities to public transport systems, schools and hospitals) is signalled by the cost of housing plus the local rate of taxation. Mobile individuals go in search of the most attractive bundle of collective goods they can afford, treating these local authorities as 'clubs' (Buchanan, 1965). Within these, members seek to share most advantageously with chosen others, and to distance themselves from fellow citizens with whom it would be more costly to share, because of their needs and disadvantages.

Public choice theorists have argued that this allows mobility to provide the counterpart to consumer sovereignty in markets for the public sector of economic life. The democratic justification is that such choices stem from the preferences of individuals, voting with their feet by moving to those local authorities whose tax rates and mix of services fit their particular incomes and tastes. The attraction of this approach for national governments is that it is claimed to 'tame the Leviathan' of government spending and official controls (Oates, 1972, 1985), by creating active, informed citizens, who take responsibility for their own welfare, rather than looking to the state for protection

However, this approach has contributed to and reinforced the tendency of First World societies, and especially the USA and UK, to polarise into districts containing residents of similar incomes and tastes (it is largely intended to do so), and in particular to create least-favoured neighbourhoods with concentrations of poor residents and social problems. Such citizens have access to more-favoured districts only for menial employment (as cleaners, cooks, refuse collectors, odd-jobbers, servants or carers), or for opportunistic informal activity and crime. In a parallel way, those who leave the poorer states in the world system, and who follow the pathways of globalisation, come to the First World as the invisible service sector staff of global cities (Sassen, 1991). Despite their often superior education and employment experience, they arrive to fill these roles as tourists or students, by clandestine channels or, in the last resort, as asylum seekers and refugees. The polarisation of First World societies, and the marginalisation of many minority ethnic residents, facilitates those processes, allowing irregular migrants who perform useful service roles a discreet anonymity in their host societies.

Hence, the concepts of 'irregular migration' and 'economic migrants' need to be defined and elaborated within a model of mobility in an integrated world economy; but citizenship as exclusive membership needs, in turn, to be analysed as containing elements of mobility within and between states. Systems for the management of migration are increasingly concerned with facilitating those forms of economic migration (intra-firm transfers and foreign recruitment, as well as business-related visits) that are required for the smooth functioning of global production and exchange, but blocking those not specifically required.

The dimension added by global terrorism cuts across this distinction. As far as can be ascertained, the people who hijacked the commercial airlines and flew them into the twin towers and the Pentagon were *legal* immigrants to the USA. Their occupations, as technicians and computer experts, or students of these subjects, made them typical of the recruits that are being sought by US and European firms. Several had spent time in Germany as students. Instead of being part of the underground of clandestine migration, or the closely supervised processes of humanitarian protection, they followed the legitimate channels of the global economy, and used its everyday instruments against it.

ECONOMIC MIGRATION

Irregular migration is generally assumed to have economic motivation; it is seen as a response to some combination of incentives through higher potential earnings and access to collective benefits and services. But economic migration is only irregular when it is in violation of border controls, and border controls have political as well as economic justifications. Hence, the analysis of irregular migration is inseparable from the evaluation of fairly complex economic and political arguments for various kinds of controls and restrictions on the transnational movement of people.

Our adoption of an economic approach as our primary framework for the book is in line with the recent shift, both in theoretical debates and in government policy deliberations in Europe, towards a more positive assessment of economic migration. As shown in Chapter 2, the highly restrictive approach to border control policies in the EU and its member states in the 1990s is giving way to cautious relaxation, especially in relation to certain kinds of labour-market recruitment. In the UK, where economic migration was officially associated with 'bogus' asylum seeking as late as 1998, government ministers have been speaking of the benefits of economic migration (Roche, 2000, 2001).

Both the activity of international capitalist corporations and the adaptations of transnational networks offer economic opportunities and incentives for irregular migrants, arising from the differentials of advantage created by state boundaries. Although stemming from impoverishment and the decay of institutional structures in their countries of origin, individual decisions to migrate are prompted by demand for labour in First World economies, and especially for supplies of adaptable and mobile low-wage labour (Portes and Guarnizo, 1990; Portes, 1996, 1998), in agriculture and domestic service, catering and garment 'sweatshop' work.

Although transnationalism and transnational communities represent responses to these common conditions under globalisation, the actual social relations in these networks, including those between irregular migrants, are extremely varied. Our empirical study of undocumented workers in London, and the reactions of host society organisations to them, reveals how differently migrants from Brazil, Poland and Turkey explained their reasons for coming, interpreted their experiences, and interacted with each other and with UK institutions. It also shows how asylum seeking is embedded in complex ways in the linkages and structures of transnational entrepreneurism, informal economic activity and the shadow labour markets of the host economy.

It may be helpful at this point to summarise the main themes and questions explored in the book, and how they are located within the text.

THEMES OF THE BOOK

1. Mobility of labour is a key element in the achievement of efficient allocations of resources through markets. From the perspective of the global economy (and global efficiency) migration across borders is simply a form of labour mobility. Yet theories of trade suggest that national economies can most efficiently specialise in production, with different ratios of capital and labour. If trade is taken into account, is it possible to reach reliable conclusions about the economic consequences of migration? (Chapters 1, 9 and 10)
2. Political units are territorial, and attempt to develop their land to its most efficient productive capacity, and to optimise distributions between members of their communities. Can the economics of welfare within political units, seeking advantage in competition with other units, be reconciled with global efficiency in production and exchange? (Chapters 1, 3, 8 and 10)
3. The opportunity and the freedom to choose in which community to live and work are key principles, both in the economics of labour markets, and in liberal theories of political justice. They are also important in public choice theory on the efficient allocation of collective goods. Are these principles compatible with national border controls? (Chapters 1, 2, 3, 6 and 10)
4. Migrants have incentives to cross borders without proper status because of global and regional inequalities of income. It is often better-educated and better-qualified people who migrate, yet the work they take is unskilled. Are there ways of channelling economic migration more efficiently? (Chapters 4, 5 and 9)
5. Welfare systems (including systems for humanitarian protection) distort economic incentives for migration in various ways, and allow governments to justify border controls. Welfare provision for asylum seekers cannot be insulated from irregular economic activity. Which institutions can promote labour-market flexibility, yet provide appropriate and effective public services? (Chapters 3, 5 and 8)
6. Irregular migration occurs because border controls restrict entry. Can border controls be justified in any version of global distributive justice? (Chapter 10)

PLAN OF THE BOOK

In Part I of the book, we present our overall framework for the analysis of irregular migration and migration control systems. The key concepts are mobility and membership. We argue that the presence of irregular migrants from the Second and Third Worlds in affluent First World countries exposes an unresolved issue in economic theory and that the economics of production and exchange knows no boundaries or borders, while the economics of welfare is about distributions among finite membership groups. It also reveals the limits of orthodox political theory of justice, which concern roles and resources in a society, conceived as a system of economic co-operation. Globalisation, which intrinsically involves accelerated mobility of people across borders, accentuates the shortcomings of both economic and political theory in these respects.

As we have already suggested, the influence of public choice theory on public policy, in the USA and the UK particularly, both clarifies the problems and highlights these deficiencies. In principle, mainstream public choice theorists can fill this gap in economic and political theory by supplying a self-regulating model of mobility and membership. Just as an invisible hand moves market actors towards optimal allocations for purposes of efficiency, so some similarly benevolent force propels them between jurisdictions, to form membership groups around collective services. The task of deciding how to regulate this process of choice through mobility, and membership based on voting with the feet, becomes a largely technical exercise, much like the task of regulating market exchanges. However, no such comprehensive theory, capable of providing a basis for migration management regimes, is yet available from this source. This is not surprising, given the preoccupations with national identity and 'race' that have dominated immigration laws and regulations of the First World states.

In Chapter 1 we set out these issues in economic theory, and the dilemmas they pose for governments, hitherto concerned mainly with managing ethnic diversity and 'race relations'. In Chapter 2 we introduce the current policy background in the European Union, the way that migration management systems have been evolving and how these relate to labour supply and welfare policies. In Chapter 3 we consider the working of labour markets, and their relation to unemployment, poverty and social exclusion. Throughout Part I of the book irregular migration is analysed as an aspect of mobility, both within and between states, and understood both as a consequence of new attempts to improve economic efficiency, and as a challenge to new versions of social justice.

In Part II we use the UK as a case study of these processes. Drawing on our empirical research, we examine why migrants who have spent time in London as undocumented workers chose to come here in the first place, how they survived and what they planned to do in future. What our research reveals is that the motives for and justifications of irregular migration are diverse, and that they vary between the migrants' countries of origin. We studied people from Brazil, Poland and Turkey, three very different societies without strong historical links to the UK (though there is a postwar refugee community from Poland, and a concentration of immigrants from northern Cyprus and from Turkey in north-east London). What all these migrants had in common was the fact that they were rather well-educated, hardworking and motivated to improve their lives. What almost all of them were doing was working in occupations which were well below those indicated by their education and previous work experience – mainly in textile factories, or in cafés and restaurants, or cleaning houses, or in construction.

What distinguished them was therefore not what they did but the kind of justifications they gave for their irregular activities. The great majority of them had entered the country and stayed legally, and their only immigration offence was to work without proper status. Others had decided to stay and work only when their visas had expired. They challenged the immigration rules, and their implicit grounding in notions of global justice, in three broad ways. The first was to claim a right to visit the UK to study and gain work experience, in order to return to their home countries with improved c.v.s; this would allow them better chances in the labour market. Most of those who made this claim were Brazilians. The second was to argue for rights to work, earn and save, in order to provide essential items (houses, cars, the funds for businesses) on their return. Poles and other Brazilians considered that they should have this right, as participants in a global economy where their chances of doing this at home were almost zero. The third was to claim political freedoms that were absent in their home countries. Nearly all the migrants from Turkey challenged the restrictiveness of systems for granting asylum applications with such claims, and argued that they were only working in breach of the regulations because these were designed to reinforce restrictions, yet at the same time supply cheap labour under exploitative conditions.

In Chapter 4 we set out in detail the migrant interviewees' accounts of why they came to London, in terms of these three justificatory arguments. In Chapter 5 we go on to analyse the consequences of their actions, and the strategies they used for survival in the UK. Here we show that irregular migration in the present context of a deregulated labour market and large shadow economy of very low-paid work has adverse consequences for the migrants themselves, and for the host society. Whichever of the three main justifications for coming they deploy, they risked becoming trapped within the world of shadow employment, and those who wanted to return were usually forced to stay longer than they planned.

In Chapter 6 we turn to the response of organisations that support immigrants and refugees to these issues around irregular migration. Here we show that they have developed strategies and structures which were shaped by two main issues – the discrimination against black and Asian immigrants in the UK's laws and policies, and the restrictiveness of decisions on asylum. Thus, although their practice put them in frequent touch with undocumented migrant workers, issues around work were seldom directly addressed. This meant that many groups of irregular migrants have little representation; indeed, migrants from Poland and Brazil were hardly ever in contact with such organisations, though those from Turkey were (as asylum seekers) far more likely to be represented, and to be members of cultural or political associations in London. But this greater involvement served to integrate them into situations of disadvantage and exclusion, within under-resourced 'communities of fate'.

In Part III of the book we analyse the response of the host society's institutions to the presence of irregular migrants, whose basic strategy was to disguise themselves as members of minority ethnic groups, and to make themselves inconspicuously useful in low-paid shadow-economy roles. What distinguishes the UK from other EU states is the less-regulated, more 'flexible', nature of the labour market, and the ease with which such migrants can get employment and accommodation on arrival. Internal controls, identity checks and systems of registration are all much lower key or absent, in comparison with Continental states. There is also a stronger culture of anti-discriminatory practice in public services, which makes it easier for irregular migrants to assimilate to minority groups.

In Chapter 7 we investigate the operation of those systems for control that act within the country, to enforce the immigration rules. These were based on a small unit in the Home Office's Immigration and Nationality Directorate (IND), the Immigration Service Enforcement Directorate (ISED). We show how the ISED's operations depended on co-operation with the police and the fraud investigation service of the Benefits Agency. However, not only was this co-operation fragile; undocumented work was also a low priority for the service, whose main targets were asylum overstayers. This was in line with long-standing government policies, directed primarily at limiting black and Asian immigration.

Other public services were suspicious of or hostile to the IND, and tried to practise in a way that combated racial discrimination. In Chapter 8 we show how staff in health, education and community services offered explanations of their practice, which precluded co-operation with the enforcement of immigration rules, for these reasons. However, welfare provision for asylum seekers was – even before the Immigration and Asylum Act of 1999 – already minimal and deterrent. Irregular migrants' accounts indicated that they were able to get health service treatment and – in some cases – education for children. But, despite the efforts made by public service staff on their behalf, welfare provision largely served to consolidate their disadvantaged economic role, while probably further weakening the overstretched infrastructures of these poverty-stricken neighbourhoods.

In Chapter 9 we briefly review developments in the recruitment of foreign labour under work permits. This has been expanding, and is promised to develop further, in the other EU states as well as in the UK. From interviews with work permit holders, we show that this process distinguishes their pay and conditions strongly from those of irregular migrants, and raises questions about how these differences can be justified. We consider the possible future modification of rules restricting economic migration, and new measures for absorbing some irregular migrants into the workforce, in the light of the UK's broader long-term strategy in the world economy.

In the final chapter of the book, we return to the theme of global justice, and the challenge to notions based on membership that is posed by migration. The right to choose in which community to live and work is fundamental to liberal democratic versions of distributive justice. Within such polities, other rights to welfare benefits and services, and other systems for economic management, have to be reconciled with this entitlement of individuals. Political communities protect their versions of distributive justice when they fear the destabilising influence of unrestricted entry. But the present threat lies chiefly in a globalised economic environment in which the 'exit option' has become a principal means by which individuals seek to improve their welfare. We argue that the pursuit of a better balance between exit, voice and loyalty (Hirschman, 1970) in political communities worldwide is more consistent with principles of justice than border controls.

This has already been an issue in the EU, as it has taken in new and poorer members from the periphery; and it is again an issue with the enlargement to include the former communist states of Central and Eastern Europe. Free movement within the EU has had to be balanced by measures that give populations good reasons to remain in their countries of origin, because their security and welfare is adequately protected. It is this approach that is likely to provide viable long-term solutions to issues of irregular migration.

PART I

Mobility and its Regulation

1. Irregular migration and mobility in economic theory

Irregular migration – crossing borders without proper authority, or violating conditions for entering another country – has been seen as a threat to the living standards and the cultures of the citizens of rich, predominantly white, First World states. In the 1990s the rise in claims for political asylum by black and Asian migrants to such countries was defined as disguised irregular migration. Public opinion polls conducted in EU member states in 2001 gave 'race relations and immigration' as the fourth most important problem facing both the UK and the other states, well ahead of education, health and poverty (*The Guardian*, 22nd June 2001).

This survey played into the stereotype of immigrants as black- or brown-skinned people, challenging both national identity and prosperity. But at about the same time, the long policy debate in Europe about how to handle issues of ethnic diversity was overtaken by a more urgent debate about the potential advantages of labour-market recruitment from outside the EU. Both fears of 'swamping' among indigenous populations, and the aspirations for civic and political equality among immigrants, were set aside, in favour of economic arguments about the flexibility this would give the labour supplies of the receiving countries, and the skills' shortages it would remedy.

In line with this shift, this book analyses irregular migration primarily in an economic framework, arguing that it is closely linked to globalisation, and very often uses the pathways of the world economy as the means for crossing borders. However, the main point of adopting this method of analysis is to clarify the weaknesses in political ideas about migration, and the contradictions in the new policies that are being adopted to manage it. Nationalism (policies based on the idea that the interests of the citizens of one state usually conflict with those of citizens of others) and 'race' (the idea of a group identity based on ethnicity or skin colour, often giving rise to definitions of nationality or citizenship) still strongly influence immigration policies. Hence economic principles are seldom consistently applied, and such migration as is allowed or encouraged often exposes problems in the versions of both membership and justice that are prevalent in the receiving countries.

The resurgence of economic arguments in favour of immigration is linked to recognition of the limits to the potential mobility of indigenous populations.

Recent policies focusing on the supply-side causes of unemployment, and aimed to 'activate' citizens claiming unemployment-related benefits, are already approaching these limits. Hence even irregular migrants working in the shadow economies of First World countries are now seen as potentially useful recruits. After all, they have already demonstrated their mobility by entering the country, their flexibility by accepting often appallingly low wages and their adaptability by surviving and sustaining themselves (almost always without recourse to benefits). They also often have skills and potentials that are being underused in their undocumented work.

However governments (and supranational bodies like the EU) still face the task of developing viable systems for migration management that allow 'useful' workers to come and go, and some to settle, while dealing consistently with irregular entrants. Economic arguments alone cannot provide the tools for this task, since it raises important questions about membership, and access to rights of all kinds in the host society. It also requires fair treatment of a number of other migration issues, such as asylum seeking, which are not directly linked to economic considerations. Already in a globalised economic environment, the concept of citizenship has gained some transnational features, and the notion of 'portable' rights has emerged in connection with the crossing of borders (Baubock, 1994). But there are reasons to doubt whether it can be stretched far enough to encompass all these new requirements.

Our analysis does not follow the approaches that are familiar from other studies of migration. It does not deal primarily in issues of race and citizenship, or of population movements from Third World, peasant societies to wealthy, urbanised ones. Although it seeks to clarify the concept of 'forced migration', it does not attempt to do justice to the range of persecutions and oppressions from which millions flee as refugees. This is not in any way meant to reject or belittle such analyses. It is that the whole concept of 'irregular migration' demands a rather different focus, collecting together all these issues, and several others ('demographic balances' on the one hand, 'terrorism and security' on the other). Our approach seeks to integrate a rather specialised topic in political science and labour-market economics into a much broader theoretical framework that can investigate the significance of mobility more generally.

In an article entitled 'Refugees from globalism', the distinguished writer about race and migration, A. Sivandandan, has rejected the distinction between political refugees and economic migrants as 'bogus'. Global capital seeks cheap labour, whether by moving production to where it is in plentiful supply, or by drawing temporary workers to the wealthy countries, through legal or irregular channels. International financial regimes (International Monetary Fund (IMF), World Bank) and trade agreements (World Trade Organisation (WTO)) impose a framework on the 'developing' countries that results in 'massive pauperisation, the erosion of educational, social and welfare provisions, the end of training and enterprise'.

> Ironically, it is also globalism, with its demand for free markets and unfettered conditions of trade, which is eroding the distinction all over the world between the economic and the political realm. ... Hence resistance to economic immiseration is inseparable from resistance to political persecution. The economic migrant is also the political refugee (Sivandandan, 2000, pp. 10–11).

Thus baldly stated, the claim is strongly rebutted by those who (like the UK Foreign Secretary) argue that globalisation benefits us all (Straw, 2001). The question remains why movement, especially movement across borders, should seem the most appropriate and effective form of resistance. Why do migrants in general, and irregular migrants in particular, choose this option, when others are still open to them? After all, every country has its history of popular struggle – for national self-determination, citizenship rights, the emancipation of workers, women or minorities, and effective democracy. Why should migration (an 'exit' strategy) replace these 'voice' strategies, and why should national and cultural loyalties be weakened for a significant minority of the populations of poorer countries?

Our argument is that it is only by focusing on mobility itself that we can answer these questions. This is why we investigate its significance in economic theory, in the politics of membership and access, and in attempts to reconcile 'flexibility' with welfare, in the first part of this book. This does not deny the continuing importance of struggles between interest groups within countries, or the continuous emergence of new forms of collective action and identity in the political sphere. Mobility has attained a significance of its own, both as a strategic asset of individuals, and as a target of government policy for gaining competitive advantage and managing internal conflict. In Part II, we use evidence from a study of irregular migrants themselves to demonstrate our thesis.

It is not only at the theoretical and policy level that mobility has become such a key concept. Mobility is one of the defining characteristics of the present-day social world, and a key feature of identities and autobiographical narratives, such as the ones that we analyse in the second part of this book (Marcus, 1992). This is linked to a transformation in which individuals shift away from communal, class or political loyalties and perceive themselves as autonomous moral agents, making choices that steer their lives. One aspect of this is to make decisions as rational economic actors, seeking the best returns on their assets (material resources or skills), a perspective encouraged by neo-liberal governments in the 1980s, and greatly reinforced by the collapse of state socialist regimes at the end of that decade. The idea that individuals should take responsibility for themselves in a competitive economic environment, and that this should include a willingness to move, especially for the sake of work opportunities, is still central to the Third Way principles of the 1990s (Jordan, 1998) that now influence European governments.

In one sense, it is obvious that stronger global market forces will promote exit strategies, since the whole logic of markets is to allow capital and labour to move to their most productive uses. But, as Hirschman (1970) pointed out, there are dangers for democracy and political justice when exit rights come to predominate over voice and loyalty. Instead of balancing the increased free- dom of movement in societies, new systems of public finance encourage citizens to vote with their feet over collective goods, rather than acting together and in solidarity to improve their quality for all. In the longer term, those who are disadvantaged by less chances for mobility within these rules exit from the rules themselves into various informal or illegal activities. Irregular migration uses the greater opportunities for cross-border movement that are afforded by a globalised environment, as a counter to the privileges and advantages enjoyed by those with more resources and assets on the one hand, and those with 'insider advantages' on the other hand.

MOBILITY AND MARKETS

By the end of the twentieth century, a quarter of the world's output of goods and services was traded across borders (World Bank, 1999, p. 229). In 2001 the ingredients of an average British Christmas dinner had travelled 24 000 miles to reach the table. Over 100 million people had been living for more than six months outside their country of citizenship (World Bank, 1995, p. 53), mostly in sub-Saharan Africa, the Middle East and South-east Asia. Movements of capital, labour, technology, raw materials and products were linked through an integrated world economy. It makes no sense to study migration in isolation from mobility more generally.

At a fundamental level, markets are claimed to achieve efficient allocations of all these things because they move; the basic language of economics is one of *shifts* and *movements*. In the simplest economic models, with perfect information, zero transaction costs and an absence of legal barriers, every- thing responds to the laws of supply and demand. In this sense, capital and labour, which move to wherever their marginal product exceeds their mar- ginal cost, are like any other commodities that are traded in a market. More complex models then go on to analyse how other factors – such as transport costs, imperfect competition or market failure – influence these decisions and flows.

In principle, employers simply hire or fire workers until the extra revenue gained by selling the output of the last one employed just covers the cost of that worker's wages. The labour market for these workers' skills is in equilibrium when this wage is equivalent to the ones paid by other firms (or industries), taking account of non-monetary considerations, such as working conditions. When demand for any firm's (or industry's) products declines, wages fall, and workers move to other employment. Conversely, when demand for other products increases, wages in those firms (or industries) rise, and this too leads workers to move elsewhere.

On the capital side, employers are treated as hiring buildings, plant and machinery up to the point where the increase in revenue from the extra output produced just covers the charge for their use. These capital goods are supplied by their owners at a price which covers their depreciation less resale value, and takes account of the real interest rate. How employers choose to combine labour and capital inputs depends on their relative prices (wages and capital charges). For instance, if overall wages rise without a corresponding increase in output, they will introduce more capital-intensive production techniques. But capital will generally flow towards those firms and industries where new technology provides the greatest scope for such substitution.

In the modern era, wages have tended to rise, and the capital intensity of production to increase, but at very different rates in different industries. During the UK's Industrial Revolution, new technology for machine production allowed both the output of manufactured goods and the output per worker (the productivity of labour) to rise. This provided the ideal basis for economic growth, as workers and capital flowed towards cities and factories from rural areas and occupations. By the end of the twentieth century, it was the newly industrialising countries, especially those of South-east Asia, that were achieving this kind of growth. In the UK, the combination of greater capital intensity and increasing employment was characteristic of banking, insurance and business services, and related to new information technology.

This shows that 'uneven development' has always been a feature of the economics of markets. The divisions between town and country, industry and agriculture, have been fundamental to the dynamic of economic development (Lewis, 1954). In models of how such specialisation within particular territories contributes to growth, the mobility of labour between sectors with different intensities of capital, and hence of productivity and wages, has been a central element.

However, theories which include national borders in their analyses of these features of economic life make very different assumptions about mobility, because they treat countries as economies, rather than specialised sectors of the same economy. For instance, in the Heckscher–Ohlin theory of trade, all the factors of production are assumed to be perfectly mobile within their own countries, but immobile between countries. Some countries are relatively well endowed with land, others with labour, and others with capital, and this affects the relative prices of these factors in the different countries. Each should therefore specialise in those methods and products in which it has comparative advantage, and all will benefit from trade between them (under a number of assumptions about transport costs and the absence of other barriers between them).

This theory of trade predicts that countries will trade more with each other the more their factor endowments differ. The alternative model proposed by Linder (1961) suggests that more trade in manufactured goods takes place between countries with similar endowments; because rich states have similarly high per capita incomes, their demand patterns are skewed towards high-quality goods. They often also trade different varieties of the same product ('overlapping demand'). Linder's model can also be adapted to allow for increasing returns to scale, characteristic of trade in manufactured goods (Grimwade, 1989, p. 17).

Migration, like trade, affects the prices of the factors of production in both sending and receiving countries. It alters both factor endowments and demand patterns in both countries. Where both trade and migration occur, the inflow of labour usually makes import-competing goods cheaper to produce in the receiving country, and lowers the demand for imports and their price, improving the terms of trade (Bhagwati and Srinivasan, 1983, pp. 249–60). However, there are circumstances in which it can worsen the terms of trade for the country of immigration. Hence 'the theoretical picture is fairly complex' and the theories available, 'taken together with the current state of empirical knowledge … identify some possible adverse consequences [of migration], but are equally adept at identifying possible favourable consequences' (Sykes, 1995, p. 168).

What we want to show in this section is that dilemmas of mobility arise because of unevenness in the development process, and inequalities between individuals and groups, and not just because of national borders. After all, the classic economic analysis of migration, in terms of 'push' and 'pull' factors, was originally a theory about *internal* mobility, not border crossings. Simply because some cities or regions have gained advantages, or have come to have specialised economic roles in the historical development process, they tend to attract both capital and labour. There may be circumstances in which it is economically advantageous, at least in the short run, to allow (or for government to promote) this uneven development. South-east and East Asia has been the most economically dynamic region of the world in the final quarter of the twentieth century, and it has exemplified all these dilemmas.

Example: China and Hong Kong

To illustrate the complexities of mobility and markets, we have chosen the example of the southern coastal region of China, including Hong Kong. From the mid-1980s, China's communist government promoted a form of market economy in these provinces that was modelled on the nearby newly industrialising economies, and based on the rapid expansion of export-oriented manufacturing. In 1997 one of these, Hong Kong, which had been a British colony, became part of China. Thus began a process of integrating two economies at very different stages of development; the southern provinces experiencing rapid industrialisation, and Hong Kong already at the stage of being a leading centre of banking, insurance and business services for the whole region, as well as a crowded island where land prices were already very high.

By 1996, the year before the handover, trade between China and Hong Kong was the world's third largest bilateral trade. Of China's exports to Hong Kong, 85 per cent were subsequently re-exported to other destinations (Zhang, 2001).

In terms of capital mobility, foreign direct investment in China increased from US$916 million in 1983 to US$25.7 billion in 1993 and US$40.9 billion in 1996 (China Statistical Publishing House, 1998, Table 16.1, p. 587). Most of this was targeted on the coastal provinces' 'open cities'; in 1990 42 per cent went to Guangdong, the province that is adjacent to Hong Kong (Smith, 2000, p. 677), which, in turn, was the largest source of this investment (Findlay, Jones and Davidson, 1998).

That province was also the leading destination for inward migration from other parts of China. In 1990 alone, 3.3 million people entered Guangdong, adding over 5.5 per cent to its population (Smith, 2000, p. 678). In addition to this, many more moved from within the province, from rural districts into the new cities (Fan, 1995; Fan and Huang, 1998). In Guangdong, the percentage of the population officially designated as urban increased from 18.6 per cent in 1982 to 36.8 per cent in 1990 (Smith, 2000, p. 679).

However, this story of rapid development is by no means simply an example of the workings of labour and capital markets. In the first place, communist China did not have such markets at all until the Deng Xiaping government introduced its 'modernisation' programme in the 1980s; such voluntary labour mobility as existed was mainly illegal migration to Hong Kong. The Chinese government still exercises strong controls on which aspects of the economy it chooses to open for competition.

Second, China's strategy for economic development is to increase its share of world production of manufactured goods by becoming a successful exporter of such products. This follows the path taken by Hong Kong in the

1960s to 1990s, when the same strategy led to real annual growth of GDP of between 5 and 10 per cent; in the past decade, China exceeded this. In order to attract the capital for this expansion, the Chinese government offered a very favourable tax and planning regime to foreign investors, and borrowed from the World Bank and Asia Development Bank.

At the same time as it seeks to attract foreign capital, the Chinese government both allows controlled internal labour mobility and blocks migration from abroad. Many peasants from Vietnam may wish to move to Guangdong to work, but are prevented from doing so. Hence the government's strategy is to capture the benefits of industrialisation for its citizens, and deny access to citizens of neighbouring states.

Meanwhile in Hong Kong, this phase of industrialisation is largely over, partly because of the higher costs of land. Its main economic role is now as a supplier of capital to Guangdong and the other coastal provinces. The wages and salaries of workers in Hong Kong are well above those in mainland China, but migration to the island is severely restricted by the government, at least for the present. The reunification of Hong Kong with the mainland may otherwise lead to excessive migration pressures; the city authorities expel even those with close family connections (*The Guardian*, 11 January 2002). Indeed, Hong Kong now receives many more migrants from the Philippines and Indonesia, who are granted work permits to act as servants in wealthy households, than it does from China (Amjad, 1996; Findlay, Jones and Davidson, 1998). Its pattern of inward migration is typical of a capitalist 'global city' (Sassen, 1991).

Now that Hong Kong and China potentially form a single labour market, there are millions of mainland workers willing to do the jobs held by Hong Kong employees for less than they are currently paid. Conversely, given the much lower rates of pay prevailing on the mainland, Hong Kong workers are being paid more than the wage needed to keep them in their jobs. In this sense, they enjoy what is called an 'economic rent' – the difference between the wage required to attract a willing worker in a competitive labour market and their current salary.

All this makes that part of South-east Asia a kind of microcosm of global dilemmas of mobility. In principle, international agencies like the WTO favour free markets, and emphasise that all gain from the growth of trade. Seen from a whole world perspective, the expansion of manufacturing production in countries like China enhances efficiency, and the gains in welfare to previously impoverished peasants, now earning factory wages, are substantial. Owners of capital can get a better return on investments in China than anywhere else in the world, and the new factories can supply goods to the world market at lower prices than would prevail if they were produced elsewhere. Those who lose their jobs in the manufacturing sectors of developed countries can be compensated and supported through social security systems until they can retrain and relocate in other employment. In other words, the mobility of capital and labour that characterises the Chinese economy at present is an example of the dynamism that markets promote, and the growth that is only possible through 'creative destruction' (Schumpeter, 1942).

Yet this is not the whole story. Unlike the developed countries of Western Europe, North America and Australasia, China has no minimum wage, and little regulation of working conditions. Unlike those countries, or nearby South Korea, China has no free trade unions to provide collective protection for workers, and balance the organised power of employers. Indeed, China has no political freedoms, and very limited civil rights. For these reasons, as well as the living conditions that still prevail in inland provinces, many still attempt to leave China, to enter the USA, Europe or Australia as clandestine immigrants, or to apply for asylum. The 58 irregular migrants who died in a container lorry on the crossing from Rotterdam to Dover in June 2000 were from an inland province of China.

Many advocates of free markets argue that the gains from all kinds of 'voluntary exchanges' outweigh the benefits of any attempts to protect the living standards of workers and citizens. In the eyes of theorists such as Olson (1982), trade unions, like business cartels, are collusions through which organised interest groups seek to gain advantage over unorganised and vulnerable individuals. From this perspective, although basic protection of human rights and economic security by government is desirable, collective action generally damages both efficiency and equity. However, such analyses seldom mention transnational migration as an issue.

One of the difficult issues of mobility in the example we have given is the question of living standards in Hong Kong. Now that it is part of China, how can the higher salaries enjoyed by those working there be justified, and why should migration from the mainland be severely restricted? These questions arise all over the world, wherever developed economies are close to poorer ones, as at the borders between the EU and the former communist countries of Central and Eastern Europe. From the perspective of those who have lost both income and security through the introduction of markets after the collapse of communism, the salaries earned by most EU workers contain a large element of 'economic rent'. If there was free movement of labour across the whole continent of Europe, they would willingly do these jobs for lower wages.

Yet in the Chinese example, the authorities have, at least in the short term, decided to underwrite the inequalities between the living standards of the residents of Hong Kong and those on the mainland. Some of the motivation for this is clearly political; this policy was part of the deal under which the

UK government handed Hong Kong back to China. But is there a longer-term case for allowing these inequalities to persist, so that Hong Kong can continue to supply much of the capital for industrial expansion in Guangdong and elsewhere? And if so, it is necessary, from an economic standpoint, to protect the living standards of workers in the Hong Kong economy?

These questions point towards other dimensions of mobility. The owners of land (the immobile factor of production) must decide how to allocate it between different possible uses. All these uses require infrastructures – transport systems, fuel supplies, the services to sustain workers and their families – and institutions for governance of these collective aspects of their exchanges. How can these infrastructural facilities best be supplied, in ways that are sustainable within a world economy driven by mobility of capital and labour, which optimises the outcomes of those movements?

MOBILITY, GOVERNANCE AND COMMUNITY

In principle, the owners of land maximise their return on this asset when they develop it up to the point where the last unit of such development costs is equal to the revenue from this expenditure. Decisions about how much collective infrastructure to supply can be regarded as being simply part of this choice; from an economic perspective; the level of infrastructural goods provided under competitive conditions will be efficient when it maximises the landowner's profits (Stiglitz, 1986, p. 574).

This is clear in the case of the Chinese government's development of the Special Economic Zones and 'open cities' of its coastal provinces, because the government owns all the land in China, and is therefore able to act as a pure capitalist developer. It has chosen to develop the peripheries of existing cities, as suburban residential districts with factory sites provided at low cost (Lin, 1997); the expansion of smaller provincial cities has been even faster than that of larger ones, and has taken the form of semi-urban 'sprawl' (Shue, 1995). On the other hand, the government has chosen to leave other parts of the province, and much of the rest of the country, in a state of impoverished rural underdevelopment (Fan, 1995).

In the advanced industrialised countries, and especially in the USA, a comparable phenomenon has been the emergence of 'private communities'. Here private developers have supplied ready-made infrastructural facilities, including libraries, hospitals, schools and residential homes, for those who could afford to pay the price for these, included in the costs of their accommodation (Foldvary, 1994). But here another aspect of this process is evident. The inhabitants of such communities have a common interest in getting together to make collective decisions about these infrastructural matters, if only to protect themselves against future increases in the amounts they are charged for them. In this way, inhabitants who have chosen to move to the community, and hence consented to a certain level of collective provision, and the price they pay for it, also take control of the governance of their collective life. On condition that they continue to pay their contributions, they become members of a self-governing community, with full control over the supply of collective goods within their territory, but free to leave simply by selling their houses. These developments are paralleled in the affluent, 'gated communities' (with extra security services) in North American and UK cities, and especially in South Africa.

What these two very contrasting examples have in common is that in both cases the owners of land make decisions about its development that attempt to optimise the gains from mobility of labour and capital. It is rare, at least in the advanced industrialised countries, for landowners to be in a position to do this. In the case of the Chinese communist government, it has the power to act as a virtual dictator, defining a territory (the 'open cities') in which competitive markets prevail, and hence these gains can be fully exploited. In the case of the developers of 'private communities', the size and positioning of their landholding allows them to create an enclave with its own exclusive infrastructure and system of governance.

But elsewhere, and particularly in developed welfare states, quite different economic assumptions inform the shape of political institutions, and indeed justify government itself. Although there may be conditions under which landowners provide the optimum collective services for a particular piece of territory, orthodox economic theory shows that neither they nor any other economic actors have the incentives to do so for a whole economy, where most resources are privately owned and traded in markets (Buchanan, 1968). This is because many features of the necessary collective infrastructure for such an economy, including the enforcement of the rules of property ownership and market exchange, are 'goods' from which all benefit, but none can be excluded. Hence there is insufficient return to a private supplier, who relies on private consumers buying products for exclusive consumption. Markets cannot produce the institutions that make markets possible; they systematically undersupply these and other infrastructural goods that are needed to make the efficient allocations they promise. Paradoxically, the avowedly communist government of China can create markets (selectively, where it chooses to do so), but market actors, especially highly mobile ones, with the whole world as their potential sphere of operations, cannot be relied upon to supply an environment suitable for their own activities.

Once government is built into the system, as a regulator and supplier of collective goods, the question becomes how final income (or utility) within the territory governed can be most efficiently *and* equitably distributed among this population, taking account of the 'laws' of production and exchange in markets. Government is assumed to take the form of a nation state with territorial sovereignty, making decisions in the collective interests of all its citizens, under some kind of 'social contract' between them. Thus, whereas the economics of production and trade is based on an open, competitive system with no boundaries and highly mobile resources, the economics of distribution – 'welfare economics' – considers issues of who gets what within a finite economy, among a fixed population of citizens. This is also the basis for political theories of justice.

The criteria under which such distributions are evaluated in welfare economics do not take account of the interests of foreigners, or even of potential immigrants. Both the Pareto criterion (that no one can be made better off without making someone else worse off) and the Hicks–Kaldor criterion (that those who benefit from a change in allocation could in principle compensate those who lose, and remain better off) refer to the effects on current residents or citizens. So, for example, a change in immigration policy could be recommended, even if it imposes losses on the sending country and the proposed immigrants (Hadfield, 1995, p. 204).

In the 'golden age of welfare states' (Esping-Andersen, 1996), it was taken for granted that citizens would look to the state for protection from the arbitrary outcomes of the market, and the contingencies of the life cycle. The bigger and stronger the state, the more it was able to persuade the representatives of capital and organised labour to agree to such redistributions through transfers and social services, and hence the better the welfare dividend to its citizens. But with the impact of globalisation, the greater mobility of capital means that states must compete with each other to attract investment, and persuade their citizens not to move their savings abroad. As a result, there are limits on states' powers to raise taxes, and to offer protection from global markets to their vulnerable populations.

However, new theory on the economics of collective goods has provided a different perspective on these issues, and one that has to some extent influenced all governments, but especially those of the USA and the UK. Instead of assuming that societies are made up of a fixed and static population, about whom decisions over the distribution of resources have to be made by governments, elected at occasional democratic ballots, this approach mobilises individuals in pursuit of their own welfare. In this way, mobility becomes the key to allocations based on the active choices of the population, rather than the outcomes of official decisions.

This theoretical model postulates not only households that are perfectly informed about tax rates and service quality in each public authority, and capable of moving costlessly between them, but also a perfectly elastic supply of jurisdictions, such that each can reproduce the most attractive features of its competitors, yet each can also exclude the residents of other jurisdictions from all the benefits of the services it supplies (Tiebout, 1956). Hence equilibrium is reached when no household can improve its welfare by moving elsewhere, and each local authority has a population size that minimises the average cost per household of providing the relevant service (Inman and Rubinfeld, 1997, p. 81).

For public choice theorists, the point of this model is that it allows heterogeneous populations, with diverse incomes and tastes, to form themselves into groups who share the costs of 'local and particular' collective goods. This is always more cost-efficient than a large central authority providing standardised services for its whole population (Oates, 1972, p. 35). Under a regime of 'fiscal federalism', the mobility of citizens between local authorities holds down tax rates and forces public servants to provide infrastructural goods efficiently. Thus voting with the feet, by moving to another jurisdiction, is the public choice equivalent of consumer sovereignty in markets (it empowers individuals in relation to producers of collective services), and competition between authorities for members requires them to improve their allocation of resources, just as market competition does among industrial firms.

However, the way in which this is achieved has other consequences. As its proponents acknowledge, the whole dynamic of mobility will encourage those with high incomes and few needs for specific services to cluster together, leaving those with low incomes and expensive special needs as far behind as possible. 'The rich tend to want to be away from the poor, but the poor want to be in the same jurisdiction as the rich' (Cullis and Jones, 1994, p. 297). The optimum size of local authorities in the model is based on the assumption that they can exclude those unable to afford their tax rates and local housing costs; in this sense, they act as 'clubs' for their residents, in the strict economic sense, because only members can benefit from their services – as in a private swimming pool (Buchanan, 1965). Again, cost-sharing demands that individuals with like incomes and tastes group together to share costs, so 'there may well be a tendency for zoning on the part of high-income groups in order to exclude the poor' (Cullis and Jones, 1994, p. 300).

This theory has been enormously influential, and was most consistently applied to the reform of the public sector in the UK in the late 1980s. For each of the services previously supplied under principles of universalism and territorial standardisation, budgets were devolved to the smallest feasible local unit, managers were given incentives to save costs and league tables were published to inform citizens about their performance. For health care, education and social services in particular, the aim was to redesign the public infrastructure so as to stimulate better-informed citizens to vote with their feet, by moving between the relevant authorities responsible for providing the collective goods they needed. Research on the outcome of this restructuring suggests that while it certainly succeeds in 'taming the Leviathan' of public spending, and in holding taxes down (Oates, 1985), it also results in more homogeneous residential districts, because it sorts populations into groups by incomes and preferences (Hughes, 1987).

So the public choice approach largely substitutes voting with the feet (the right to leave one jurisdiction for another) for collective action to demand better services, and redistributes power in terms of capacities and opportunities for mobility. It shifts the emphasis off political decisions about the distribution of roles and resources by central governments, and leaves issues of justice to a kind of invisible hand that moves people between local authorities, in search of low taxes and efficiency.

Whether this causes a 'race to the bottom' (states and local authorities competing with each other to produce the leanest, meanest welfare provision) is still under debate (Brueckner, 2000). In principle, public choice theory could supply a global model of 'fiscal federalism', in which welfare gains were claimed from mobility within an integrated world economy, and migration between countries. However, no such model has yet been developed. What is clear is that the public sector reforms already undertaken within First World states have had many consequences for migrants, some of which were not intended by the reformers, as shown in the next section.

Once voting with the feet becomes the main mechanism by which populations express their choices over collective goods, the least mobile and the poorest are at a grave disadvantage. On the other hand, those who are willing to take the risk of moving, including moving across borders in breach of immigration rules, are able to take advantage of some of the unintended consequences of the new situation.

MOBILITY AND SOCIAL EXCLUSION

From the perspective of the individual or household, decisions about mobility have several dimensions that are not fully taken into account in the economic models discussed so far. What has also to be explained is why (especially in Europe) so few people move, and those who do move short distances, often within the same city. Hence – at least for large parts of people's lives – immobility is the dominant strategy, and many people spend their whole lives in the same location.

Part of the answer to this question is that local people have 'location-specific insider advantages' (Fischer *et al.*, 2000) – assets that have accumulated through living and working in the same place, and that would be lost or devalued by moving. The most obvious of these is an 'insider' job, where the employee's salary reflects his or her value to a particular firm, and this value in part reflects specific links with networks in the community, colleagues and the local infrastructure. But it also includes leisure-oriented advantages, such as social capital built up through participation in local clubs and associations, and access to informal support and long-standing friendships.

For most people, however, this constraint does not limit their mobility within a travel-to-work area, since improved transport facilities allow them to commute further, as well as belong to more widely-spread groups and organisations. At certain points in the life cycle, they are likely to consider moving – to study, to take up their first jobs, on forming a household, in search of the best schooling for their children and on retirement (Jordan, Redley and James, 1994). It is at these points that their strategic decisions express votes with their feet, over the collective amenities of the districts that they can afford to live in, as well in their choices of employment.

The redesign of public infrastructures discussed in the last section has been partly aimed at facilitating geographical and social mobility. Especially in the Anglo-Saxon countries, there has been an attempt to redefine the social elements in citizenship, with a stronger emphasis on individuals' responsibilities to provide for themselves and their families through their earnings. Instead of aiming at 'equality of outcome', income maintenance and other systems promote 'equality of opportunity' (Brown, 1997). This implies accelerated movement of people, for the sake of equity as well as efficiency. In a culture of achievement and choice, people pursue 'positional advantage' (Hirsch, 1977). They move to more favoured districts, with better recreational and cultural facilities. Those who can afford to cluster round the best public services – schools, hospitals, health clinics and care homes. Each town or city organises itself into relatively homogeneous districts, where residents of like incomes and tastes congregate (Jordan, 1996, chs. 4 and 5).

However, another consequence of this form of mobility is the deterioration in the life-chances of those left in the least-favoured districts. As studies in the USA have shown (Wilson, 1989, 1997), concentrations of poverty, unemployment and many other social problems occur where both capital and skilled labour move out of a particular district, leaving neither work opportunities nor the resources to create them. Social exclusion occurs when the least skilled, with the fewest material resources, are left behind in districts with the worst infrastructural facilities. Their immobility is a consequence of not being able to afford the housing costs of living elsewhere, but also of their reliance on informal networks in these neighbourhoods for their survival strategies. For men, these are networks of informal economic activity, including those that deal in drugs, and engage in other forms of crime, to fill the economic void left by market failure. For women they are networks of mutual support over child care, and the support of older relatives and disabled kin

(Jordan *et al.*, 1992; Jordan, 1996, ch. 5). These districts become 'communities of fate' (Marske, 1991) on the margins of society – inner-city ghettos or bleak outer-city social housing estates (Power, 1997).

It is easy to see how the market-oriented reforms of the social services in the UK have facilitated these processes. Under such new arrangements as the devolution of budgets to local schools, hospitals and support facilities, and funding local authorities to buy services from local commercial providers, the managers of such units have an interest in attracting high-yield, low-cost pupils, patients and clients, and excluding low-yield, high-cost ones (Jordan, 1996, ch. 6). Thus the interests of citizens, moving to find the best possible bundle of collective services, and of managers seeking the service users giving the best return for their budgets, coincide. The strategic actions of mobile middle-income households and public-sector staff combine to produce league tables of the performances of such facilities corresponding closely to the income levels prevailing in their localities, which, in turn, provokes a further twist of the same cycle. At the other end of the scale, managers of public services in the most disadvantaged districts are left to deal with pupils, patients and clients with multiple problems, who also have the fewest household and wider communal resources.

In the UK, these processes are now recognised as having contributed to inter-ethnic conflicts, as 'white flight' from least-favoured districts, and *de facto* segregation between the poorest white and minority ethnic communities, led to rivalry and mistrust. Both spontaneous concentrations and local authority policies were blamed in official reports on the race riots in Oldham, Burnley and Bradford in 2001 (*The Guardian*, 12 December 2001). Irregular migration may contribute to this segregation process (see Chapter 8).

The main policy response (in the USA and the UK especially, but also in Europe – see Chapter 3) has been to try to increase the labour-market participation of residents in these districts, through programmes of 'activation' including training and other 'welfare-to-work' measures, together with reforms to improve work incentives (Jordan, 1998). But exclusions of this kind cannot be overcome by policies that are confined to employment and law enforcement. Those countries that have most vigorously pursued policies for increased mobility in the name of 'equality of opportunity' – the UK, the USA and New Zealand – have also experienced the largest increases in income inequality in the final 20 years of the last century, with corresponding growth of homelessness, prison populations and other indicators of exclusion. The UK and USA now have the highest labour-market participation rates in the world, and also the longest working hours among the developed economies, yet also the highest rates of social exclusion in such societies by these measures.

Furthermore, the recent increases in participation rates have been achieved by growth of service work, often in low-paid occupations (such as cleaning, catering, retailing, social and personal care work), usually taken by women, employed part time. The same trends are clear from other countries that have expanded employment, such as the Netherlands (Hemerijck, 2001). When governments induce more claimants of income maintenance benefits to take work, the kinds of jobs they are able to get do not enable them to live in districts with better amenities; instead they have to travel daily to work there. This is recognised in the UK government's assessment of its measures to tackle unemployment in deprived neighbourhoods (the Employment Zones and Action Teams). The staff of these programmes are:

> ... identifying suitable vacancies in neighbouring areas and bringing the two together. Additionally, they are tackling barriers to employment, including funding for transport to enable people to access nearby vacancies (HM Treasury, 2000, sect. 4.34).

In other words, residents of poor districts will be required to work in more affluent ones, to serve the needs of communities of which they are not, and probably never will be, members. This is not inclusion. Poor people not only endure the highest risks and costs associated with such social ills as pollution, the degeneration of the urban infrastructure, housing squalor and social disorganisation; they also receive the worst in education, health care and social services, because higher-income groups act to attract most funding and the best professional staff for their facilities.

But even this process of mobility is becoming problematic, because – as the costs of housing in desirable districts where residents are able to earn high salaries continues to rise faster than house prices elsewhere – even these public service professionals cannot afford to live nearby. It has been calculated that the disposable incomes of nurses and teachers (as well as those of other modestly paid occupations such as drivers, secretaries and construction workers) are between £1300 and £3900 lower in London than the average for these groups in rest of the UK, after housing and travel-to-work costs (Centre for Economics and Business Research, 2001).

Hence in London, and in other cities and districts in the UK, the local authorities have turned increasingly to recruitment from abroad to fill vacancies in the public sector professions. Teachers and social workers are recruited from such countries as Canada, Australia, South Africa and Zimbabwe, to join doctors and nurses from all over the world. Public sector professionals are the largest category of foreigners given work permits to work in the UK. They provide a supply of staff who are adaptable, and willing to live in very modest accommodation (such as hostels) – hence ideally suited to the requirements of an economy with huge inequalities in housing costs.

This example shows how the economics of residential polarisation may influence mobility in labour markets. From the standpoint of the local authorities in affluent districts, and of those who elect them (the members of such communities), it is preferable to be able to attract low-paid staff to travel from poor districts to do menial work, and to recruit public service professionals from abroad, than to have to pay more local taxes, to provide affordable housing for these groups of workers. And even if there are enough workers with these skills in the economy as a whole, the local supply will be determined by a combination of house prices and travel costs.

Where both accommodation costs and distances to the poor districts where unskilled workers live are high (as in many of the great metropoles), another solution to this problem quickly emerges. Saskia Sassen (1988, 1991) drew attention to the phenomenon of irregular migration providing a whole segment of service sector, shadow employment in global cities like New York, London and Tokyo. Our research, reported in the second part of this book, provides the first detailed evidence of this phenomenon in London. Irregular migrants from Brazil, Poland and Turkey, most unable to speak any English, were able to get work within days of arriving in the country, mainly behind the scenes in restaurants, cafés and fast-food outlets, in textile 'sweatshops', or in work renovating wealthy houses. Far from encountering resistance and hostility, these arrivals were welcomed as a supply of cheap labour for such work, and found it rather easy to conceal themselves among the city's minority ethnic populations. Hence, irregular migration provided a remedy for the increasing problems of the new infrastructure, as the rich moved further and further away from the poor, and the latter were trapped in the most deprived districts by rising costs of travel and accommodation.

It is not too fanciful to see how such a combination of factors may lead to a rather different division of social policy responsibilities between the levels of government in Europe. For the local authority, the task would be to provide the infrastructural facilities and services suitable for the range of business sites and accommodation it can provide. This is only a slight variation on the profit-maximising strategy of the landowner-developer, planning a private community – a community of choice – in the previous section. For the national government, the main remaining functions would be to sustain those people unable to gain secure access to such communities of choice, to train and motivate them to be flexible and mobile service workers, moving between them according to demand. For the supranational authority (the EU), the main task would be to guarantee a supply of still more mobile and adaptable transnational migrants, to be recruited wherever skills shortages or short-term, seasonal or crisis work appeared. The implications of these developments for social exclusion is explored in Chapter 3, and in the conclusions to the book (Chapter 10).

People who migrate across national borders through their own choice, or flee from political persecution, do not fit easily into such a framework. Even if they are acting rationally, as bearers of skills in search of better-paid employment in a global economy, their status does not fit the work categories allotted to citizens and denizens of local, national or regional polities. These authorities are required to create some kind of niche for asylum seekers, and to deal with foreigners caught working in the shadow economy. But these people are uncomfortable reminders of unresolved issues in the systems they have established for managing mobility.

CONCLUSIONS

At first sight, economic theory might seem to point unambiguously to open borders, and hence to free migration, as a contribution to the mobility that could maximise the unimpeded increase in global welfare. However, patterns of economic development that have led to enormous disparities in income between neighbouring regions and states, and the global mobility of capital owned by international corporations, create complex issues over the mobility of people. Both movement within countries and migration between countries therefore reflect the strategies of companies, governments and migrants themselves, attempting to capture gains from mobility. Irregular migration is one of the means by which migrants counter states' strategies.

Economic theory seeks to explain population movements in terms of wage differentials caused by imbalances in the supply of and demand for labour. We have seen from the example of China how a developing country has transformed its economy by establishing a manufacturing base to serve the world economy. This attracted from its own hinterland the workforce for a relatively labour-intensive form of manufacturing. Other newly industrialising countries in the region had followed the same strategy, but lacked the same abundant internal labour supplies. Countries like South Korea, Taiwan and Malaysia quickly came to rely on migrants from the less-developed economies of the region, like the Philippines, Thailand and Indonesia. Hence a 'migration system' developed in East Asia, with over three million foreign workers migrating legally each year from one country to another, for an average stay of two years (Abella, 1995; Jones and Findlay, 1998), and many others crossing borders without proper status.

An important element shaping this migration system was the global movement of capital. Without foreign direct investment, China would not have been able to establish its export-oriented manufacturing zones, nor would the other newly industrialising countries of the region have been able to accomplish the transformations of their economies. Capital mobility and the activities of international corporations, in turn, required the restructuring of cities and city states in the region, which emerged as headquarters for these companies, and financial centres for the regional economy. These global cities, including Tokyo, Hong Kong and Singapore, attracted different kinds of migrants – low-paid service and construction workers on the one hand, and high-paid professionals and managers on the other (Boyle, 1996; Findlay, 1996). The former type of movement was substantially fed by irregular migration.

In principle, the gains in global welfare from migration could be used to compensate those who are losers in these processes. But in practice the only systems that exist to provide such compensation are internal to national polities. In the First World countries, and especially in Europe, systems that protect the earnings of workers, and provide social protection for those out-side the labour market, are used to justify rules that restrict access by migrants, even where this would be, from a world perspective, both welfare-enhancing and income-equalising (Begg, Fischer and Dornbusch, 1991, pp. 644–5). Thus although such restrictions are, from a global standpoint, like tariffs and quotas, ultimately a form of protectionism, they may remain as bastions of national sovereignty under global regimes for removing other kinds of barrier to mobility, and alongside schemes for recruiting specific kinds of foreign workers to meet shortages in particular sectors.

This is paradoxical because, as we have seen in the second half of this chapter, mobility has come to be regarded as a much more important consid-eration in the provision of collective goods within polities. The influence of public choice theory has been towards the development of a diversity of public infrastructures, competing to attract mobile firms and individuals, and hence reaching more efficient allocations of these goods. In emphasising the benefits of choice expressed through mobility, this new approach is in tension with a system of nation states that are communities of fate with fixed mem-berships and restrictive conditions for entry.

In practice, both the forms of social protection that consist in minimum wages, social insurance systems and other public services, and the social polarisation that occurs in regions that promote mobility between diverse local authorities, create niches for irregular migration. Under the former, employers (especially marginal entrepreneurs) have strong incentives to hire irregular migrants at lower wages, in worse conditions, and without paying social insurance contributions. Within the latter, wealthier individuals and households seek services for which labour may not be available in the dis-tricts where they live, except through the work of irregular migrants.

This chapter has illustrated the disparities between membership systems in which mobility is seen both as an important right and a necessary condition for economic dynamism, and border controls which restrict and select mi-grants. In some ways, irregular migration might be seen as a form of 'safety valve', allowing the tensions and pressures created by this non-congruence to be eased – a 'crime without victims'.

... because illegal aliens participate only minimally in entitlement programs, do not vote, and usually pay taxes, it is by no means clear that their presence should be viewed as a 'problem' (Sykes, 1995, p. 159).

In the next chapter, we show how new opportunities for mobility between states were a central focus for the creation of the EU – but how new freedoms of movement gave rise to greater concern about irregular migration into the EU from the post-communist and developing countries. In Chapter 3 we turn to the specific concerns of policy-makers about the effects of migration in general, and irregular migration in particular, on labour markets and welfare systems.

2. Mobility and migration in the European Union

This chapter investigates the relationship between mobility and membership in the European Union. The primary rationale of the EU has been to create a single market among member states, with free movement of capital, labour and goods. This has involved redefining migration between countries as mobility within a single market, creating rights of European citizenship, and agreeing common policies on immigration from outside the Union (Geddes, 2000). In order to understand how current measures to control irregular migration, but allow recruitment of 'useful' workers, have emerged, we need to analyse the relationship between these elements in the evolution of EU institutions.

As the original European Economic Community has grown to include 15 states, it has embraced countries with increasingly diverse systems of membership, and traditions of migration. The core states had relatively homogeneous versions of citizenship, and drew in migrant workers mainly from the Mediterranean region – Spain and North Africa especially in the case of France, Yugoslavia and Turkey in that of Germany. With the accession of the UK came a different form of welfare state (more concerned with individual economic freedom), and a wider reach for its recruitment of immigrant workers, from the New Commonwealth countries. Finally, the expansion included both Scandinavian countries with more homogeneous populations and stronger social citizenship rights (Finland, Sweden), and Southern European states with more fragmented welfare systems, and long histories of supplying migrant labour for the more prosperous economies of Northern Europe (Spain, Portugal, Greece).

On the face of it, the creation of a single market might have been expected to accelerate mobility of workers between the member states, and especially from the poorer periphery towards the richer centre. In fact, migration of this kind, which had already been slowing in the 1980s, began to go into reverse, with Southern European countries that had been suppliers of migrant labour drawing back some of their members from the north, and Ireland some of its members from the UK.

As we shall see, this was partly because of slower economic growth at the heart of Europe; partly because of the emergence of new political freedoms and social rights in Spain, Portugal and Greece; and partly because of new measures by the EU to promote 'social cohesion', by redistributing resources towards the poorer regions. But, at the same time, the new institutions of the EU were challenged by migration from further afield, both in the shape of growing asylum applications, and in irregular entries.

These population movements were clearly related to the new world political situation after 1989. The collapse of the Soviet bloc regimes, and the catastrophic consequences of the impact of market forces on their economies, were one source of new migratory pressures (Castles and Miller, 1993). The other was the wars that flared up on the fringes of Europe, with the break-up of the former Yugoslavia, and the conflicts in the Caucasus. Finally, the impact of both globalisation and the new geopolitical order on the developing world contributed to an increase in migration as a strategic response to a combination of economic and political constraints.

This was the first period in which international movements of population 'can be said to have become truly global. With the spread and advancement of modern communications, the expansion of the global economy, and the intensification of regional and international economic and demographic disparities, every continent in the world is now touched by this phenomenon' (Collinson, 1994, p. 4). It was estimated that the total number of people living outside their country of citizenship in the early 1990s was over 100 million (Russell and Teitelbaum, 1992). It was also the time when the nature of globalisation was being recognised – that the strategies of international economic actors were breaking down the distinctions between the political and economic realms, and the mobility of capital stimulating movement of people (Sassen, 1988).

> Much of this migration is driven by economic and political forces – such as world trading patterns and capital flows – which have become increasingly global in their genesis and development. The global causes and impacts of international migration have become increasingly intertwined (Collinson, 1994, p. 4).

The 1990s can be seen as a period of ambivalence about mobility within the EU, and resistance to immigration from outside. On the one hand, there were fears about the possible negative consequences of increased mobility, both in further decline of less-developed regions, and in damaging the life chances of less mobile people – 'mobility is socially divisive' (European Foundation, 1990, p. 10). On the other, there was growing concern about the 'European social model'; its 'inflexibility' was partly reflected in the unwillingness of unemployed people to move in search of work. Thus the barriers to immigration that were hastily erected in the aftermath of 1989 were beginning to be questioned by the end of the decade.

In 2000 the European Commission issued a 'Communication on a Con-certed Strategy for Immigration and Asylum', which laid down the framework under which these 'separate but closely related' issues would be addressed (European Commission, 2000). In this chapter, we trace this strategy to attempts to harmonise EU immigration and asylum policies under the Maastricht Treaty of 1991; to the evolution of a European model for the processing of asylum claims and the reception of applicants; to the successive transfer of Justice and Home Affairs matters from national to Community competences under the Amsterdam Treaty of 1997; and to the acknowledge-ment of the need for future immigration at the European Council's Tampere Summit in 1999.

The declared aim of this new approach is to open up channels for legal immigration from outside the EU, while maintaining control over migratory flows, according to assessments of the 'social, economic, legal and cultural' issues at stake. But at the same time, a new strategy for combating irregular migration is being put in place, that sees it as linked with transnational crime, racketeering and trafficking, and hence as undermining the proper function-ing of the single market order.

In the relationship between mobility and membership, it is clear that the establishment of the right of free movement of workers in the EU gave a major impetus to the development of a concept of European citizenship (Meehan, 1993). There has been an attempt to balance the 'exit right' of mobility (seen as an extension of freedom of choice, and as allowing indi-viduals to adjust more rapidly to changing economic circumstances) with voting rights in the member states where migrants were living (Day and Shaw, 2001). Social cohesion and social inclusion became important goals of EU policy. But the main focus of immigration measures has been the more narrowly economic one of reducing skills' shortages, and meeting seasonal or specific demand for unskilled labour. In this way, an immigration regime is coming into existence in the EU which uses outside recruits to tackle prob-lems of mobility in member states' labour markets – such as the difficulties of the south-east region in the UK, where two-thirds of this country's foreign workers are employed (Salt and Clarke, 2001, p. 479). It is in this context, rather than as an abuse of humanitarian protection or a manifestation of international crime, that irregular migration can best be understood.

LABOUR RECRUITMENT AND THE FREE MOVEMENT OF PEOPLE

The years since the Second World War can be divided into two very contrast-ing periods of immigration policy in Europe. Between 1945 and 1973, there was almost unrestricted labour migration into Northern European countries. Large numbers of immigrants served as replacement populations following war losses; initially they came mainly as refugees from new communist regimes in Central and Eastern Europe. They supplied labour for reconstruction and industrial development, and contributed substantially to the postwar boom (Kindleberger, 1967; Herbert, 1986).

Migration of labour from the south peaked in 1970, when over 700 000 new foreign workers entered the Federal Republic of Germany (nearly 125 000 from Turkey and over 200 000 from Yugoslavia) and over 300 000 (of which 140 000 from Spain) entered France (Böhning, 1972, pp. 30 and 34). By then these countries were already trying to restrict immigration through bilateral agreements with sending countries, but only around half of those entering were recruited in this way. The oil price crisis of 1973 marked the turning point, as growth of these economies slowed down, and they introduced stronger measures to try to stop immigration (Collinson, 1994, pp. 50–1).

Although the subsequent period has been characterised as a regime of 'zero immigration' (European Commission, 2000, p. 3), it was the recruitment of foreign workers, rather than immigration itself, that was frozen. Spouses and dependants of migrants continued to enter Northern European countries, and the Federal Republic took in large numbers of people of German descent from the Soviet bloc countries. Overall, however, the stocks of foreign population in the main receiving countries did not increase significantly in the 1970s and 1980s, because immigration was balanced by voluntary return migration, especially to Southern Europe (Collinson, 1994, p. 55). By the time that Spain, Portugal and Greece entered the European Community in the 1980s, they were receiving substantial numbers of returning migrant workers (aided by programmes of financial assistance in France), and also beginning to experience immigration from outside the EC.

Meanwhile, the initial agreements for the free movement of workers within the EC had been reached in the 1960s, with the right to cross borders in search of work implemented in 1968 (Böhning, 1972, p. 15). The accession of Spain, Portugal and Greece to the EC was facilitated by the fact that economic growth in those countries had accelerated, just as it was declining in the north, so that the collapse of fascist and military regimes in the applicant states coincided with improved economic prospects. Even so, the European Commission, in its Milan White Paper of 1985, was keen to emphasise that the right to free movement embodied in the Treaty of Rome and in the Single European Market would be balanced by measures:

... to maintain social cohesion and regional balance across the Community and to avoid some of the negative effects of previous migrations, particularly by encouraging economic development in the regions of emigration and underdevelopment (European Foundation, 1990, p. 73).

These fears reflected theoretical models in which a large advanced economy, with increasing returns to scale, attracted labour from a smaller, more traditional economy, with constant returns to scale (Markusen, 1988; Krugman, 1991). Movements of workers under these conditions widen the gap between the centre and the periphery as the latter come to specialise in traditional production, and to lose competitiveness (Straubhaar, 2000, p.19). The fear was that centre might gain permanent economic advantage, because of its concentration of highly qualified labour, and capacity to attract skilled workers from the periphery, leading to more and more movement from the less-developed regions.

The Cecchini Report (1988) concluded that the Community's Structural Funds would have to be doubled to offset the negative consequences of the single market for these regions. Following the decision of the Council of Ministers of 11–12 February 1988, the emphasis of cohesion policies was to be equally on the promotion of workforce mobility, the establishment of minimum social regulations and the support and development of marginal social groups and regions.

In retrospect, it can be recognised that these policies were brought forward in a relatively sheltered economic environment. In many ways, the Iron Curtain protected the EU from the effects of global economic changes, at the same time as it shielded the Soviet bloc countries' economies from these forces. Far greater movements of population, especially from the countryside to the towns, and in the explosive rise of megapolises, had been happening in the Third World. Relatively few asylum seekers, from Vietnam and Chile, the Ugandan and Kenyan Asians to the UK, or East Timorese refugees to the Netherlands, reached Europe. In the 1980s conflicts in Sri Lanka and Turkey, and the beginnings of political struggles in Central Europe (especially Poland), increased these numbers (Zolberg, Suhrke and Aguayo, 1989). After 1989 the collapse of communist regimes, along with the development of global travel infrastructures and cheaper air flights, exposed Europe to new migrations; once initial communities were established, chain and secondary migration patterns followed (Sassen, 1996).

All this gave much greater significance to the tentative beginnings of a co-ordinated European migration policy that were stirring in the mid-1980s. The Trevi working groups extended their remit from terrorism and drugs to migration matters, and five member states (France, Germany and the Benelux countries) set up the Schengen Agreement as a parallel structure within the EC, and a pacemaker for developments to come. By the time that the Agreement was fully implemented in 1995, abolishing internal border controls and initiating a concerted approach to immigration, asylum and the external borders, all the other member states had joined the agreement, except the UK (Seiffarth, 1997). From the time of the Palma Document of 1989, the fight against 'illegal migration' had been one of the priorities of the participants (Group of Co-ordinators, 1989); freedom of movement within the Community was to be combined with the exclusion of outsiders (Bunyan, 1993).

IMMIGRATION CONTROL AND EXTERNAL BORDERS

The collapse of the Soviet bloc regimes in 1989, and the sudden movement of around a million people across the borders that had constituted the Iron Curtain, provoked an urgent reappraisal of migration policies among EC member states, and the development of new institutions for co-operation on border control issues in the Community. When the Treaty of Maastricht created the EU in 1991, this meant that the control of immigration to the EU was one of the main political issues around which this new supranational entity was organised.

> The market-making project and free movement unavoidably made immigration and asylum issues common interests for EU member states, which raised the salience of external frontier control at the borders of the single market and internal security policies within (Geddes, 2000, p. 3).

Seen from the inside of the EU, free movement of citizens between states was like the circulation of memberships between a federation of clubs. Members were entitled to use collective facilities, and benefit from collective cost-sharing, contributing through both national and EU taxes, and voting at both national and EU elections. But, in relation to outsiders, the marginal gains from allowing large-scale entries from the east and south were seen as far smaller than the costs (in terms of training, integration and the effects of competition, crowding and congestion). As a provider of collective goods to its citizens, the EU defined itself as an exclusive club, saw itself as too attractive to would-be migrants who could not afford its membership dues, and set about making its facilities less accessible.

At first, fears about uncontrolled migration focused on the recognition that enormous economic, social and demographic imbalances between EU member states and their neighbours (to the east and the south) could lead to a mass exodus from these poorer and less stable countries. This soon shifted to anxiety about mass movements from inter-ethnic and inter-communal conflicts, especially those in the former Yugoslavia. Finally, the upsurge of anti-immigrant and xenophobic actions in the EU, and especially the attacks on asylum seekers in Germany in the early 1990s, fuelled fears of new racist political movements, and was used to justify restrictive measures (European Commission, 1990). Thus the new institutions were developed in a context of tighter control policies, reacting to short-term fears, and shifting member states' concerns into systems at the supranational level (Collinson, 1994, p. 63).

This was specifically linked to the establishment of the internal market, and to the anticipated free movement under the Schengen Agreement. A Communication on Immigration in 1991 noted that:

> ... the suppression of internal frontiers ... could entail a risk that the absence of checks at internal borders will render any control of immigration impossible. ... This has led Member States to recognise the need for a common approach (European Commission, 1991, p. 8).

This was followed by specific efforts to co-operate over the development of border control regimes (especially in the Southern European member states), to harmonise visa policies and asylum laws and admission policies (Lavenex, 2001). However, whereas free movement of citizens had become an integral part of the 'constitution' of the EU, immigration and asylum remained issues for intergovernmental co-operation. This led to a 'muddled, confused and confusing transfer of competencies' over the latter questions (Geddes, 2000, p. 3). Since 1991 high-ranking officers from national police forces, customs and immigration authorities have been meeting as a Co-ordination Committee, and set up Centres for Information, Discussion and Exchange. These focus on the sharing of data and intelligence over irregular migration and its control, including the alleged 'abuse' of the asylum system (Ad Hoc Group on Immigration, 1992). Subsequently, a number of executive bodies have been created, such as automated fingerprint systems (EURODAC), a databank on False and Authentic Documents (FADO), an International Border Police Conference (IBPC), the Schengen Information System (SIS) as well as EUROPOL, which is actively involved in 'the prevention of and combat against clandestine migration' (European Council, 1999).

At the same time, the EU became engaged in bilateral negotiations with sending countries and transit states for migration. Ostensibly, these were concerned with assisting the balanced development of these states, and to prevent damage to their economies and societies from unregulated migration. In practice, they were focused on control measures. This has been particularly clear in relation to the transit role of Central European countries. In 1991, the Visegrad Group (Poland, Hungary and the then Czechoslovakia) offered co-operation on migration issues as a kind of opening bid in the process of accession to the EU (FFM, 1997). The EU then employed its PHARE programme to fund the training and development of border management regimes, and the enforcement of safe Third Country regulations over asylum. Similarly, in relation to the newly independent states of the former Soviet Union, the TACIS programme funding included 'border management to fight illegal migration at the Ukrainian–Moldovan border' (Statewatch, 2001).

All these initiatives served to increase the number of border crossings classified as illegal. For instance, on the one hand, the previously permeable borders of the Southern European member states were redefined as external borders of the EU, which it was important to secure. Of all the estimated 2.6 million undocumented foreigners in the EU in the early 1990s, as many as a million were thought to be in Italy and Spain (Collinson, 1994, p. 14). These had formed part of a large informal sector of those economies, which functioned partly as an alternative to social protection systems for their most vulnerable populations. The new EU measures thus had important implications both for creating new 'immigration offences', and in attempts to impose internal regulation on these economies. On the other hand, they enforced restrictions on mobility between the post-communist countries, at a time when their economies were supposed to be introducing freer trade and more open competition.

Taken together with the growing inequalities between EU member states and the sending countries, these restrictions increased pressures for migration through irregular channels. Since there remained a demand for irregular labour – especially for certain kinds of service sector work – in the EU, it was not surprising that organisations sprang into existence, especially in the former communist countries, to supply such workers. This, in turn, fuelled further restrictions, and the perception by EU security organisations that irregular migration was a criminal activity, reflecting the interests of racketeers and traffickers, rather than the decisions of migrants.

IMMIGRATION 'CRISIS'

These measures to strengthen border regimes were the counterparts to the ones that established free movement of people, now defined as European citizens rather than workers, within the EU. The Maastricht Treaty marked the beginning of a decade in which attempts were made to give legitimacy to the EU by granting democratic rights to its more mobile citizens (Day and Shaw, 2001), while severely limiting access from outside the Union. Within this new 'Fortress Europe', mobility was to be seen as part of citizenship, but its benefits were to be reserved for full members of the EU states. Even long-standing legal residents who were not citizens of member states (such as 'guest workers' from the 1960s in Germany and their children) did not qualify for rights to free movement – indicating an inconsistency in policies claimed to be aiming at 'social inclusion' (Geddes, 2000, ch. 7).

The problem for this strategy was that it was seeking to balance the effects of globalisation in Europe at a moment when its impact on the post-communist and developing worlds was almost uncontrolled. All over the globe, political and economic structures were collapsing, as the barriers to international production and trade were pulled down. In the aftermath of this devastation, displaced populations – whether fleeing from new outbreaks of inter-communal violence and ethnic cleansing, or from the ravages of economic breakdown – were on the move (Sivanandan, 2000). Europe's stability and prosperity were equally attractive for those able to make the journey there.

There were still legal channels for migration into EU member states, despite the co-ordinated efforts described in the last section. In Germany, for example, the laws allowing families of ethnic German origin, many of whom had been living in the Soviet bloc countries for several generations, to 're-turn' gave opportunities for hundreds of thousands to become full German citizens in the 1990s. There were also schemes for seasonal and temporary workers from post-communist Central Europe, and for allowing secondary migration, mainly from Turkey (Cyrus and Vogel, 2000). In the UK, schemes for working holidaymakers (mainly from the Old Commonwealth), for seasonal agricultural workers, for students and *au pairs*, and family reunion, allowed legal access. Some work permit holders were allowed to switch from temporary status to indefinite leave after four years. For the Southern European countries, the inexperience of the new authorities in controlling inward migration provided continuing opportunities, especially since large-scale amnesties and regularisation schemes were occasionally offered (Collinson, 1994, p. 136).

However, the other main channel of migration to the more prosperous North European member states was asylum seeking, and because this had grown so sharply after 1989, it was seen as the main focus for tighter control policies (Lavenex, 2001). Applications peaked in Germany (500 000), France (60 000), Belgium and Luxembourg in the early 1990s, but were already falling by the middle of the decade, as new measures to restrict benefits and impose accommodation regimes were introduced (European Commission, 1997). By contrast, the UK was later to introduce such changes, and hence had rising applications until the late 1990s.

Tighter controls focused on welfare provision for asylum seekers. It was assumed that relatively liberal benefit regimes attracted applicants, so that restrictions would not only deter them, but also placate citizens who resented generous treatment of outsiders, and particularly of black and Asian applicants. Member states borrowed ideas about deterrence from each other, while becoming intermeshed within a framework of co-operation (Lavenex, 2001, p. 148) so that something like a European model emerged, consisting of dispersed accommodation, often in camps (pioneered in Sweden and Germany), in-kind assistance and fast-track procedures (introduced by France). At the same time, the EU authorities were seeking to harmonise asylum regulations, establish common standards for procedures and reception conditions, and determine which state was responsible for assessing applications (European Council, 1999).

The model of dispersal and camp-style accommodation resulted all over Europe in highly visible institutions, exposing asylum applicants to xenophobic attacks, especially when these were located in peripheral areas, with no traditions of ethnic minority settlements (Düvell, 1996; European Race Bulletin, 2000; Institute of Race Relations, 2000). Yet as long as asylum provided the only legal framework under which migrants could seek entry, the numbers of applications to EU member states remained high.

Another consequence of tighter controls was that they made irregular migration a relatively more attractive option. Estimates of the numbers of irregular entrants and those overstaying their permitted entries are inevitably vague and unconvincing. Sassen gave a figure of four to five million for the whole of the EU in 1993 (Sassen, 1996); more recent estimates are as high as eight million, which is comparable to the USA (Düvell, 2002). Another figure offered is that 500 000 enter the EU illegally each year, while it is acknowledged that there are 'practical difficulties in returning people to their countries' (European Commission, 2000, p. 13).

In Part II of this book, we use the UK as a case study for investigating the processes by which irregular migrants gain entry, survive undetected, and (in some cases) regularise and settle. The strategies employed by irregular migrants vary, in line with the rules and practices of immigration control authorities, and internal regulation systems. However, some features contribute strongly to the choice of destination, and to the ways in which migration is accomplished, irrespective of these particularities. The most important is the existence of informal networks, based on kinship and transnational communities, providing 'underground support structures' (Alt and Fodor, 2001). As we show in Part II, friends, relatives and associates played a key role, especially on entry and in the early part of irregular stays, even for rather individualistic migrants, who had little trust in fellow nationals (see pp. 116–27). Hence the existence of a core population from the migrants' countries of origin was an important precondition for these strategies.

Within the receiving countries, refugee and immigrant support organisations also play an important part in sustaining irregular migration. Within EU member states, many citizens actively oppose harsh treatment of asylum seekers from poorer countries, and the rules under which they are denied refugee status. In Germany, thousands of refused asylum seekers have been protected by churches (Just, 1993); in Italy, Centri Sociali provide shelter for large numbers, including many illegal immigrants. As we show in Chapter 6, the UK has a vibrant culture of grass-roots organisations, mainly focused around questions of asylum and racial discrimination. Although their policies are not geared to issues of irregular migration, their practitioners do offer advice and support to migrants who are in breach of immigration rules, as well as to asylum overstayers.

However, of at least equal importance were the changes that accompanied globalisation itself. In a social and economic environment in which mobility (including border crossings) is a taken-for-granted feature of everyday life, the opportunities for irregular migration increase. As we show in Chapter 5, a 'global city' like London provides a particularly favourable milieu for migrants willing to make themselves inconspicuously useful, and to blend into a cosmopolitan population. In such 'transnational social spaces' (Pries, 1996), a combination of shadow markets and informal support structures supply the means of survival, as migrants assimilate to minority groups and marginal citizens, often adopting the strategies of fellow outsiders within the host society.

As we illustrate in Chapter 3, some of these niches for irregular migrant labour were created by the policies through which EU member states sought to protect their citizens from the effects of globalisation. From the standpoint of transnational capital, systems for income redistribution, social housing and welfare services represent potential barriers to the adaptability (including mobility) of labour. Whereas Continental governments, and the EU itself, sought to preserve the core elements of the European social model, the logic of the single market pointed to the advantages of competition and deregulation, and demanded a workforce that was ready for these challenges.

In the late 1990s a plentiful supply of capital was in search of profitable investment opportunities in Europe, especially in the service sector (Bischoff, 1999; Huffschmid, 1999). Business lobbies began to demand a relaxation of labour recruitment regulations, both for high-tech occupations, and in certain kinds of unskilled work. In 1999, the General Agreement on Trade in Services (GATS) provided fresh impetus for importing labour for this sector, as a solution to an impasse over reducing both wages and non-labour costs, such as social insurance contributions (George and Gould, 2000; *The New York Times*, 4 September 2000). A minority of voices were already emphasising the benefits of immigration, even during the period of 'crisis' restrictions (Corry, 1996; Sassen, 1996). This change of direction is analysed in the next section.

FROM 'ZERO MIGRATION' TO MIGRATION MANAGEMENT

The announcement of this shift took place in 2000, in speeches by ministers in member states, and in Communications from the European Commission. In Germany it took the form of a 'Green Card' scheme for information technology experts; in Italy, the establishment of a Commission for the Integration of Foreigners; and in the UK, a series of speeches in which the Home Office minister, Barbara Roche, redefined 'economic migration'. As recently as the White Paper of 1998, this had been treated as synonymous with 'bogus' asylum seeking (Home Office, 1998, para 1.7). Here it was represented as an important element in a new, integrated global labour market, in which states must compete for the 'brightest and best' talents, in order to achieve economic dynamism.

> Many immigrants, from all over the world, have been very successful here, bringing economic benefits to Britain as a whole. ... The evidence shows that economically driven migration can bring substantial overall benefits both for growth and the economy (Roche, 2000, pp. 3–5).

For the European Commission, the task of bringing together policies for recruitment from outside the EU to meet labour shortages, the harmonisation of the asylum system and the control of irregular migration was a delicate one. Its Communication on 'A Concerted Strategy for Immigration and Asylum' accepted that 'immigration will continue and should be properly regulated, ... to maximise its positive effects on the Union, for migrants themselves and for the countries of origin' (European Commission, 2000, p. 3).

In the next chapter, we argue that this was an attempt to introduce greater flexibility into European labour markets, without losing the security and social cohesion provided by welfare provision for EU citizens. The sudden recognition of 'urgent needs for both skilled and unskilled workers', at a time when there were still some 18 million unemployed citizens of EU member states, signalled problems in the regulation and management of mobility. Immigration was redefined as part of the solution to these problems, but new management systems were designed to deal more toughly and effectively with irregular migration.

The main principles of the new approach had been agreed at the Tampere meeting of the European Council in autumn 1999 (European Council, 1999). The Commission accepted that 'immigration will continue and should be properly regulated' because 'migrants can make a positive contribution to the labour market, to economic growth and sustainability', and to meet labour shortages in agriculture, manufacturing and some business services (European Commission, 2000, p. 3).

the benefits of a more open and transparent policy on migration movements, together with the co-ordination of policies designed to reduce push factors in countries of origin and greater efforts to enforce labour legislation in the Member States, could also help reduce illegal immigration, in particular the worst forms of smuggling and trafficking. Member States will be in a better position to address the problems of irregular migration if they are equipped with a broad range of migration policies going beyond measures to curb the perceived or real misuse of their asylum systems (EC, 2000, p. 14).

The new approach to economic migration attempts to balance greater flexibility with a continuing need to regulate labour markets and protect citizens' wage levels and working conditions. On the one hand, the Communication recognised the need 'to respond quickly and efficiently to labour market requirements at national, regional and local level', and for 'greater mobility between Member States for incoming migrants' (p. 15).

EU legislation should therefore provide a *flexible* overall scheme based on a limited number of statuses designed so as to *facilitate* rather than create barriers to the admission of economic migrants. The aim should be to give a secure legal status for temporary workers who intend to return to their countries of origin, while at the same time providing a pathway eventually to a permanent status for those who wish to stay and who meet certain criteria (EC, 2000, pp. 17–18).

On the other hand, the Communication was concerned about 'the existence of a demand for clandestine manpower of the exploitation of such undocumented migrants' (p. 6), seeing this as 'fuelling unfair competition in the Union' (p. 14). Migration management should be seen as part of 'the development of economic and social policy for the EU', which included wages and working conditions. Hence the enforcement of both labour market regulations and border controls was an essential element of this system.

The attempt to develop a common immigration policy for the EU relied on the notion of assessing and agreeing upon 'the economic and demographic development of the Union and of the situation in the countries of origin' (EC, 2000, p. 5), as well as the integration of migrants, and effective measures against racism and xenophobia (p. 6). But these ambitious aims were to be achieved – as far as possible – by gaining the full advantages of free mobility and economic liberalisation within the Single Market. The management of migration was one instrument among others, such as 'modernising social protection systems', developing the services sector and increasing raising the employment rate among EU citizens:

In Lisbon the Council set a new strategic goal for the EU for the next decade namely that it should become the most competitive and dynamic knowledge-based economy able to sustain economic growth and create more and better jobs with greater social cohesion. ... In fact, the ability of different countries and regions in the EU to compensate for demographic effects and to mobilise unused labour resources varies considerably and immigration, therefore, will have a contribution to make in offsetting these problems in some countries as an element in the overall strategy to promote growth and reduce unemployment. While procedures are already in place at EU level to co-ordinate the free movement of goods, capital, services and EU workers and other citizens, sufficient attention has not yet been given to he role of third country nationals in the EU labour market (European Commission, 2000, p. 26).

RESISTING IRREGULAR MIGRATION

The concept of managed migration in the common EU strategy (closely mirrored, with some variations, in the policies of the largest member states) was located within the notion of 'an area of freedom, security and justice' in the EU. This phrase, derived from the Treaty of Amsterdam of 1997, was constantly repeated in the policy documents, and especially in the justification of measures to deter, prevent and combat irregular migration. However, it is difficult to see how freedom, security and justice can be fenced off in a single political space, when the whole logic of global markets is to promote mobility, and unleash the forces of 'creative destruction' (Schumpeter, 1942) on the world's weaker economies.

The phenomenon of increased migratory pressures, in the form of both asylum seeking and irregular migration to the EU, was a dim reflection of those events in the most distant corners of the earth. As globalisation gathered pace, movements of people became elements in the economic strategies of states as well as individuals. By the late 1980s, the total value of international remittances (estimated at US$60.9 billion in 1989) was second only to trade in crude oil, as migrants sent parts of their earnings home (Collinson, 1994, p. 4). Some developing countries began to specialise in exporting labour; between 1975 and 1987, over three million citizens of the Philippines worked abroad, representing some 5 per cent of the population (Asian Regional Programme on International Labour Migration, 1990). Nearer to Europe, Turkey and the North African countries, which had made bilateral labour recruitment agreements with Germany and France in the 1960s, reached such agreements with the oil-rich gulf states in the 1970s and 1980s (Collinson, 1994, ch. 5). Over two-thirds of the world's labour migration occurred within systems in sub-Saharan Africa, the Middle East and South-east Asia (OECD, 1992).

The European Commission's Communication 'On a Common Policy on Illegal Immigration' acknowledged the need for 'the promotion of peace, political stability, human rights, democratic principles and sustainable economic, social and environmental development of the countries of origin'

(European Commission, 2001a, p. 6). However, this was the only sentence on this topic; the rest of the Communication dealt in detailed measures to restrict unauthorised entry and overstaying, while fulfilling obligations to protect those 'genuinely in need' of humanitarian protection.

The EU was able to exert some influence on migration process through its relations with those post-communist countries applying for membership. Since the Central European applicant states have been transit countries for much irregular migration (as well as being sending countries themselves), the adoption of EU rules on combating illegal immigration could be made a condition for early accession in the first wave of enlargement. The Communication added that 'the candidate countries are also required to produce detailed national Action Plans for implementation of the Schengen acquis' (European Commission, 2001a, p. 9).

Enforcement of the legal framework against irregular migration, and adequate sanctions against trafficking and smuggling, were also seen as essential elements in the strategy. Common penalties for trafficking of at least eight years' imprisonment were specified. However, the Communication also mentioned 'employers of illegal residents' as targets for sanctions. As we show in Chapter 7, present enforcement and prosecution in member states is far from uniform, with the UK giving low priority to action against this group.

The Communication acknowledged that there was no way of assessing 'the exact proportions between the different categories of illegal residents' – those who enter through the actions of 'organised facilitators', and those who enter with valid travel documents for a short-term stay, and then either overstay, or work in breach of entry conditions. 'It seems clear, however, that each one represents a significant part of the whole phenomenon of illegal immigration and that any future action needs adequately to address each category' (European Commission, 2001a, p. 7).

In practice, the measures proposed focused almost entirely on the issues of trafficking, smuggling, clandestine and fraudulent entry, as problems of policing and border security. Proposals for new measures of information exchange (CIREFI), a European migration observatory to monitor migratory flows, an early warning system (EWS) on facilitator networks, and even the development of a European Border Guard, with its own system of training, first within a police school (CEPOL), and eventually a European Border Guard School, all reflected this emphasis.

Indeed, in all its relationships with the wider world, the priority of restricting irregular migration enters the EU's agreements, treaties and conventions. As a party to the G8 Stability Pact for the Balkans, it stipulates illegal immigration as one of the elements (European Commission, 2001b). And even for the Stability Pact for South-east Europe, for those not joining the EU it claims a 'decisive role ... in particular on issues of human trafficking, illegal migration and border control' (European Council, 2000). The topic was included in the Barcelona Declaration with the North African countries (Statewatch Bulletin, 1996), and in the Lome V Convention with the 77 African, Caribbean and Pacific states. Some 300 EU member state police officers are employed outside their national borders, half of them outside the EU, and some as far away as Moscow or Bangkok (European Commission, 2001c).

CONCLUSIONS

In an integrated world economy, governments – like individuals – must find new strategies for pursuing their interests. In joining together as the EU, member states sought to gain some of the advantages of free movement within a single market, while protecting their citizens from the adverse impacts of global economic forces. Migration was for almost 30 years seen as one of those negative factors – the threat of competing away the protected wages and conditions of European workers, and of crowding and degrading their welfare and environmental systems. In the new international division of labour, the EU sought to establish itself as a region of capital-intensive industrial production, financial and business services, with a high-quality collective infrastructure of public amenities.

However, the logic of such a strategy does not point unambiguously to a certain set of policy measures, nor is the context for decisions stable and constant. The break-up of the former Soviet bloc presented a whole range of new issues, while fundamentally changing the range of options. The strategy of allowing former communist countries to join the Union now involves far greater challenges of membership and inclusion than previous enlargements, and the new common approach to migration is in part a reflection of the rethinking that is taking place around this major structural shift.

As it became more difficult to protect their citizens' living standards and their social infrastructures, states had varying reasons for entering the EU. In the case of Scandinavian countries like Sweden and Finland, accession to the single market allowed them to open their economies to more competition, and their governments to justify less spending on social protection (Fernandes, 1999). For the Southern European states like Spain, Portugal and Greece, the EU Structural and Cohesion Funds helped them to establish more generous welfare provision. In rather the same way, inward migration could be deployed as part of an overall strategy in face of globalisation, leaving member states enough discretion over how to channel it in relation to their particular versions of these common issues.

In this sense, migration pressures could represent an opportunity for the EU to discover institutions for turning a source of potential conflict and threat into one of dynamism and development. It has been argued that one strength of European polities has been their capacity to find ways of harnessing the antagonisms and tensions generated by capitalism through systems of modernisation and reform (Negri, 1984). Keynesian economic management systems were eventually able to do this in relation to class conflicts after the Second World War (Tronti, 1966). From this perspective, globalisation has transformed class conflicts into even larger-scale struggles involving populations in the developed and the developing worlds. Perhaps the emergence of a global migration regime might allow some such process, rather in the way that the USA's economic dynamism was fuelled by labour migration from Europe in the late nineteenth and early twentieth centuries (Hoerder, 1985).

The attempt to establish some such regime has indeed been signalled by a number of initiatives, by the World Trade Organisation (WTO), the North American Free Trade Area (NAFTA) and in Australasia (Hollifield, 1998). The EU's most recent policy innovations on migration can be seen as part of such a proactive process, in parallel to measures by the International Monetary Fund (IMF) and World Bank for restructuring and steering global capitalism (Hirsch, 2001). However, it is still far from clear whether such a regime has been successful. Intensification of efforts to combat irregular migration, and now the 'war against global terrorism', signal that the poor countries' mass movements to resist inequality and injustice, and the antagonisms associated with the regime itself, are not easily suppressed.

Straubhaar (2000) argues that there should be an international General Agreement on Movements of People, because 'global games need global rules'. It would be founded on the idea that free international movement of people is beneficial for both countries of origin and those of destination, and hence would promote free entry and exit of migrants. However, it would also seek to deal with the externalities and market failures associated with cross-border movements of people in an equitable way (Straubhaar, 2000, p. 29). This is further discussed in Chapter 10 (p. 251).

Interactions between emerging migration management systems and irregular migrants are inherently difficult to study and analyse. This chapter has introduced the broad outlines of the new EU common policies, but their interpretation varies in each member state. For example, in Germany the announcement of a Green Card system for foreign IT workers, and of a new independent immigration commission, has been accompanied by the publication of a restrictive bill to regulate other aspects of migration. The latter adversely affects asylum seekers' access to welfare benefits, appeals and permissions to work, and abolishes the concessions through the 'Dulding' or 'Tolerance' status of those served with deportation orders that could not be executed, numbering 250 000 to 350 000 people. This could drive many of these into illegality. The contradictory effects of the rapid changes in rules and their implementation, and the variations between member states' inter-pretations of the common policies, make for problems in assessing the impact of the new measures. It also makes for inconsistencies and injustices, and often, also for unintended consequences, which Straubhaar's proposal of an international regime would aim to reduce.

Our approach is to look first in more detail at the issues on labour markets and social protection that confront member state governments, and how migration policy and irregular migration influence reform programmes. This is the subject of the next chapter. In Part II, we turn to the UK as a case study in the impact of irregular migration, and in Part III to an analysis of how public policy deals with it.

3. Irregular migration, labour markets and social protection

So far we have analysed migration mainly as the interaction between relatively poor and oppressed populations of developing and post-communist countries, and governments of relatively rich and free ones. However, migration and its management must also be understood in terms of interactions between owners of capital and those who supply the labour used in production, with governments setting the rules under which these take place. Mobility is again a key element in the power relations that shape these interactions and these rules.

In an integrated world economy, having the freedom to move is a key advantage in power relations, and having the access to mobility is an important determinant of status. *Power* consists in imposing one's choices on others; power is institutionalised when the rules of competition allow one to restrict the range of choices open to others (Lukes, 1974). Mobility allows capital to hold over labour the constant threat that it will withdraw, and go elsewhere in search of profit (Cohen, 1995). This, in turn, enables capital, through the rules imposed by governments, to regulate and channel the mobility options open to workers. Labour markets have been made more 'flexible' in line with capital's requirements, as the restrictions on the opportunities of the many are tightened, giving more freedom to the mobile few (Bauman, 1998, pp. 69–73).

As full-time industrial employment for men in the First World countries has declined, and service employment has expanded, employers have drawn on supplies of part-time female labour, and have developed new strategies for the creation of a peripheral workforce of the occasionally semi-employed. At the same time as immigrants have supplied many of the workers in this latter section (Wrench, Rea and Ouali, 1999), recruitment from outside the First World has allowed an expandable workforce, growing or shrinking according to demand conditions. In this way, migration becomes an element in the 'flexibility' of labour markets, and is shaped by employers' requirements, rather than the choices of workers.

All these developments, in turn, give rise to niches for irregular migration that arise partly as a result of new social relations among indigenous populations (such as the need for domestic workers in two-earner households); and partly because of the unintended consequences of government systems for creating flexibility in the supply of indigenous labour (such as benefits systems and training schemes). Irregular migrants move in to take advantage of these opportunities, and are able to do so partly because they are more mobile than indigenous workers and have lower housing costs (Breuer, Faist and Jordan, 1996).

Neoclassical economic theory of production purports to show how workers' skills are allocated to their most productive uses. In each firm or industry, the extra revenue from hiring the last worker employed should be equal to the costs of his or her wages, and wherever this is not the case, workers should move to other jobs until it is. In this way, an equilibrium should be reached where the level of wages would balance the number of hours offered by workers with the work required by employers, and there would be no voluntary unemployment.

In this branch of economics, potential workers are treated as deciding how many hours of work to offer employers at a given wage by choosing between the utility of earnings and that of 'leisure'. But 'leisure' includes the whole range of activities for which no wage is paid – everything from sitting at home trading on the stock market through the Internet to looking after a frail elderly relative. Households with heavy responsibilities for unpaid caring – sick or disabled relatives, or several children – are relatively immobile. Women, who do most of this unpaid work, are less mobile than men. Strong ties with a community or kinship network, where unpaid mutual help is given, also limit mobility.

Between the early 1970s and the end of the century, there were few shortages of skilled or unskilled male industrial workers in the rich First World countries. As corporations shifted their labour-intensive production to the newly industrialising states, and redundancies in traditional industries grew, governments were required to find some balance between activation, retraining schemes and unemployment benefits, and to finance these out of social insurance contributions rather than direct taxation (Scharpf, 1999). In Europe, the wages and conditions of the remaining workers were protected; in the USA average earnings of 'non-supervisory' workers fell – from $8.40 an hour in 1978 to $7.66 in 1997, at constant prices (Luttwak, 1999, pp. 95–6).

European governments gave relatively generous unemployment benefits, and provided fairly high-quality retraining schemes. In this way, the rules still encouraged employers to pay 'efficiency wages' to their remaining staff, reflecting the value of the best of them, whom the firm wished to retain. This extra wage, paid to keep 'insiders' in, created a barrier to 'outsiders' not in work – but their social insurance unemployment benefits reduced their incentives to try to compete wages down (Solow, 1990). In the USA, less protection for those outside the labour market meant more competition, and lower wages.

In the service sectors of these economies, firms sought to create a 'secondary labour market', made up of married women, older workers, younger people and members of ethnic minorities, most of whom were not the main earners in their households. Here again, where employers were able to persuade governments to change the rules so as to give greater incentives for these kinds of employment contracts, or to drive such people into paid work, service employment grew rapidly – as in the USA, UK and Australasia throughout this period, and in some European countries, such as the Netherlands and Denmark, in the 1990s. But where governments continued to uphold the traditional division of labour in households, and to discourage married women from paid work – as in Germany especially – service employment grew much more slowly (Esping-Andersen, 1990, 1996, 1999).

Irregular migrants found spaces for work within both these types of labour market. In the relatively 'rigid', high-wage and regulated employment markets of the European countries, there were opportunities for those willing to enter the informal economy of small manufacturing companies, petty trading, seasonal work and hidden, behind-the-scenes tasks, such as domestic cleaning. In this way, they remedied some of the 'inflexibility' that neoclassical critics condemned in these systems (Garson, 2000). In these economies, the incentive to hire irregular migrant workes were greater for employers, facing high minimum wages and social insurance contributions (Tapinos, 2000). In the more fluid, less-regulated labour markets of the USA and UK, irregular migrants could quite easily evade internal controls, which were rather thinly spread and little enforced, and take their place among the fragmented and casualised employees of the secondary labour market, self-employment and the service sector.

LABOUR-MARKET REGULATION: FLEXIBILITY AND MOBILITY

The labour-market policies of First World governments – including the recent policies on immigration and recruitment discussed in Chapter 2 – can therefore be seen as responses to the implicit or explicit threats of mobile international capital, and the opportunities for attracting investment in competition with other states and regions. In Continental Europe, where capital was one of the 'social partners', along with organised labour, in corporatist arrangements over macroeconomic decisions, 'flexibility' was balanced by protection of living standards, but at a price, in terms of high unemployment. In the USA, UK and Australasia, governments pursued strategies aimed at subsidising or improving incentives for low-paid, part-time work, and driving claimants into accepting it (Jordan, 1998, chs. 2, 3).

Especially in the latter countries, these policies tried to encourage workers to move to where employment was available; but often this work was on less favourable terms than their previous employments. In this sense, governments channelled mobility, emphasising self-responsibility and the need to adapt to the new economic environment. It was often a kind of forced (or at least unchosen) mobility of the dispossessed, from regions where better-paid jobs and the prospect of such jobs had disappeared, to the uncertainty of new, often temporary and insecure employments elsewhere. This kind of mobility was conducted in parallel with the ones promoted by residential polarisation, and the redesign of the public infrastructure discussed in Chapter 1. Local authorities and regions attempted to attract capital investments, to match their provision of infrastructural and collective services, in an overall environment of greater mobility. Public choice theorists argued that the mobility of workers under 'fiscal federalism' (see pp. 27–8) operated as a hedge against regional recessions, making both private and public schemes for unemployment insurance redundant (Wildasin, 1995; Devillanova, 2001).

The goals of labour-market policy have shifted through both competition and comparison. Policy has evolved through comparing the performance of national and regional labour markets in these regimes, and attempting to emulate the success of those countries that seem to have adapted best to new global economic conditions. In this search for supply-side solutions, in terms of training, motivation, flexibility and incentives, the goals of 'full employment' and an adequate 'family wage' for male breadwinners have gradually been replaced by ones of 'almost full part-time employment' (Hemerijck, 2001, p. 189), and increased participation by women in all but a few countries.

Neoclassical economists have focused their critical attention on the systems through which governments tried to maintain the earnings of employees and the incomes of those outside the labour market, especially minimum wages, and the rates, the terms and conditions, and the duration of unemployment, sickness and disability benefits. They have also been concerned with the activities of trade unions in protecting their members' interests, and the strategies of those politicians, bureaucrats and professionals with stakes in the public sector, and interests in sustaining high levels of employment and job security in public services (Minford, 1991).

In the mid-1990s labour-market economists drew attention to structural differences between regions of the global economy. In Continental Europe, with high rates of unionisation of labour, well-regulated working conditions and job security, short working hours and high replacement rates of social security benefits, unemployment rates were high and rates of economic growth low. In the USA, with less unionisation, longer working hours, lower social security contributions and benefits and lower costs for employers in hiring and firing workers, both job creation and economic growth were currently faster, though inequalities of earnings greater. Japan, with rates of unionisation and social security contributions even lower than the USA, greater job security and even longer working hours for workers in the major enterprises, unemployment rates were lower still; at that time, growth remained healthy (Tachibanaki, 1994, pp. 2–3). They drew the conclusion that it was the *flexibility* of US and Japanese labour markets (the USA through wage differentials and easier hiring and firing, Japan through the operation of a secondary labour market in smaller firms, but both because of limited social security systems) that led to lower unemployment and faster growth. Although there were some differences in mobility between global regions – with US workers most mobile, especially geographically, and Japanese least – this was not considered the crucial factor. The leading authorities of this school of thought argued from a comparison of the OECD countries:

> Our broad empirical conclusions indicate, first, that the levels of unemployment and size of the unemployment response to shocks depends on the structure of the unemployment benefit system and the mechanism of wage determination. Second, the persistence of unemployment depends again on the benefit and wage determination systems, and also on the degree of employment flexibility (Layard and Nickell, 1994, p. 284)

Hence, the problem to be addressed was that of 'Eurosclerosis' – the over-regulation of the European economies, the over-generosity of their welfare systems, and the excessive costs of social insurance contributions, all of which made these countries' economies less dynamic, and their labour markets less suitable environments for the creation of new jobs. But by the later 1990s two other issues strongly influenced the policy debate. On the one hand, it became apparent that, even in a labour market that was allowing new employment to be created, and drawing new workers into these posts, there were many households with no working members. The UK was a clear example of this; in 1997 some 20 per cent of households headed by a person of working age contained no member in employment (DSS, 1998, p. 7). Linked to this was the informal economy of economic activity not recorded in official statistics, and especially the part of it which attracted claimants of benefits. This shadow work and benefit fraud had come to be seen as a response to problems of incentives and barriers for entry to the formal labour market (DSS, 1998, ch. 9).

The case of the UK was striking, because in other respects it differed from the Continental European regime, and its labour market functioned well in terms of the new policy objectives. Overall employment, at 28 million, reached a record high in 2000, and participation rates were among the highest in the world – at 75 per cent, compared with an EU average rate of 64 per cent. Over 20 per cent of employees changed their jobs (though not necessarily their employers) in any year (DfEE, 2001). Yet, despite all this – including the flagship New Deal programme, under which the New Labour government trained and activated beneficiaries – there were still just under a million unemployed claimants, and another four million work-ing-age claimants of benefits for sick and disabled people, or lone parents (DSS, 2001).

In UK labour-market policy, issues of mobility were therefore subsumed under issues of flexibility during the 1990s. The task was defined as drawing citizens out of 'inactive' roles – either in the unpaid household and commu-nity economies, or as benefits claimants – and out of the informal economy of shadow work, into formal, paid employment. The issues at stake were identified as those of wage differentials and income inequalities, incentives ('making work pay'), and barriers to employment (including those arising from the structures and conditions of benefits).

Each of these issues, however, contained disguised problems of mobility, both between employments and between locations. These began to emerge at the beginning of the new century. In particular, skills' shortages in particular occupations appeared, and triggered the reappraisal of immigration policies that was discussed in the previous chapter. But of course they also related to irregular migration, because shadow labour markets, employing foreigners without proper status, supplied many of the demands for mobile and adapt-able workers, especially in unskilled work. In the rest of this chapter, we show how within each of the concerns of labour-market policy there are important issues about the deployment of undocumented immigrant workers. This allows us to illustrate the relevance of our case studies of Brazilian, Polish and Turkish undocumented workers in London, which form the sub-stance of Part II of the book.

INEQUALITY OF EARNINGS

Inequality of earnings (or 'wage differentiation' as it is politely known in labour-market economics) varies between national labour markets and over time. For example, the corporatist systems of economic management estab-lished in the Scandinavian countries followed policies for equality of earnings of industrial workers (mostly men) and public sector staff (mostly women). France, Germany and other European countries had somewhat similar sys-tems, but did not use them to implement such policies. The USA and the UK both relied more on markets and the collective bargaining of trade unions to determine wages, but those of the UK moved in the direction of greater equality of earnings up to the 1970s, faster than those of the USA.

If equality of earnings is measured in terms of the ratio of the gross wages of a worker in the bottom decile of earners relative to the worker at the median, Sweden (76 per cent in 1979) was the most equal of the OECD countries, followed by Denmark (71 per cent). Germany stood at 60 per cent, the UK 60 per cent and the USA 54 per cent. But between 1980 and 1989, Swedish and Danish earnings became only 1 per cent less equal, while the UK's became 4 per cent and the USA's 5 per cent less equal. In Germany, equality *increased* by 4 per cent in that period (Iversen and Wren, 1998, Table 2, p. 518).

These changes were connected with shifts between sectors of employment, between regions of economies, and the decline in male and rise in female participation. In the UK, and especially in the USA, there was a large rise in private service employment – but not in those other countries. The special features of service employment will be discussed in the next section. Those countries with the highest ratios of inequality of earnings also had the largest expansions of private service employment (Iversen and Wren, 1998, pp. 522–3).

Studies in the USA have shown that, in the absence of active policies to equalise earnings, wages can fluctuate quite considerably between regions of the same economy. For instance, during the US 'jobs' miracle' of the 1980s, in the booming New England region average wages of men increased by 17 per cent, while in the 'rustbelt' Midwest they fell by about 8 per cent (Juhn, Murphy and Topel, 1991). This reflected changes in demand for certain skills; the growth of information-based production in New England raised demand for workers with these aptitudes, while the decline in production of manufactured goods in the Midwest depressed demand for male industrial workers. However, it also indicated that the supply of workers could influence regional earnings significantly. At this time, both the supply of women entering the labour market (often to supplement or substitute for falling male earnings), and the supply of immigrant labour were relevant for changes in earnings inequality in the USA.

With the shift from manufacturing to information-based production nationally, the earnings of better educated and more skilled workers were raised relative to those of less skilled in all regions of the US economy. However, the decline in less-skilled workers' wages varied between regions. In New England, the wages of less-skilled men fell by 10 per cent, but those of less-skilled men in the West (Pacific) region fell by 19 points. Topel (1994) concludes that '*if women's participation had not changed there would have been no decline in the relative wages of less skilled men*' (p. 125, emphasis in the original). This was because, as production methods changed, employers preferred to hire the women who were entering the labour market in large numbers at the time, rather than men who were being made redundant from declining industries. This substitution did not occur in highly skilled work, and in fact many highly educated and skilled women were employed in low-skilled jobs, because employers could choose them in preference over less educated and skilled men.

Although studies of US cities indicated little effect of immigration rates on wage levels (Altonji and Card, 1991; Borjas, 1987, 1990), Topel found that in the West 'the largest decline in relative wages of less skilled men appears to be closely linked to an increase in labour supply of less skilled workers, which is driven by new immigration' (1994, p. 121). He found that Hispanic and Asian immigrants increased the pool of less-skilled workers most in the West, and his econometric modelling of the effects on relative wage rates in the US regimes concluded that these immigrants 'account for the greater increase in wage inequality in the West than in other regions' (p. 124).

Furthermore, what has to be explained is the *overall, absolute decline* in wages in non-supervisory employment in the USA between the early 1970s and the late 1990s (Brenner, 1998; Luttwak, 1999). Household incomes in this period rose by no more than a few percentage points at constant prices, and then only because more partners were working (Madrick, 1997). Given that immigration to the USA was at a high level in this period, and far higher than that of the EU, it looks as if it contributed to this process.

This should not be seen as surprising, or as contradicting the general rule that migration has economic benefits. It has long been recognised that some of the indigenous population will have interests that are complementary to those of immigrants, while others will have interests which conflict, for instance because migrants supply substitute labour. What was unusual about the US case in this period was that both women and immigrants were providing substitutes for men, across a broad range of manual and clerical occupations, so it was only holders of capital, and those in managerial jobs, who benefited from these shifts.

This suggestion appears to be at odds with other evidence about the basis for the US 'jobs' miracle' in the 1980s. Others have demonstrated that immigrants from Latin America and Asia 'brought their jobs with them'; they set up small businesses, often supplying niche markets for consumers from their own minority groups. Hence, 'the creation of 25 million jobs in the USA over a period with little if any net job creation in Western Europe from 1972 to 1986 is inexplicable without this supply-side contribution of the migrants. ... This can either be as entrepreneurs and workers in the very bottom tiered subcontractors of, for example, the garment industry, or in small commercial shops in the ghetto and elsewhere' (Lasch, 1994, p. 163). But of course this does not contradict Topel's findings. Such firms are likely to pay very low wages by US standards, and those immigrants who do not work in such enterprises are available for recruitment by indigenous companies.

Part of the explanation of the success of small immigrant businesses in the USA and the UK has been their merging of household and commercial production, kinship and commercial relationships, which enables them to compete with indigenous producers on more favourable terms. In the USA, for Asian and Hispanic families 'work is based on a pre-modern family structure, in which women typically do unpaid work in the (informalised) public sphere' (Lasch, 1994, p. 163). We found echoes of this in our study of undocumented workers from Turkey in north and east London. Turkish-owned coffee shops, kebab outlets and cafés, as well as small textile factories, used family members and recruited kin from Turkey, often mixing together unpaid household labour, formal employment and the informal employment of workers without proper immigration status (Düvell and Jordan, 1999).

This link between immigrant entrepreneurs and workers, and the blurring of the distinction between formal and informal economic activity, is an important part of our investigation in Part II of this book. It has already attracted considerable scholarly attention, starting with the studies of informal activity that sprang from Portes and Sassen-Koob's (1987) work. They pointed out that economic activities that escape legal regulation, such as the taxation system and the benefit rules, are not simply the resort of poor and marginal people seeking survival, but constitute a characteristic sector of an advanced industrial economy. Workers in this sector are not necessarily worse paid than those in formal employment. Immigrant entrepreneurs and workers find places in their host countries' informal sectors; they do not bring such activities, or all the cultural practices associated with them, from less-developed economies.

Saskia Sassen (1991) has argued that the informal production associated with immigrants is characteristic of 'global cities', with concentrations of headquarters of international companies and finance houses, and of administrative and professional activities. As manufacturing becomes more capital-intensive, and the earnings of skilled employees rise, all these post-industrial developments require servicing by flexible but low-skilled workers, and this increases the demand for goods and services from the informal economy of shadow activity – including sweatshops using undocumented immigrant workers, and cleaners and nannies without proper immigration status. This explanation of how immigration is linked with both 'informalisation' and greater inequality of earnings is echoed in studies of unemployment among immigrants, who become trapped in the informal economy because there are fewer manual and semi-skilled jobs which can be stepping stones into formal employment. Kasarda, Friedrichs and Ehlers (1992) compared US and German cities, and found that this process was related to post-industrial development. Local studies in large cosmopolitan cities add evidence to this view. In one district of Amsterdam, Bijlmer, with a high concentration of unemployed immigrants, Van de Bunt (1992) found a flourishing informal economy, with 100 illegal taxi drivers, 200 (Afro) hairdressers, 150 car mechanics, 20 handymen, 35 caterers and many other contract clothing workers and other 'odd-jobbers'. Other studies (Rath, 1999) revealed an almost perfect match between the 80 Turkish garment manufacturers' numbers of employees (Tap, 1993) and the number of people of Turkish origin registered as unemployed in the early 1980s in that city (Bloeme and van Geuns, 1987). Although Amsterdam is not a 'global city' in Sassen's sense – it is far smaller than London, New York or Tokyo – it does have some of the characteristics of post-industrialisation and cosmopolitanism.

The garment industry can be taken as an instance of the complexities of these processes. In many advanced industrialised economies, both production and employment in this industry declined dramatically in the 1980s, as manufacturing was relocated in factories in the newly industrialising countries (Scheffer, 1992). However, firms that designed and marketed products contracted out work to small specialist enterprises, geared to producing in small quantities for the rapidly changing fashion market. Between 1981 and 1986 in the Netherlands, the share of Turkish contracting companies in the industry rose from 25 to 72 per cent (Tap, 1993). Rath (1999, p. 130) reviews the coverage of these developments in the reports of the Board for the Garments Industry and in the Dutch Parliament, where estimates of irregular migrants employed in '1000 illegal sweatshops' were around 12 000 to 14 000 workers, or up to 43 per cent of the total workforce in the garment industry in the country. In Amsterdam, such estimates by the tax and labour relations' inspectorates were of up to 600 sweatshops and 10 000 workers in 1994 (Rath, 1999, p. 131).

Descriptions of such sweatshops emphasise their pre-industrial features, derived from Turkish workshop systems (White, 1994) – their use of cultural capital, in household labour practices, kin and communal networks (Bovenkerk, 1982). These features may give them advantages in competition with other kinds of firms. However, they operate under conditions of great insecurity, with constant shifts in demand, as well as in their costs. Bloeme and van Geuns (1987) estimated that in Amsterdam the average lifespan of 'sweatshops' was less than a year, with 41 per cent closing within six months. Our researches in London showed that such enterprises not only recruited undocumented labour through kinship and communal links in Turkey, but also shifted production between Turkey and London very rapidly, according to market prices, labour costs and contractual conditions. In other words, they represent an example of the rapid mobility of both capital and labour, as well as the blurred boundaries between the formal and the informal economies (Portes, 1998).

As we show in Part II of the book, none of this can be adequately analysed without reference to the host society's systems for labour-market regulation, immigration control and social protection. Decisions by entrepreneurs about the location of production and the wages offered, and by immigrant workers about their choice of destination and to whom to supply their labour, are all deeply influenced by these considerations. Whether this informal economy substitutes for potential indigenous production, employing citizens who are currently unemployed or being trained at public expense for other occupations, and whether it provides a bridge for immigrants into the host economy and society, are related to those institutional features of the host environment (Rath, 1999).

Inequality of earnings contributes to the growth of informal production and exchange, as well as being fed by it. In the UK, the fall in relative (and in some cases absolute) wages of unskilled workers and the decline in secure, long- and full-time employment in manufacturing, construction, mining and the utilities, have contributed to the casualisation of much unskilled work (Jordan, 1995, 1996). During the 1990s, there was evidence of extensive informal economic activity by claimants of social assistance benefits (Evason and Woods, 1995; Rowlingson *et al.*, 1997), side by side with 'moonlighting' by regular workers (Jordan *et al.*, 1992; MacDonald, 1994; Jordan and Travers, 1997). Immigrant enterprises and workers may add a twist to this vicious circle of work casualisation, and the depression of wages, but they do not initiate it. The actual shape of their economic relations, with fellow immigrants and with the host economy, is strongly influenced by wages and conditions at the lower end of the host economy's labour market, and its informal, shadow sector. This is illustrated in Part II.

SERVICE EMPLOYMENT, WOMEN'S PARTICIPATION AND UNDOCUMENTED WORK

Present-day policies for 'well-functioning labour markets' in the advanced industrialised countries must take account of an issue that was only indirectly addressed by postwar welfare states and Keynesian economic policies. The 'breadwinner-housewife' model of household relations, which formed the background assumption for these institutions outside the Scandinavian countries (Lewis, 1992), sought to improve the earnings and working conditions of male workers, and especially male industrial workers, as the basis for raising standards of living in the economy as a whole. Men were taken to be the earners of a 'family wage', which not only provided for their partners and children, but also supplied their entitlements for their incomes when they were outside the labour market (because they were unemployed, injured, sick or retired) through social insurance contributions. Industrial (and especially manufacturing) jobs for men had, since the UK's Industrial Revolution in the early nineteenth century, been expanding as a proportion of all employment in these economies, and were seen as providing the most reliable basis for the continuation of the economic growth that characterised the postwar period. The service sector was seen as supporting industry, and its employment levels as largely determined by the performance of the industrial sector. Women, in turn, were perceived at most as secondary earners of household income, and the structure of labour-market regulation, trade union representation and social protection reflected these priorities, in many ways protecting male employees from what was seen as potentially damaging competition from women workers, and providing them with income and services for their unpaid domestic and child care roles.

Industrial employment of men has declined as a proportion of all employment in all the OECD countries since the early 1970s, and in absolute terms in all except the USA since then. Hence the focus of labour-market policies has gradually shifted towards the service sector, and towards the employment of women. By the early 1990s, policy analysts were commenting on the very different performances of national labour markets in relation to these factors. For example, the liberal Anglo-Saxon regimes of the USA, the UK, Australia, New Zealand and Canada had fast-expanding private service sectors, and fairly high and growing participation rates of women; the Continental, predominantly Christian Democratic regimes of Western Europe had much smaller and slower-growing public and private service sectors, and lower rates of women's participation; and the Scandinavian social democratic regimes had large public sector services and the highest rates of participation by women (Esping-Andersen, 1990). By the end of the 1990s, these features were being linked with overall economic performance. The liberal, Anglo-Saxon countries were seen as having flexible labour markets, and hence lower unemployment rates, the Continental European countries as suffering from rigidities that contributed to high unemployment, and the Scandinavian countries as having possibly unsustainable tax and social protection regimes and levels of public service employment (Esping-Andersen, 1996).

However, these categories and connections were by no means straightforward. On a country-by-country basis, for example, the performance of the European economies did not produce a simple correlation between less regulation of labour markets, more expansion of private sector services and women's employment, and low unemployment rates. For instance, Austria in the late 1990s still had the second lowest unemployment rate in the EU (4.5 per cent of the total labour force in 1997), despite its regulated labour market, on the German model (Marterbauer and Walterskirchen, 1999). Furthermore, two-thirds of its job growth in the previous ten years had come through public sector employment. Both Denmark and the Netherlands had achieved considerable employment growth since the early 1980s, and had reduced their unemployment rates, against the trends in their Scandinavian and West European neighbours; but only in the Netherlands was this associated with increased labour-market participation by women (Hemerijck, 2001, pp. 152–5). Hence, we must look in more detail at the dynamic of service sector growth, and the processes by which women become more active in the labour market, before exploring the ways in which undocumented work by immigrants has influenced and been influenced by these changes.

The service sector is extremely diverse, consisting of some high-paid jobs in financial and business services; a middle range of educational, health and social services, some of which are professional in nature, others relatively unskilled and labour-intensive (such as the care of frail elderly and disabled people); and a very heterogeneous group of distributional, leisure and domestic services. This last category, in which employment has been fastest-expanding in most advanced economies, presents a particular problem. There are serious technological limits to the potential improvement of the productivity of workers in tasks like cleaning, catering, retailing, hairdressing and gardening; it has not been possible to raise output per worker significantly by new machinery, so these activities have remained labour-intensive. This is even more obviously the case for personal care, including the care of people needing help in everyday tasks because of illness or disability. Hence, wages must tend to fall, relative to those in occupations where new technology can improve productivity, and which are hence more capital intensive. Although demand for these and other services has increased more rapidly than demand for manufactured goods, the net effect is to intensify the economic pressures leading to greater inequality of earnings (Iversen and Wren, 1998, pp. 509–12).

One way in which employers can achieve greater efficiency in the production of labour-intensive services is through the organisation of the work process. This can be done partly by having a larger periphery of part-time workers, whose shifts are staggered so as to provide for more intensive activities at certain periods in the day or night, and partly by hiring short-term workers from employment agencies, in line with fluctuations in demand. These trends are reinforced on the demand side by consumers' expectations of greater convenience of access and service use – for instance, longer opening hours of shops, bars and restaurants, or the availability of care assistance in the evenings and at weekends. All these factors have contributed to employment patterns that have included a marked growth in part-time jobs, taken mainly by women (Hemerijck, 2001, pp. 155–7). Women's part-time hourly wages have been lower than men's full-time wages in the same occupations and industries.

From the perspective of government, the decision about whether or not to facilitate these processes was quite complex. Under neo-liberal administrations in the 1980s and early 1990s, both the USA and the UK did pursue polices to deregulate labour markets, privatise public services, weaken the influence of trade unions and allow earnings inequality to grow. For households with two partners, women's employment allowed rising earnings where the men's was secure and well paid, and income to be maintained when the men's earnings were low or falling; the two-earner household became the norm, and the incomes of these households rose steadily, even though women's pay lagged behind men's. In the Scandinavian countries, women's employment was already high, relatively well paid, and mainly in public services; only Denmark was able to achieve a significant shift towards private service expansion and overall employment growth. In Western Europe, policies and performance were more varied, with France and Germany sacrificing employment growth for the maintenance of relative equality of earnings, and having low rates of female participation and private service growth (Iversen and Wren, 1998), and the Netherlands promoting women's employment in both public and private sectors, achieving overall jobs growth and unemployment reduction without significant increases in inequality (Hemerijck, 2001, pp. 151–8).

What these changes concealed was the way in which households themselves had to reorganise their supply of unpaid work for maintenance and mutual care to allow increased hours to be supplied to the formal labour market, and to recruit paid workers into the domestic economy to compensate for those spent in employment. For example, in the UK in the early 1980s, when male employment was declining, there was evidence of men spending more time on home improvements, to take advantage of the boom in house prices in that decade (Gershuny, 1983). There were also signs that men were undertaking more child care tasks when their partners were in full-time (but not part-time) employment (Martin and Roberts, 1984). However, there was also a substantial increase in paid work, in cleaning, maintenance, gardening and child care, as women's participation in the labour market increased. And it was here that the contribution of immigrant workers, including those without the appropriate status, became significant.

Domestic work is structured by gender and race as well as by the relative incomes of employer and employee. The typical domestic worker is young and female, and often from particular ethnicities (Asian, black African, South American or East European). A total of almost 15 000 domestic employees and nearly the same number of *au pairs* entered the country legally in 1999 (Dobson, McLaughlan and Salt, 2001, p. 67); a support organisation interviewed in 2000 estimated an equal number of irregular migrant domestic workers in the UK (see p. 160).

Migrant domestic labour is a clear example of how the categories of chosen and forced migration, economic migration and asylum seeking, legal and irregular migration, are extremely difficult to distinguish. Some workers are educated, young and adventurous women, who use the immigration status of *au pair* to gain the advantages of mobility. Others are lone parents, desperate for employment to feed their children and kin back home. Some use the same immigration status to flee political instability (see pp. 137–8); others come as indentured (often virtually slave) labour to wealthy mobile families, including diplomats.

Domestic work takes place under special conditions. Migrant workers often live as part of their employers' households, are paid in kind as well as cash, and are hence more reliant upon the personal quality of their relationship with employers, as well as 'selling' their whole person, rather than simply their work skills. Domestic workers are more vulnerable to personal and sexual abuse than other workers (see pp. 141–2).

It is difficult to legislate for or regulate work of this kind. Migrant domestic labour is seldom adequately covered by industrial relations, health and safety or immigration law, and many domestic workers end up without proper status, as undocumented workers, either because they do not have a status outside the families with whom they entered, or because they have fled from unbearable living and working conditions (Anderson, 2000).

This dynamic is relevant for our study of undocumented immigrant workers in London in Part II. On the one hand, a significant proportion of women from Brazil, Poland and Turkey worked as cleaners, carers or nannies, enabling UK women to take more hours of paid work. On the other hand, the unregulated nature of the UK labour market allowed more of them to work in cafés, kebab shops, bars or restaurants than their counterparts in Berlin, where an even higher proportion were employed in households, and thus invisible to the regulatory authorities. In both kinds of role, they formed part of the infrastructure that sustains the lifestyles of better-off UK households, and keeps down the costs associated with two-earner patterns (reduced unpaid household hours, more reliance on paid services, including meals out). In this sense, undocumented work by immigrants may depress wages at the lower end of the labour market, but it certainly increases the disposable incomes of higher-earning households.

INCOME MAINTENANCE, EMPLOYMENT AND IMMIGRATION

If the goal of postwar income maintenance policies (social insurance and social assistance) was to provide adequate replacement incomes for workers temporarily or permanently outside the labour market, for their 'dependants', and for others unable to work, the aim more recently has been to encourage employment, enterprise, saving and self-responsibility and hence improve the functioning of the labour market. As we saw in the first two chapters, the approach pioneered in the USA, and closely followed in the UK (DSS, 1998 – see pp. 30–31) has now influenced the European strategy for modernising social protection (European Commission, 1999 – see pp. 36 and 41). Although there has been some convergence around a set of measures, no one country illustrates the application of all of these, because their starting points at the beginning of the 1990s – in terms of institutional systems and labour-market profiles – were so varied. However, the following policy goals and technical instruments have been extensively adopted.

(a) *Improving incentives for employment* ('making work pay') The problem of income maintenance systems was that (rising) benefits for those outside the labour market discouraged claimants from taking available employment with (falling) wages, less security, more variable hours and deteriorating working conditions, and from setting themselves up in self-employment in a competitive market with high rates of business failures. At the same time – especially in the Continental European states – rising social insurance contributions discouraged employers from hiring new workers. For example, in Germany, France and the Netherlands, the sum of workers', the state's and employers' contributions amounted to 15.5 per cent, 20.4 per cent and 18.3 per cent of gross domestic product (GDP), respectively, in 1996, compared with 6.2 per cent in the UK, 2.1 per cent in Australia and 0.4 per cent in New Zealand. This added cost to each unit of labour was part of the explanation of the greater success of the Anglo-Saxon countries in creating new employment; it also helped to explain the relative success in this respect of Denmark, with a proportion of 1.8 per cent of GDP compared to Sweden's 15.5 per cent, despite an overall taxation rate of the same (50 per cent of GDP) as Sweden (Scharpf, 1999, Table 5, p. 18).

Most states tackled the problem of incentives by containing or reducing the rate of unemployment-related benefits, and shortening the duration of eligibility. However, this was politically easier to do in the UK and New Zealand than in Continental European countries, with elaborate earnings-related benefit systems and corporatist social insurance bodies. Where trade unions had no formal role in the determination of social policies, income maintenance issues could be decided without negotiation through such corporatist institutions. Even so, Denmark, which had both generous and extended (seven years) unemployment benefits before 1993, reduced the coverage of these to one year by 1997 (Jordan and Loftager, 2001), and most countries removed entitlements from some groups or lowered replacement rates.

In the USA, the incentives for claimants to take jobs with problems of low wages, insecure employment and irregular working patterns were addressed through the tax system, as well as through limitations on eligibility for benefits. Tax credits provided income subsidies for low pay and unreliable earnings. In particular, tax credits could be used to make it worth while for long-term claimants of social assistance, such as lone parents and unemployed people with large families, to come off benefits and enter the labour market. They could be set at such a level that someone taking a part-time job on the minimum wage would be significantly better off, thus breaking the 'unemployment trap' – the disincentives for leaving benefits schemes, when gains would be small, and workers who lost employment after a short period faced daunting delays and difficulties in re-establishing their claims for social assistance (Jordan *et al.*, 1992). However, such 'solutions' do not give adequate medium- or long-term incentives to increase earnings incrementally, because the amount paid to the worker through the tax credit is reduced as hours are increased or wages rise. Hence, the technical advantages of tax credits, and their effects on the equalisation of incomes, rely on a buoyant labour market, with plenty of opportunities for recruits at the lowest end to move quickly into better jobs (Jordan *et al.*, 2000, chs. 2, 3). These 'ladders' are just what are missing from many markets for unskilled work in advanced industrialised countries. In their absence, there is a danger that wages subsidies add a further twist to the casualisation of employment in this sector, and the increase in wage inequality, since tax credits give employers an additional incentive to make more work part time, to make hours more variable and to reduce wages further. There is also evidence that tax credits encourage some workers to supply fewer hours to the labour market, while inducing others to supply more (Blundell *et al.*, 1999).

Despite these difficulties, in the USA, Earned Income Tax Credit had become the largest assistance programme for US citizens, outstripping both social insurance unemployment benefits and social assistance for poor people (Haveman, 1995). This influenced the UK's New Labour government to adopt this approach to 'making work pay' when it took office. Its Working Families Tax Credit scheme had attracted 1.1 million claimants by 2000, and helped increase the number of lone parents in the labour market by 15 per cent (HM Treasury, 2000, sect. 4.41). Initially confined to workers with children, the principle of tax credits is now to be extended to couples without children and single people over 25 years of age (HM Treasury, 2000, sect.

4.43). In this way, income maintenance can be focused on people in low-paid work rather than those outside the labour market, since the government is committed to increasing the value of tax credits with the rise in wages in the economy as a whole, while benefits are to continue to be pegged to more slowly rising prices (Jordan *et al.*, 2000, ch. 2). Extrapolations from Treasury forecasts indicated that by 2003–4 total spending on tax credits would be £10 billion (*The Independent*, 26 December 2001).

In principle, any income maintenance system that supports citizens and legal recruits from abroad advantages them over irregular migrants who are not eligible for such programmes. Tax credits have the additional feature of helping those in formal employment or self-employment, whereas benefit systems may, by reducing incentives to take such work, create niches in the informal economy of shadow work, for claimants and for undocumented workers from abroad. However, tax credits also contribute to the fragmentation of employment, and in doing so may unintentionally increase the scope for undocumented work. Their goal, of creating a 'flexible' labour market, with very variable working hours, conditions and wage rates, has certainly been achieved in the UK, but this relies on less regulation than in Continental European countries. Comparing undocumented Brazilian workers in London with their counterparts in Berlin, our study found that it was much easier for those who came to the UK to find shadow employment quickly, and without help from UK citizens (Jordan and Vogel, 1997a). Furthermore, the existence of tax credits in the USA for many years now has not reduced that country's high rates of illegal immigration.

In the Continental European countries, the high costs of social insurance contributions mean that the obvious strategy for governments keen to improve incentives for employers to expand their workforces, and new firms (especially in private services) to enter the market, is to try to reduce these, or to provide rebates for lower-paid, labour-intensive work (Scharpf, 1995, 1997). The latter policy has been introduced in France. However, there are two factors operating against such measures. First, it is not by coincidence that the cost of social insurance contributions rose sharply in the 1980s and 1990s in these countries. Governments faced severe constraints on taxing personal and company incomes, because individuals and firms could move their resources to more favourable tax regimes in other countries. This 'tax competition' explains why the rates of these forms of taxation stayed rather stable and uniform in Western Europe during this period (Scharpf, 1999, Table 5, p.18), and the UK's rates were in line with these. On the other hand, with unemployment rising fast, and a rapid increase in early retirements and people classified as disabled (more acceptable ways of shedding older workers from the labour force), the costs of income maintenance schemes were growing. Hence social insurance contributions were the only option for funding these costs, so long as governments wished to sustain the incomes of those outside the labour market.

The second factor was the nature of the corporatist institutions that governed social insurance systems. These contained members from the employers' federations, trade union federations, social insurance funds and employment services of the government (responsible for retraining schemes for claimants). All these had a stake in maintaining the efficiency wages and good working conditions enjoyed by labour-market 'insiders', the 'sound finance' of the insurance funds and the high-quality (but expensive) benefits and training regimes for claimants. In Germany, where social insurance contributions represent 50 per cent of the costs of employing a worker at the minimum wage, and where retraining costs the taxpayer DM45 billion (£15 billion) per year, all these interest groups turned down an attempt to introduce social insurance contributions rebates for low-paid, labour-intensive employment, proposed by the Chancellor's office in 1998–9.

(b) *Activation of benefits claimants*   The second set of measures to improve labour-market functioning has also been pioneered in the USA, though a very different version of it was built into the Swedish welfare state in the postwar period. This is the attempt to increase the supply of labour by motivating, educating, training and (in the last resort) threatening claimants, who prefer the passive security of remaining on benefits to the risks of taking available employment. The 'workfare' approach, introduced in the USA in the early 1980s, was primarily targeted at black 'welfare mothers' – women with (often several) children, and without the support of partners, claiming Aid for Families with Dependent Children – and young black men, considered to be in danger of becoming cut off from the labour market, partly through involvement in drugs and crime (Mead, 1986). The notion of an 'underclass' of claimants of social assistance justified measures including the tough enforcement of ever more restrictive work and training conditions linked to these benefits, aimed at cutting expenditure on 'passive' systems, and transferring it to ones that focused on 'activation' and 'work-readiness', even if these cost as much or more.

In the other Anglo-Saxon countries, activation took rather different forms, and – as an approach to benefits administration – was more gradually and cautiously adopted. In the UK, it was closely associated with a reinterpretation of the 'contract' between the state and citizens, and a higher expectation of 'independence' and self-responsibility by the former of the latter (see pp. 30–31). In so far as the New Deals, Employment Zones and Action Teams, the flagship programme of the New Labour government of 1997–2001, rested on an attempt to redefine the moral basis for income maintenance provision, the line taken by the government was very open to question (Jordan, 1998; Levitas, 1998). It seemed to rely, for its ultimate justification, on the notions that citizens had a duty not to burden their fellow citizens unnecessarily, that the costs of income maintenance payments were an unnecessary burden in many cases and that the state had a duty to enforce work to minimise these costs. But – apart from the difficulty of distinguishing avoidable from unavoidable claims – the argument over costs cuts both ways. Welfare-to-work measures, in-work benefits and tax credits, educational courses and training programmes are often equally or more costly, especially when the claimant population shrinks to a residuum of seriously disadvantaged and disabled people, and those with child care responsibilities. If it comes down to a question of cost, 'passive' benefits may be the cheaper option, and if it is not the costs as burdens to the taxpayers, what other moral basis (other than an unacceptably paternalistic one) can there be for such approaches?

In spite of these difficulties, activation has proved politically popular in the UK, and the approach has influenced most other European regimes (Cox, 1999; Hemerijck, 2001). But the reappearance of skills' shortages and vacancies in unskilled employment raise serious doubts about the economic value of these programmes for labour-market functioning. For example, in the UK there are still nearly one million claimants of unemployment-related benefits, over four million of incapacity and disability benefits and 700 000 of lone parent benefits. If there are would-be immigrants willing to take this work without extra training costs, would it not be more efficient to allow them to do so? It is just this question that has inspired the new debates and new policies described in the last chapter.

These questions are also linked to ones about pockets of extreme deprivation (especially inner-city ghettos and outer-city social housing schemes), depressed areas and problems of social exclusion. Policies for regeneration of such districts and areas imply that capital should move to them, and workers be recruited locally. But here again there must be doubts about the extent to which government should subsidise these programmes, and whether they represent the best available strategy. Rather than trying to bring new employment to these areas, it might be better – at least for the medium term – to develop schemes through which residents would improve their own physical and social infrastructure, according to their own priorities (Jordan and Jordan, 2000, chs. 6, 7).

Once the option of recruitment from abroad is opened up, it becomes possible (perhaps even necessary) to compare the costs of activation programmes with those of immigration. In principle, it should be possible to compare the returns on a given government expenditure on welfare-to-work training, or urban regeneration, with those on a cohort of overseas recruitment. It seems likely that the latter will do well in such comparisons, especially when activation measures are dealing with only half-willing workers, or people with severe physical or emotional problems. It has been estimated that a 1 per cent increase in immigration to European countries increases both GDP output per head by between 1.25 and 1.5 per cent (Glover *et al.*, 2001, p. 6). It is dubious whether the same can be claimed for a unit of spending on activation.

In the case of irregular migration, the outcomes are much more difficult to measure. However, the fact that it happens at all indicates that there are opportunities within the economy for labour to be advantageously supplied. The existence of schemes such as those for seasonal agricultural workers from abroad to come under temporary visas indicates a grey area between regular and irregular immigration. In the UK and European countries, such legal immigrants are often found working side by side with ones without proper status, and they frequently overstay or apply for asylum at the end of the scheme. This is further discussed in Part II.

(c) *Reduction of Working Hours* Policies for reducing working hours, as a way of widening labour-market participation, are taken seriously in the Continental European countries, but not in the Anglo-Saxon ones. Average annual working hours have fallen by some 350 hours in the Netherlands between 1973 and 1996, by 300 in Germany, 250 in France and 200 in the UK in the same period. But working hours in the UK in 1996 were still higher than those in the Netherlands in 1973, and higher by 200 hours than those in France and Germany in 1996. During those years, working hours in the USA increased slightly, and in 1996 were over 200 hours higher than in the UK (Hemerijck, 2001, Table 7.8, p. 157).

There is little correlation between average working hours and rates of participation or unemployment. In those countries, like the Netherlands, which previously had low rates of female participation, the increase in part-time employment has been an important factor in enabling jobs growth. By contrast, in Germany neither part-time work nor women's employment have grown so quickly (Hemerijck, 2001, Table 7.5, p. 155), and unemployment has remained higher.

As far as irregular migration is concerned, labour-market regulation is a more important factor than working hours. A country with a highly regulated labour market provides more limited scope for shadow activities. In the Netherlands, working time reduction is seen as part of a process of labour-market regulation; in the UK, the increase in part-time work is an aspect of deregulation.

(d) *Wage Restraint* The countries which have exercised wage restraint through corporatist institutions most effectively in the 1980s and 1990s have been Ireland and the Netherlands (Jordan *et al.*, 2000, ch. 1; Hemerijck, 2001,

p. 154). This has certainly been a factor in the success of both in achieving jobs growth and unemployment reduction. However, this success has depended on achieving *positional* advantage. It is because labour costs have risen more rapidly in other competitor economies that Ireland and the Netherlands have gained from wage restraint.

High labour costs create opportunities for irregular migration where marginal employers and new entrepreneurs can save money by hiring workers for less than minimum wages, and without paying taxes and social insurance contributions. In this respect, Germany is a clear example, since it had the highest overall increase in labour costs in the period 1980–94 among the larger OECD countries. This explains why there are opportunities in Germany for people from the former communist countries of Central Europe to work without proper status, and especially for workers and entrepreneurs from Poland.

CONCLUSIONS

Government policies, aimed at improving the functioning of labour markets, do not take account of the effects on people working in other countries, and facing quite different opportunities and constraints, wages and costs. Policies intended to increase flexibility, participation or protection of workers may have the unintended consequence of increasing the numbers of undocumented immigrant workers in the economy, some of whom may (in the longer term) come to rely on income maintenance systems when they legalise and settle.

Policies in the 1990s were mainly concerned with lowering or abolishing the barriers to labour-market participation that were built into postwar welfare state institutions. In general, countries with less comprehensive systems of social insurance, lower replacement rates in benefits and more reliance on social assistance schemes, went furthest in these directions, giving priority to improving incentives, reducing eligibility for benefits and activating claimants. But deregulation of labour markets, aimed at increasing flexibility and mobility, also created conditions in which irregular migrants could make their way as unskilled workers or entrepreneurs. This, in turn, contributed to the casualisation of employment, the depression of wages and the growth of the shadow economy.

Conversely, those countries which were most reluctant to adopt these policies, where social insurance systems were strongest, and social insurance contributions rose most, were least likely to see the casualisation of formal work, but created niches for informal activity, by citizens and by foreigners. Germany was a clear example of this second kind; irregular migration was related to the rigidity of a highly regulated labour market, high labour costs and more generous income maintenance provision. Employers had strong incentives to hire irregular migrant workers, because of high minimum wages and social insurance contributions.

Neoclassical economic theory models the labour market as an open system, where mobility is determined by demand and supply. If the whole world formed an integrated labour market, there would be no differentials between the wage rates of particular skills in different countries, other than those associated with the costs of moving from one to another (Chiswick, 1999, p. 4). Seen from a whole world perspective, 'as long as the marginal productivity of labour differs in various countries, the migration of labour is welfare improving' (Zimmerman, 1994, p. 14). However, the eventual equilibrium produced by this migration would result in all the 'economic rents' enjoyed by First World workers being competed away. Hence, even the optimistic, positive authors of an assessment of the economic and social consequences of migration to the UK sound a note of caution:

> In general, migration increases the supply of labour (and human capital); this is likely, in theory, to reduce wages for workers competing with migrants, and increase returns to capital and other factors complementary to migrant labour. In general, this redistribution will favour natives who own factors of production which are complementary to migrants, and hurt those who own factors of production which are substitutes … ' (Glover *et al.*, 2001, p. 4).

Irregular migrants take account of the costs of crossing borders in breach of immigration rules. Part of these costs is a calculation of the risks and consequences of being detected; another part is made up of learning a language and a culture, and finding suitable accommodation; and another is isolation from kinship and neighbourly support in their home country. But the choice to cross borders is also an *investment* decision (Chiswick, 1999, p. 3). Irregular migrants make sacrifices in short-term welfare for the sake of long-term increases in their earning potential. If wages are falling and opportunities narrowing in the migrant's country of origin, and they are rising and expanding in the country of destination, the rate of return on that investment increases. This is the background to the study of irregular migrants – why they came, and how they survived – in the second part of this book.

PART II

The UK as a Case Study

4. Why they come

The UK provides the opportunity for a case study of all the issues identified in Part I of the book, because of the changes in official thinking on economic migration in the years that we were conducting our research (1996–2001). In the first three years of this period, the focus of government policy was on the asylum system, and on stopping it being used as a channel for economic migration.

> … economic migrants will exploit whatever route offers the best chance of entering or remaining within the UK. That might mean use of fraudulent documentation, entering into a sham marriage or, particularly in recent years, abuse of the asylum process. … The Government's aim is to create an efficient asylum system that helps genuine asylum seekers and deters abusive claimants (Home Office, 1998, paras 1.7–8).

By the year 2000 the Home Office Minister with responsibility for immigration policy, Barbara Roche, was arguing that 'economically driven migration can bring sustainable benefits both for growth and the economy', because 'in the UK we are now seeing the emergence of labour shortages in key areas' (Roche, 2000, p. 3). A Home Office publication pointed out that, according to economic theory:

> If all markets are functioning well, there are no externalities, and if we are not concerned about the distributional implications, then *migration is welfare-improving*, not only for migrants, but (on average) for natives … *migration is most likely to occur precisely when it is most likely to be welfare enhancing*. Countries which are abundant in labour will have lower wages than countries which are abundant in capital; workers will, if labour is mobile, have an incentive to migrate from the former to the latter, improving resource allocation overall (Glover *et al.*, 2001, p. 4).

This fairly cautious and qualified endorsement of economic migration could easily be used to justify selective recruitment of highly skilled workers, and continued restrictions on other forms of migration. That, in turn, could legitimate tough enforcement of immigration rules, and increased efforts to identify and expel irregular migrants. However, at the same time, voices began to be raised for more open borders, and a more liberal interpretation of the potential benefits of migration of all kinds. These changes were proposed as ways of ensuring fair outcomes from the globalisation process. For example, a leader in *The Guardian* argued:

> Greater labour mobility can bring benefits to both donor and recipient countries, and is a precondition for making globalisation work. ... A lop-sided system where capital is free to move at will while labour absorbs all the economic shocks is what gives globalisation a bad name (*The Guardian*, 11 December 2001, p. 15).

In this part of the book, we look at who did come without proper status, or stay without keeping the conditions of their entry to the UK, and how they survived as underground members of their host society. This study, of course, says as much about the UK economy and its collective institutions as it does about those individuals who breached its immigration rules. But it is necessary first to look in detail at why these migrants came and how they stayed, before considering in Part III how the UK authorities and public services dealt with them, and what impact they had upon the host society.

Because of this shift in perspective (from a long-distance analysis of migratory flows to a close examination of the behaviour of individual migrants) and of focus (from a long-lens study of economic forces acting on large populations, to subjective accounts of motives and decisions), this chapter will contain sections on the reasons why this particular research study was chosen, the problems in conducting the study and the methodology employed. We then go on to describe the factors which led the irregular migrants interviewed to come to London, rather than choose another destination, either closer at hand or further away.

Our interviews were carried out as part of research studies conducted in London, under grants from the Nuffield Trust, the Economic and Social Research Council (ESRC) and the European Community. The first and third of these contained a comparative element; interviews with immigrants from the same countries were conducted in Germany and (in the third project) in Italy and Greece. During the period of the research, as well as rapid change in the law, policy and practice, and there was also a crisis in the immigration service's administration (over computerisation – see Chapter 7), and a 'moral panic' over asylum.

The interviewees comprised all kinds of irregular migrants – clandestine entrants, people who had been smuggled, students not pursuing their courses of study, asylum seekers who had overstayed following the failure of appeals – across the range of working-age groups, who had been in the UK for periods of three months to ten years. The great majority of these men and women came as tourists, some later converting to student visas and a few applying for asylum. This suggests that most economic migration uses the channels open to 'passengers' - the visitors that public policy aims to facilitate – rather than criminal intermediaries or the asylum process. Worldwide,

it is estimated that between 15 and 30 per cent of irregular migrants emp
traffickers or smugglers (Stalker, 2000). These have attracted particular att
tion from policy makers (see pp. 48–50); there has also been some research
on people smuggled to the UK (Morrison, 1998). The only 'immigration
offence' committed by most of the interviewees was working without proper
status. However, they had often spent a lot of money, taken considerable risks
and showed great persistence and ingenuity, to come to London to work.

Our aim in this chapter is to disentangle their motives for travelling to
London (often via other countries), and how their reasoning led them to
choose a particular immigration status for entry into the country. By comparing the accounts given by migrants from three countries (Brazil, Poland and
Turkey), each with a quite different political history, economic trajectory,
ethnic mix and relationship to the UK, we seek to show the common characteristics – in terms of perceptions of the UK as a potential host society – and
the differences in terms of experiences and outlooks in their countries of
origin. Each individual's account is both a personal narrative of a transnational
journey, revealing complex processes of decision-making, and the factors
influencing choices, and also a version of how the UK appears to those
coming from outside its borders, as a country with external and internal
controls, a political society with rights and obligations, a community with a
cosmopolitan population and an economy with opportunities and dangers.

What such qualitative research cannot show is the extent of the phenomenon
'irregular migration'. Usually, these methods are employed to complement
large-scale surveys, resulting in quantitative analyses of the scale and composi-
tion of the relevant population. Despite the huge literature of this kind in the
USA (Bratsberg, 1995; Espenshade, 1995; Martin, 1998), the considerable
body of work in Continental Europe (Häussermann, 1997; Eichenhofer, 1999),
and new studies by international organisations (OECD, 1999; Garson, 2000;
Tapinos, 2000), there has been no comparable research in the UK. The Home
Office is only now consulting with academics about how to estimate the 'illegal
population', and currently no satisfactory methods have been agreed. Guessti-
mates vary between 200 000 and over a million.

The first question to be answered is therefore why no such survey research
has ever been done, and why only a few qualitative studies, by members of
voluntary organisations (Refugee Council, 1997b; Anderson, 1999), and none
by British academics, have been recently undertaken. This seems to imply
that there is something of a taboo around the topic, and the reasons for this
reveal something about the politics of immigration in the UK, and the delicate balance of power that sustains the present rules, their enforcement and
the pace of change. Before looking at the experiences of those who come as
irregular migrants, it is important to examine these factors, which have both
defined their entry as against the law, and put their lives outside the scope of

investigation by researchers in the UK. Why is immigration (and specifically irregular migration) an important issue in UK politics, yet so selectively researched by government agencies and UK academics?

THE RESEARCH QUESTION

The question 'why do they come?' is deceptively simple. It implies that there are discernible 'push and pull factors', that can be demonstrated to give rise to a certain volume of immigration. In the 1990s the UK popular press proclaimed that the poverty of certain groups in Central-Eastern Europe, and of whole populations of countries in the developing world, plus the availability of social assistance benefits for asylum seekers, made the UK a 'soft touch' compared with other European countries, and led to a disproportionate number of applicants for asylum. All other issues about economic migration were subsumed under this one, and government policy documents reflected the same perspective. The Home Office's White Paper on the 'modernisation' of the Immigration Service *'Fairer, Faster and Firmer'* (Home Office, 1998) started from the proposition that asylum was the only category of immigration to the UK that had risen in the 1990s (ibid., para 1.2), and inferred both that most claims for asylum were attempts at disguised economic migration, and conversely that most economic migration was carried out through the medium of 'bogus' asylum claims:

> ... modern communications and modern travel have been significant factors in changing the nature and extent of economic migration, facilitating the genuine traveller but also creating opportunities for those who seek to evade immigration control. ... People living in countries with weaker economies receive daily images of the potential economic and other social benefits available in richer countries across the globe. The knowledge of such opportunities ... provides an incentive to economic migration, but it is now available to a much larger population. ... The desire to move is obviously strengthened where relative poverty is combined with political instability.' (Home Office, 1998, paras 1.3–4)

The White Paper went on, after documenting growth in asylum claims since 1988, to show that asylum seekers were mainly young, came from all over the world and embraced more countries as well as individuals than in the 1980s. It also showed that the rise was part of a pan-European phenomenon. This quickly led to a section on 'abuse of the asylum system' in which it was argued (with evidence from a few anonymised 'case studies') that 'there is no doubt that the asylum system is being abused by those seeking to migrate for purely economic reason' (ibid., para 1.14). It went on to put part of the blame for this on 'unscrupulous "advisers"' (ibid., para 1.14) and 'immigration racketeers' (ibid., paras 1.17–19). This then justified 'reforms' that focused mainly on deterring asylum seeking, by further restricting the availability of cash benefits for applicants, and dispersing them to 'no choice' accommodation in peripheral areas.

The clear implication of this analysis was that the push factor in economic migration was poverty in developing countries all over the world, that better transport and information provided the means, that the principal medium for this migration was the asylum system, and that one of the main pull factors was the availability of social benefits. Yet historical and recent analyses of economic migration showed that patterns could not be adequately explained in this way. There have been long periods when there was very little migration from poor countries to richer ones, and some poor countries still have very little. Often, increased mobility has coincided with rapid rises in standards of living in the countries of emigration. And the routes followed are clearly influenced by trade and investment, creating 'migration systems' among a group of states at different stages of economic development (see Chapter 1, pp. 33–4).

One example of such a system was the movement of capital, labour and products between the UK, the USA and Germany in the nineteenth century (Thomas, 1973). Another encompassed the USA, the Caribbean Basin and South-east Asia from the mid-1960s. In both these cases, a sudden surge of emigration on a large scale to the USA accompanied processes of industrialisation in the sending countries; economic migration could not be understood in isolation from flows of investment and exchange.

Saskia Sassen (1988) has argued that high levels of immigration to the USA from Mexico, the Philippines, South Korea, China, India, the Dominican Republic, Jamaica and Colombia correlated closely with the increase in direct investment by US companies in those countries in the 1970s and 1980s. Between 1970 and 1980 the Asian population of the USA increased by 100 per cent, and the Hispanic population by 62 per cent.

> While the redeployment of manufacturing and office work to less developed countries has contributed to conditions that promote emigration from these countries, the concentration of servicing and management functions in global cities has contributed to conditions for the demand and absorption of the immigrant influx in cities like New York, Los Angeles and Houston. *The same set of basic processes that has promoted emigration from several rapidly industrialising countries has also promoted immigration into several booming global cities* (Sassen, 1988, p. 22).

London was one of these cities, whose economy was analysed by Sassen in her later book (1991). But immigration to the UK, and to London in particu-

lar, was already part of an older system, established in the 1950s, and involving links with the New Commonwealth countries of the Caribbean, the Indian
Subcontinent and Africa. In 1970 the UK's share of foreign direct investment
in developing countries was (at US$5912 million) second only to the USA's,
and 13.8 per cent of the total investment by OECD states (Sassen, 1988,
Table 4.1, p. 100). Although the UK's investment in these countries rose
rapidly in the 1970s, its share of this total actually fell, as Germany and Japan
in particular increased their investments even more rapidly. In other words,
UK investment in the developing world was part of the legacy of its imperial
past, rather than a new phenomenon, associated with globalisation and the
relocation of industrial production. Both the immigration of the 1950s and
1960s from the New Commonwealth, and the measures for restricting and
managing it from the Commonwealth Immigrants Act of 1962 onwards, can
be understood only in terms of this history. The immigration system that
centred on the UK was shaped by a colonial administration, and an economic
regime of 'imperial preference', under which the countries of the empire
supplied manufactured goods for British consumption, as well as providing
mass markets for UK products.

It was as part of the transition from a colonial Empire to a Commonwealth
of independent states, and from imperial preference to global free trade, that
the UK advertised for workers from the Caribbean to fill labour shortages,
and allowed others from India and Pakistan to settle in the UK in the 1950s
and early 1960s. It was also in this period that the UK's politics of immigration came to be seen through the lens of race relations, and the restrictions on
further inward migration to be justified in terms of promoting racial equality
among citizens in a multi-ethnic polity. From this time onwards, a tough
approach to policing the UK's borders and controlling entry was directed at
black and Asian people, as indicated in the 1998 White Paper:

> The Government believes that a policy of fair, fast and firm immigration control
> will help promote racial equality. One of this Government's central themes is
> tackling the problem of racism and creating a society in which our citizens,
> regardless of background or colour, enjoy equal rights, responsibilities and oppor-
> tunities. (Home Office, 1998, para 2.3)

This has meant that both the politics of immigration and the academic
study of immigration policy and its consequences have come to focus on
issues of race, racism and racial equality, to an extent that is absent from
such debates and studies in most European countries, and particularly in
Germany. The central issues have been the rights to settlement of New
Commonwealth migrants, and access to full citizenship by black and Asian
people (Layton-Henry, 1989). Because of the relatively good opportunities
for immigrants who enter legally to gain full political rights, their organisa-

tions and lobbies have focused on improving their position in relation to other rights of citizenship, and combating discrimination in the economy and civil society, while more conservative forces in the white UK community have used notions of 'good race relations' and equal opportunities as trade-offs for a series of measures tightening controls around New Commonwealth immigration.

One outcome of the use of this framework for the immigration debate has been that issues of illegal entry have either been ignored, or treated as particular problems associated with controls related to race. Both immigration policy and resistance to it have been seen in terms of racism and attempts to combat it. This explains the enormous volume of publications on immigration and race, and the apparent taboo on research into irregular migration; the topic raised too many contentious issues in such a context. The few articles in *Race Today* (Maldonado and Esward, 1983) or *Race* (Dahya, 1973), and an article in the *Morning Star* (Maldonado, 1982), were eventually followed up in a book by Ardill and Cross (1987), based on 25 interviews with unauthorised migrant workers in London the previous two years. It was sponsored by the Trade Unions TGWU, NUPE and GMB, had a focus on Filipinos, Colombians, Turks and Kurds, and was sympathetic to their situation. It drew attention to the UK's 'structural dependence on cheap labour', and that 'weak trade unions allow this to happen' (p. 61). This was taken up in a short article in *Labour Research* in 1989, while the implications for women were briefly explored by Bhaba and Shutter (1994), who emphasised undocumented immigrant workers' roles in restaurants, hotels and smaller factories (ibid., p. 164) and as servants in rich households, where they had no protections or rights (ibid., p. 181).

Our research question attempts to move the investigation onto the new terrain of immigration policy in the 1990s, without getting trapped in the specific issue of asylum, that dominated the debates leading up to the 1996 Asylum and Immigration Act, and the 1999 Immigration and Asylum Act. In fact, it was very difficult to do this before the shift in UK policy on economic migration that took place in 2000, and was marked by the speech of Home Office Minister, Barbara Roche, in September of that year (see p. 47). Our goal, as described in Chapter 1, was to analyse irregular migration in an overall context of the mobility of capital and labour, and the specific context of the UK labour market and welfare state regime. But the political context was shaped by the asylum issue, and there were ethical problems for us over publishing our findings in the midst of these disputes, and especially during the 'moral panic' of summer 2000. It has only been since the European developments described in Chapter 2 that the UK's policy context has changed, making it much easier to engage with the issues now recognised as needing debate by the UK government.

We chose the groups of immigrants to be interviewed with the conscious intention of avoiding those whose situation could be framed within the laws and policies of the period 1962–81 – New Commonwealth migrants. We wanted to look at people from other countries, without colonial or other historical ties to the UK, who were not native English speakers, and who might have been expected to go elsewhere rather than to London. In the case of *Brazilians*, they were coming from a distant continent, and most of their fellow nationals who left were migrating to the USA and Canada – indeed, there were many more Brazilian immigrants in Japan than in the UK (Weiner, 1995, p. 62). An important criterion in this case was that there were similar numbers of Brazilians in Berlin to those in London, and the first research study was a comparative one. In the case of *Polish* migrants, they represented the most important group of immigrants from the post-communist countries of Central Europe, whose migration was not related to war or political persecution. Unlike Brazilians, they were also seen as a problem, related to economic migration, by the Home Office. Hence they were relevant to the specifics of the post-1989 situation over migration in Europe, though the UK was one of the most distant EU member states from their homeland. Finally, migrants from *Turkey* (both of Kurdish and Turkish origin) could be expected to include a number of asylum seekers, and hence allowed us to try to understand the relationship between political and economic motives in migration decisions (Düvell and Jordan, 2001).

The second innovative element (in terms of UK research) was that we took as the common element in all the migration accounts we sought the fact that the interviewees had – at some time in their stays – done paid work without proper immigration status. This included work done by asylum seekers before their permission to work was granted, by students in excess of the hours allowed in their visas and by overstayers and clandestine entrants. In other words, our research question was directed at economic activity by immigrants, whatever the context of their entry to the UK, and how it related to their other reasons for coming. In fact, the great majority of the interviewees from Brazil and Poland told us that their main or only reason in coming to London was to work, and most of those from Turkey said that paid work (almost always in the shadow economy, even when they had permission to work) was a necessity for most or all of their time in the UK. Hence, we were able to show how this economic activity was understood, described and justified by people who knew they were risking deportation in undertaking it.

In this way, we aimed to analyse the economic element in migration from the three countries, as part of the processes described in Part I of the book. However, before going on to show what the interviewees revealed about why and how they came to London, we need to distinguish between the different contexts of migration from the three countries.

MIGRATION FROM BRAZIL

Brazil is an enormous country, whose population grew from 50 000 in 1950 to 144 000 in 1989, and which emerged in the final quarter of the twentieth century as a regional power, and the world's eighth largest economy. However, its evolution in this period was part of a distinctive phase in global economic development, in which an authoritarian regime had harnessed investment by international companies to a project of modernisation, based on industrialisation, urbanisation and state control.

> The new authoritarianism was a strategy to accelerate development of Brazilian capitalism, but also a strategy of the state for the state itself. ... It was ... a condition for consolidating and expanding the leading role of the state – under the tutelage of the Armed Forces – understood as the only actor capable of accelerating modernization through rational planning' (Becker and Egler, 1992, p. 83).

This process, which began in the late 1950s, was hailed as a 'Brazilian economic miracle', and sustained rates of growth comparable to those of Japan, Mexico and the newly industrialising countries of South-east Asia. It involved attracting foreign investment from all over the world; by 1982, less than a third of this was from the USA, with rising proportions from Germany (14 per cent) and Japan (nearly 10 per cent) (Becker and Egler, 1992, p. 113). Furthermore, Brazil sold almost exactly the same proportion of its exports to the EEC as to the USA. However, the outcome of this rapid growth under 'conservative modernisation' was continuing inequality, greater than in many poorer countries. In the mid-1980s in Brazil, the bottom 20 per cent of the population received only 2.4 per cent of national income, and the top 10 per cent 46.2 per cent, compared with 9.8 per cent and 25.4 per cent in India, and 4.4 per cent and 35.8 per cent in Peru (World Bank, 1990).

Brazil's economic programme of this period involved 'forced migrations' of large populations, as rural workforces were displaced by mechanisation of agriculture, which, in turn, were drawn towards the new semi-urban settlements, and to the informal sectors of the large cities. By 1989 almost 75 per cent of the population was classified as living in urban areas. This transformation led to both the emergence of urban poverty (squatter settlements) and the growth of the urban middle class – the latter being crucial for subsequent emigrations.

> The diversification and expansion of the middle class has been one of the most remarkable transformations of Brazilian society in the 1960s and 1970s. The middle class expanded in association with the secondary and tertiary economic sectors and the state apparatus. The situation of the middle class is unstable. ... The heaviest tax burden of the 'official economy' falls directly upon this class (Becker and Egler, 1992, p. 124).

This proved to be an important factor in the outward migratory flows that occurred after the debt crisis of the mid-1980s (Griffith-Jones and Sunkel, 1986). Brazil was plunged into political turmoil, and was required to undertake substantial structural adjustment, switching from a strategy for import-substitution to one of export expansion, and imposing severe controls on state spending and on wage and salary levels (Dinsmoor, 1990). The middle classes were adversely affected by all these factors, and migration – especially to North America – accelerated sharply in the subsequent period. Goza's (1994) study of Brazilian migrants living in one Canadian and one US city found that most of them were well educated and qualified, but were working in unskilled occupations, typically as janitors. Migration to the UK therefore has to be understood in terms of this history.

The Brazilian irregular migrants that we interviewed in London were mainly from this educated and qualified sector of that society, who found their aspirations blocked by the lack of opportunities in the Brazilian economy. Their decisions to migrate were taken either in the face of immediate frustrations, or as attempts to improve their long-term prospects. But London was not a major destination for the many middle-class Brazilians in this situation; only 3000 people of Brazilian origin were registered as living in London in 1993. Their presence bore witness to the diversity of the origins of those who now supply labour for the services that sustain a global city, and the complex mixture of motives adding these migrants to the cosmopolitan mix of its population.

MIGRATION FROM POLAND

Poland has been a country of emigration since the mid-nineteenth century; 3.5 million people left between then and the First World War, and 1.5 million between the wars. One-sixth of Poland's population left in 1944–6, after a net population loss (through deaths in combat, concentration camps and slave labour as well as migration) of 5 million in 1939–45. The communist years of isolation from the West culminated in an increasing flow of illegal emigration in the 1980s, mainly of educated, prime-age citizens, and mainly to Germany (Okólski, 1996).

After liberal border regulations were established in 1989, Poland soon established the highest net emigration rates in Europe. About one million Poles go abroad for less than 11 months in any year, many under special arrangements for subcontract agricultural and construction workers (Faist *et al.*, 1998) to Germany, which still takes the highest percentage of migrant workers at 76 per cent. The USA takes 13 per cent and Canada 9 per cent (Okólski, 1996). In this flow of legal short-term migration for increased earning power, they are partly sustained by family networks in the long-established Polish diaspora, but more especially by those who left illegally in the 1980s, and by the 500 000 Poles who 'rediscovered' German ancestry and since 1989 'have returned' as ethnic German *Aussiedler*. Most of these have retained Polish citizenship and passports, and have become an important source of remittances and inward investment, often owning property or business interests in Poland (Okólski, 1996, p. 47). In all, some 12 million people of Polish descent live abroad as part of 'Polonia', including 1.5 million in Germany and one million in France.

However, in addition to these flows of migrants with work permits, there are also large numbers (probably more) travelling to Western Europe to work without proper status (Cyrus, 1996). The first democratically elected Polish government adopted a 'shock' approach to economic reform with the Balcerowicz Plan of 1990, resulting in an early and sharp reduction in national income and rise in unemployment. Even though this strategy was subsequently heavily modified, and Poland's economy has grown impressively since the mid-1990s, a pattern of illegal migratory flows was established, both of Poles travelling westwards, and of those coming to Poland from the even more economically devastated countries of the former Soviet Union. All this reflected the relatively rapid adaptation of Polish citizens to economic transition – a willingness to take responsibility for themselves, and plan as rational economic actors in an entirely new situation, taking the whole world as their framework for choice, and calculating the costs and benefits of activities in the informal as well as the formal economies of each country. The ratio of *per capita* income in Germany and Poland in 2000 was 11:1 (Stalker, 2000).

Polish migration to the UK occurred in three rather separate phases. The first of these took place during and after the Second World War, as part of the refugee movement from Eastern Europe, including some 120 000 Polish members of the Allied forces. These immigrants were welcomed, as part of the war effort, and for postwar reconstruction (Harris, 1987). The second was the small number of asylum applicants during the political turbulence of the 1980s – 2,900 in all between 1986 and 1996 (Refugee Council, 1997c). The third was the economic migration of the 1990s – Polish nationals were identified as the third largest element in illegal entry to the UK in the middle of the decade (Hansard, 19.12.1996). There seems to have been little interaction between this new wave and the 74 000 people of Polish birth registered in the 1991 census; though some new migrants did make links with relatives from the earlier waves, as we show (p. 124).

The economic motivation of the new migrants was well reflected in our interviews with Polish undocumented workers in London. They took for granted the limited opportunities available to them in their home country, and the better prospects for earning that they could enjoy abroad. Their accounts of their decisions provide evidence of an approach to economic activity based on the assessment and management of risk (Beck, 1992). For example, they weighed up the chances of getting through the UK border controls, of becoming ill, having an industrial accident, or being arrested for a non-immigration related offence, and adopted strategies for dealing with such possible contingencies. Above all, they knew that they might well be caught by the authorities and removed from the country, and they took this risk into account, having a plan of what action they would take in the circumstances. In this sense, far from being typical post-communist actors with 'mental residues' of that system (in a need for greater security and protection), they were members of the *avant garde* of global capitalist relations – advocates of open borders, who pioneered the outer limits of labour-market flexibility and personal insecurity, insisting on taking their chances against global market forces without any shelter from collective organisations, government regulation or the rights of citizenship.

MIGRATION FROM TURKEY

Historically, issues of migration were even more prominent for Turkey than for Poland. Because of the extent of the Ottoman Empire, migration between Turkey and the Balkans in particular was a major feature of the nineteenth century (as that Empire went into terminal decline) with exchanges of population between Greece and Turkey early this century. The recent Kosovo War – in which many Muslims went to Turkey as refugees – was a reminder of the continuing legacy of those population movements.

Conversely, modern Turkey has pursued policies for dispersing or expelling ethnic minorities, and the foundation of the Turkish Republic at the beginning of the last century led to accelerated internal migration, due to these programmes and to urbanisation and industrialisation. Some 4.2 million people migrated from the rural provinces to the cities between 1950 and 1970, causing squatting and the erection of illegal suburbs (*gececondus*) with 2.5 million inhabitants in the latter year (Sever, 1984).

Work-oriented emigration from Turkey began in the 1960s, encouraged by the military government, and enabled through reciprocal contracts with several European countries (chiefly Germany, Switzerland and the Netherlands). By 1983 over a million Turks were officially working abroad, but the real numbers were estimated to be twice as high (Kleff, 1985). Remittances of Turkish migrant workers soared to around 5728 million US dollars per annum in the mid-1980s, when unemployment in Turkey stood at about 20 per cent (Pamuk, 1986, pp. 49, 78).

Most of the literature on the Kurdish minority in Turkey is in German and highly political, because discussion of this issue is banned in Turkey, and Germany is the main country of immigration. In practice, it is difficult to distinguish between refugees, expelled people, dispersed populations and economic migrants. Out of some 20–30 million Middle-eastern Kurds, inhabiting six countries, about 12 million live in Turkey. Kurds speak five different dialects, all quite separate from Turkish, and often as their only language (Mönch-Bucak, 1988). It is estimated that two million Kurds live as displaced or expelled people, or as internal refugees in non-Kurdish cities or west Turkey (Medico International, 1994). The Kurdish diaspora in Europe comprises some one million people, out of around 2.7 million emigrants from Turkey (though some are Kurds from Iraq and Syria, mainly as a result of the persecutions of 1975–8 and 1985); of these, some 300 000–500 000 are in Germany. They are the largest group of asylum seekers, and come mainly from peasant backgrounds, with no experience of urban life (Blaschke and Amman, 1988). There is virtually no research literature on Kurds in the UK, and no reliable estimates of the proportion of the probable 90 000 Turkish-speaking people in London (Karmi, 1992) who are Kurdish. About 5000 Kurdish asylum seekers from one area, Karaman Maras, arrived in Haringey in 1989–90, and about 10 000 others are assumed to be in London.

The flow of immigrants from Turkey to the UK has always responded chiefly to political rather than economic factors. In the 1960s a modest-sized settlement began in Hackney, as the effective partition of Cyprus led to the emigration of many with Turkish origins. The largest increase to subsequent flows occurred in the late 1980s, with the sudden growth in asylum applications from both ethnic Turkish and Kurdish people. This reflected Turkish government activity in suppressing internal political opposition and organised labour resistance, as well as its police and military campaign against Kurdish separatism. Hence, the asylum seekers arriving – and congregating mostly in Hackney – were mainly members of organised political groups in Turkey, and this was reflected in the formation of strong (and often ideologically committed) associations to support and sustain these immigrants. The Turkish/Kurdish community is now the second largest minority group in Hackney, with about 10 per cent of the population, organised around a number of groups and community centres, each with its campaigns directed at Turkish politics, and its agenda for improving the lot of its members in the borough. The role of these associations and support organisations is analysed in Chapter 6.

As migration from Turkey has progressed, so the community in Hackney has become increasingly active in developing its own enterprises, both in manufacturing and services – mainly textile and plastics workshops, and small catering firms. This development has been characteristic of ethnic minority groups in the USA, who have become both the entrepreneurs and the workers in new small businesses and subcontract suppliers (Lasch, 1994). These enterprises have – in their early stages – often been characterised by a pattern of household-style production, with unpaid female labour power supplied by members of the extended family (Lasch, 1994, p. 162). However, larger enterprises have increasingly employed a variety of workers, and taken on the characteristics of small UK businesses on the margins of the productive economy. One of the most unexpected findings of our study was that Polish immigrants were extensively employed in Turkish-owned enterprises (factories and catering outlets). Anecdotal evidence had it that, soon after the change of 1989, two young Polish women were seen in Hackney with backpacks, looking for accommodation. A Turkish café owner offered them a room and employment as waitresses in his coffee shop. Soon this gained him a competitive advantage over his rivals, and all Turkish coffee shops began to employ Polish waitresses. Whatever the truth of this story, there are now extensive links – including marriages – between members of the Turkish/ Kurdish business community and Polish workers. Our Polish interviewees described involvement in both Turkish factory and hospitality work as a major component of their undocumented employment histories.

The Turkish/Kurdish interviewees we recruited were comparable in age and education to those from Poland, had been in London on average slightly longer, and had broadly similar undocumented work histories. However, the reasons they gave for coming to the UK and the social relations of their life in London were entirely different. Out of 25 men and women (half of whom were Kurdish) 18 were or had been asylum seekers; of these, several had been smuggled to the UK by organisations, others had entered on false passports, and many had come after stays in other European countries. But not one said that he or she had come to London primarily to work. Their undocumented employment was described as a means of survival – that sometimes developed a logic of its own – but not the original purpose of their migration.

One ironic feature of these accounts was that many who were asylum seekers had since received work permits, yet they were still working in the shadow economy, doing undeclared work while claiming income support. They accounted for this by emphasising the systematic nature of their exploitation in the workplace, and of the UK government's immigration and social policies. They saw the solution as lying through stronger and more unified trade union organisation, yet some recognised the enormous barriers such action faced. In a sense, their very presence in London, and the structural nature of their economic marginalisation, bore witness to the problems of a New Labour government that is trying to re-regulate the labour market and suppress shadow economic activity.

ETHICAL ISSUES

In researching sensitive topics (Lee, 1993), ethical issues of several kinds arise. The most obvious are ones of confidentiality, but these are usually also relatively easy to deal with. The central principle is that the researchers should be able to offer guarantees to the subjects that they will not disclose their identities or act in any other way to damage their already jeopardised security. In our study this was clearly important, because we were dealing in prejudicial material that could be the stuff of legal actions against interviewees.

These guarantees, in turn, rest on the principle of academic privilege, and the immunity of the researcher from obligations to testify in cases of official action against subjects. This is not an abstract principle: it has been tested in the courts. In British Columbia, Canada, in 1995, a coroner's court subpoenaed a MD student, Russel Ogden, to give evidence in a case where (as a result of a newspaper article) the coroner was investigating the assisted suicide of an unknown person. Ogden was known to be conducting research on AIDS victims and assisted suicide, and to have some knowledge of the identity of this person, and of those who assisted him or her to die. However, in the witness box, Ogden claimed academic privilege, and refused to answer questions on these matters. The coroner adjourned the case, to consider whether to imprison Ogden for contempt. During the ensuing months, with the prospect of a sentence of gaol hanging over him, Ogden sought the support of his university, but this was refused, on the apparent grounds that such support could bring the university into disrepute on this sensitive issue – despite the fact that Ogden had gained specific ethical approval to conduct the research, and had been required to publicise it in academic journals and the press. In the event, the coroner decided not to take action against Ogden, respecting his scruples and courage, and the principle at stake. Ogden subsequently sued his university in a civil court for his legal fees, and although his claim was unsuccessful on a technicality, the judge roundly condemned the university authorities for their pusillanimous response on the issues of academic freedom and privilege. Subsequently, a committee of professors endorsed the legal logic of the courts' support for Ogden's stance, and the university's ethical guidelines were rewritten to take account of this.

It is important to distinguish between the issues at stake in that case, and the ones that arise from the publication of articles and books in which researchers use interview material in which they admit illegality. One of the authors has in the past been criticised on the grounds that such material might lead to the prosecution of an interviewee. This is not the same question, since all Ogden's writing contained such quotations, but it was his immunity from the duty to identify the interviewees, not the inferences that might be drawn from his scholarly or journalistic work, that was at stake. Researchers have an obligation to take care to disguise their interviewees' personal details (names of themselves and others, places and so on) so as to avoid such identification, as we have done in this study. However, this obligation applies to a broad swathe of research, and not merely to that which involves illegality.

Part of the misplaced criticism of research which breaks the taboos of the academic community is usually of this kind, and reflects the fact that this community has – usually for quite different reasons, to do with its own interests or commitments – avoided the topic. And part of the defence that can be mounted against it by taboo-breaking researchers is that in real life, public authorities dealing in very widespread illegality like undocumented work (as opposed to very serious and uncommon events such as assisted suicide) do not sit around reading academic journals to get leads for their investigations. There are several reasons why they do not. First, by the time that research gets published, the individuals interviewed are seldom if ever still involved in the same sort of activity. Second, enforcement officers in services like the police, the benefits fraud squads or the immigration service need evidence to prosecute offenders, and research reports are not evidence. Third, enforcement staff in these services are far too busy responding to emergencies, recent denunciations and 'hot' evidence to take time out to review a small amount of very 'cold' material, embedded in long and tediously academic research reports.

However, what is a serious ethical question for researchers in these topics is the possibility that interviewees' *strategies* (for keeping their actions concealed from the authorities, or for survival) will be revealed in their accounts, and that the publication of a research report will therefore jeopardise them and others like them. Of course, in our research the same was true for the enforcement authorities – in revealing *their* strategies for catching immigration offenders, we could make it easier for the latter (or at least those of them who read journals like *Policy and Politics* or *The Journal of Refugee Studies*) to escape detection.

It was therefore a considerable relief for us to discover that all the strategies revealed by the interviewees' accounts were well known to the Immigration Service enforcement staff. For example, in our pilot study, several Brazilian migrants revealed that they used enrolment in bogus language schools as a way to change their immigration status from tourist to student, both to prolong their permitted stay, and to relax the conditions around work. Our interviews with senior enforcement staff indicated that they were well aware of this loophole, and even of which 'schools' exploited it for their gain, but that it was of low priority in their very pressured schedule of work, and they seldom had time to do more than respond to denunciations of individual 'bogus students'.

Conversely, the interviews with undocumented immigrant workers revealed that they were knowledgeable about the Immigration Service's strategies for apprehending people coming from abroad to work, and that the point of entry and denunciation by a fellow national were the situations of greatest risk (the latter applying to Brazilian and Polish but not Turkish/Kurdish migrants). This explained why the enforcement staff were rather relaxed and open in their dealings with us as researchers, and gave us excellent access to the roles and situations we wished to investigate. Despite the atmosphere of official security surrounding their tasks, and the absence of the kinds of community liaison and public relations work now undertaken by most police forces, they were not in this sense a 'secret service', being neither specially suspicious about publicity, nor worried that greater public knowledge about their methods would jeopardise their success rates.

Finally – and most significantly for this topic – there are serious ethical issues around the political use of research findings. Researchers have a responsibility to try to take every possible step to obviate the partisan exploitation of distorted versions of their findings, especially when these are used to incite xenophobia or racism. However, in the last resort there is no way in which any such steps can be guaranteed success, and there is always a risk of this, especially around this topic. No doubt this provides part of the justification for the taboo on such research already discussed. But we would counter this by pointing out that New Labour's populism around issues of asylum was facilitated by the absence of research evidence (for instance about the fact that benefits have played an insignificant role in the motivational accounts of *all* the interviewees who chose to come to this country). We accept the responsibility to do our best not to present our findings in a way that could be misused. At the same time, the Home Office now commissions a good deal of academic research on various topics. Since it funds this work, there must be doubts about how independent it can be. In view of the danger of 'policy-led evidence' rather than 'evidence-led policy', it is important that an independent, critical stance is available.

METHODOLOGY

The methods used in this project were based on those deployed by the authors in earlier research (Jordan *et al.*, 1992; Düvell, 1996), and particularly in the pilot study on Brazilian migrants (Jordan and Vogel, 1997a, 1997b). It was important to ask questions about the topic of irregular migration in a neutral way that allowed the interviewees to contextualise it in their accounts. The objective of the interviews was therefore to produce *accounts* (Silverman, 1985) of immigration experiences, in which the significance of irregular activity could be understood. In all such accounts, the speaker reveals an *interpretative repertoire* (Wetherell and Potter, 1988) for describing the events in question – a set of linked ideas through which he or she explains and justifies them to the interviewer. This is because it is a central feature of all such face-to-face interactions (Goffman, 1969) that speakers feel *accountable* to those to whom they are giving versions of their experiences, and specifically they feel required to give a *morally adequate* account of their actions and omissions (Cuff, 1980). This seems to be an inescapable aspect of the way in which we all, as members of any human community of interactants, make the world intelligible and meaningful to ourselves and others, and create a sense not just of binding obligation (and hence *moral* intelligibility) but even of *external* (and hence predictable) reality itself (Hilbert, 1992).

The interesting thing about interviews with undocumented workers, of course, was that most of them did not share in membership of the formal institutional structures of UK society, and some were there completely illegally, and did not even 'exist' in official UK records. Hence, what was created by the exchanges in the interviews was an *informal* order (Rawls, 1989), accomplished (Jordan, Redley and James, 1994) between the interviewee and the interviewer themselves, and yet still in some sense accountable to the formal order of UK society (immigration rules, employment law and so on). The interviewees still felt required to give a morally adequate version of their immigration experiences, and to legitimate them by some standards that they felt reflected the relevant features of such 'realities' as the laws of economics, the current employment situation in their home countries and the UK, international migration trends and so on. To fail to do so was somehow to 'lose face' (Goffman, 1969), even though the encounter was taking place in a shadow world of illegality, and the interviewee might share few norms with the host society, or the researchers themselves.

In order to facilitate such exchanges, in which the interviewees would feel supported and enabled in creating such an 'informal order' in the interview situation, and safe to reveal the shared cultural assumptions, practices and resources of undocumented workers from their country, we employed interviewers who were fluent in the languages of the interviewees. In the pilot study, this meant that Kylza Estrella, a Brazilian doctor doing a postgraduate degree in complementary health studies, was employed to trace and recruit the original group of undocumented workers in London. She pioneered the methods, and showed great patience and persistence, in tracking down and persuading a variety of Brazilian workers, aged between 18 and 51 (Jordan, Vogel and Estrella, 1996). For our Polish interviews, we appointed Emilia Breza, who graduated in Poland, came to London to visit her brother, met and married her husband (from the Turkish/Kurdish community), and now works as an interpreter in the health service, having both residence and work permits. As a native Polish speaker who had lived in London for some time, she was able to use her networks to make contact with and recruit the group of Polish workers soon to be described.

For the interviews with Turkish and Kurdish migrants, we employed two interviewers. One of these was Thomas Stapke, a German graduate in social work, who spoke Turkish and a number of Kurdish dialects. He had the advantage of being perceived as neutral by the various political groups that made up the Turkish and Kurdish communities. The second was Agkül Baylav, a health advocate and translator. She was able to gain access to more women interviewees, and to a slightly different constituency and age range among the Turkish population.

The point of this methodology was to see how the interviewees made sense of their migration experiences, and how they integrated the different aspects of their lives as largely invisible members of the host society. Did each national group share certain interpretations of their activities, and what variations were there between subgroups within each nationality, and between individuals? The same method was applied to the analysis of accounts given by representatives of support groups and organisations for refugees and immigrants (Chapter 6), by the internal enforcement authorities (Chapter 7), and by the staff of public services (Chapter 8), to see how they made sense of their work, and of their exchanges with irregular migrants.

In the context of the UK legislation of the time, what was controversial about irregular migration was not merely that these interviewees had broken immigration rules, either to enter the country or to survive within it; it was whether they were motivated by economic gain, and specifically by access to the public infrastructure of benefits and services. Our aim was to see how those who did undocumented work accounted for their activity, and how they explained this economic aspect within their overall interpretation of the migration experience. In giving their versions of why they came and how they survived, they would also be asked how they used the welfare benefits and public service systems, if they did not mention these specifically in their accounts of their decisions.

Of course, these methods could not provide us with an unambiguous answer to questions about the motivations behind their actions, or even with a perfectly accurate picture of their activities. But the fact that interviewees were willing to speak quite openly about their breaches of the regulations, and to explain and justify their actions, could give important indications of the factors influencing migration decisions and strategies.

One of the most important advantages of the method was that it revealed how many irregular migrants were quite willing to say that they broke the rules in order to earn, and that they felt justified in doing so because the rules

were unreasonable and unfair. This interpretation was common to almost all
the Polish respondents, and several of the Brazilians. The other significant
finding was that, once the culture of a national group allows this interpretation to be adopted, it is relatively easy for individuals to mobilise within the
available immigration statuses – tourist, student, *au pair*, business visitor and
so on – in order to enter the country to pursue these aims. It was clear that the
interpretative repertoires of justified irregular work (which benefited the UK
as well as the migrants) were among the cultural resources that sustained
these travelling to London, especially from Poland. It allowed them to gather
resources and support within their countries, and make contacts with those
already in the UK.

However, by confronting the question of their irregularity solely in terms
of the rules against working and earning, migrants from Poland were able to
sidestep the other controversial issue, of the impact of irregular migration on
the collective infrastructure. In fact, most of them had used the National
Health Service during their visits, and those who settled – for instance,
through marriage to a UK or EU citizen – gained access to benefits also (see
Chapter 5, pp. 143–4). In this, and in their impact on the economic circumstances of unskilled UK workers, their presence was therefore not necessarily
as unambiguously beneficial as they claimed. But the method did allow us to
reveal their reasoning about this issue, and how it influenced their use or non-
use of the public services.

Far more delicate and difficult to investigate was the situation of interviewees from Turkey. On the one hand, from an ethical standpoint many critics
would question the appropriateness of research that looked behind the claim
for political asylum, and tried to investigate possible economic motivations
for entry into the UK. On the other, sceptics would doubt whether the version
given by interviewees claiming asylum would reveal the extent of incentives
in the UK infrastructure, and especially its welfare system (benefits for asylum seekers were still available at the time most of these applicants from
Turkey made their claims).

In fact, our methodology allowed us to show the sophisticated way in
which these issues were resolved within the interpretative repertoires of
migrants from Turkey. Their political versions of their reasons for leaving the
country were closely integrated with their accounts of economic exploitation
in the UK, and they were able to link these through transnational explanations of the capitalist dynamic. What they were fleeing in Turkey was therefore
part of an economic as well as a political system of oppression, the other end
of which (as it were) they then encountered in London. Far from acting as a
magnet, the UK benefits system played a part in this transnational process
that affected them as workers as much as refugees. In this interpretation of an
oppressive political economy, these interviewees were sustained by the cul-

tural resources of their associations and support groups in London, which, in turn, supported their claims for asylum. Even most of those not involved in these associations, or not claiming asylum, put forward similar versions of the overall context of their migrations. Migrants from Turkey demonstrated clear examples of migration as collective action (Bach and Schraml, 1982) and of transnational communities (Vertovec and Cohen, 1999).

While these methods do not demonstrate conclusively the 'push and pull factors' in migration decisions, they do indicate how the strategies for entering and staying revealed in their accounts are embedded in cultural understandings, justifications and practices. This, in turn, is relevant for the responses of the host country institutions that are examined in Part III of this book.

REASONS FOR MIGRATING AND CHOOSING THE UK

The interviewees told of their lives before migration in ways that fitted the kinds of account they were giving of their experiences as undocumented workers in London. Hence, their version of the factors in their countries of origin influencing their decisions to migrate was strongly moulded by the interpretative repertoire (Wetherell and Potter, 1988) within which they described coming to the UK, working and living in London. For example, those Brazilians who gave *learners' accounts* of their migration experiences – emphasising personal growth and investment in themselves and their future careers – focused on the limited opportunities for self-development and work experience in their home country; Poles who gave *workers' accounts* of their goals in terms of earning and saving for cars or houses in Poland referred briefly to the impossibility of achieving these aims in their home labour market; and migrants from Turkey who gave *political accounts* of their journeys in search of freedom and safety emphasised the dangers and threats of the Turkish political environment. Thus the content of the information they gave about their previous lives, and the amount of detail on different aspects of it, varied with the kind of narrative version of their migration experiences they were giving, and with what they regarded as the taken-for-granted cultural knowledge, shared with the interviewer, about why people from their countries undertook such costly and risky ventures.

BRAZILIANS

Most of the 21 Brazilians interviewed were recruited by a kind of snowball technique, one contact leading to another; a minority were contacted through

Table 4.1   Interviewees from Brazil

Occupational background in Brazil	
Professionals (teachers, journalist)	7
University or college students	6
Managers	2
Technician	1
Post office worker	1
Shop assistant	1
Musician	1
Unknown/unclear	2

Age and time spent in UK			
Age		*Time in UK*	
Under 20	1	Less than 6 months	3
20–24	4	6 months–1 year	2
25–29	10	1 or 2 years	4
30–34	3	3–5 years	9
35–39	0	over 5 years	3
40–49	1		
50 and over	2		

cafés and restaurants frequented by people from their country, and through a Brazilian church. They were aged between 19 and 52, and had been working without proper immigration status for between three months and ten years (Table 4.1).

One group of these interviewees explained their motives for coming to London as part of a 'traveller's account' of leaving Brazil, emphasising personal growth and development. They had usually come through other European countries, and had little intention of staying for long; however, several who said they came as part of such a trip had actually remained longer than they intended.

I didn't have any intention of staying here, I was on a trip. What happened I can't even explain to you, I sort of took a liking to London, ending up living here [for 7 years]. … I really like it here, I like my friends and my life (Marcos, p. 2).

On the whole, it is almost as if I've given myself time to grow and change. I had just finished university in Brazil, … beginning to work as a professional. I lived in

the USA as a teenager, and found out, at that stage, how interesting and challenging it is to live abroad. I think I wanted a bit of that spiciness back in my life
again. ... I think I came here because I wanted to live in a really foreign culture to
me (Lucia, p. 1).

Another version was that the interviewee had come to London to gain
knowledge or experience that would be valuable to them in the Brazilian
economy on their return. This might include learning English, or gaining
other qualifications, but it also consisted in work experience.

I was in my second year in a Business Administration course. ... My Dad works in
the same institution. ... He advised me to take the course and learn English. I
thought I would put the two together, come to learn English and see a bit of the
world. ... I would also like to take courses in computers and different softwares
(Alex, p. 1).

I never came here to make money. That has never been my intention at all. I want
to struggle for a better future, that is why I decided to come (Carlos, p. 1).

I will go back to Brazil in the long term, but now I want to enable myself to be
more productive here, develop my c.v. and to go back to Brazil (Joana, p. 1).

The third type of account emphasised earning, and the opportunity to save
for the future.

I wanted to buy a house, and with the money I used to earn in Brazil I would never
be able to do that (Cris, p. 1).

We are going to make money. We are very focused on our plans (Dina, p. 2).

However, despite the different reasoning in these three types of accounts,
one of the common reasons for choosing to leave Brazil, and come to London
was the fact that it was easier to get undocumented work in the UK than in
other countries (either in Europe or in North America).

It is not possible to work in Switzerland. The only work that you can do there is
prostitution. And that is what people do. Here they are more tolerant. You can
work without a work permit. In Switzerland it is very difficult, it is such a small
place anyway, and the police is always watching (Rosa, p. 1).

... I think it is more difficult to work in the USA ... I think it is more difficult
there to work and study (Alex, p. 2).

Comparing the accounts given by irregular Brazilian migrants in London
with a group recruited at the same time in Berlin, the German group relied
much more heavily on work in private households (especially cleaning), and

depended more on help from legal immigrants and German citizens (Jordan and Vogel, 1997a). This was because more and better enforced labour-market regulation made it too risky for them to seek the kind of work available to Brazilians in London. Those who came to the UK, whether as travellers, to improve their long-term prospects or to save from earning, were aware of this difference. Furthermore, those who gave travellers' and learners' accounts of why they came were often unable to sustain these in explaining why they stayed, often for many years. The accessibility of the shadow labour market was both an opportunity and a trap for them (see pp. 130–31).

MIGRANTS FROM POLAND

The interviewees from Poland were recruited by a similar snowball method, and through contacts at a health centre. Their age range was from 22 to 45. Their educational level and work experience was generally in the higher range of achievement in Poland; 13 of them were women and 12 men (Table 4.2).

Table 4.2   Interviewees from Poland

Education and previous employment	
Student or recent graduate	10
Businessman/professional	2
Dressmaker/dressmaking teacher	2
Skilled manual	4
Other manual	1
Romany/unemployed	1
Unspecified/no previous work experience	5

Age and time spent in UK			
Age		*Total time in UK*	
Under 20	1	less than 6 months	2
20–24	9	6 months–1 year	5
25–29	9	1 or 2 years	9
30–34	0	3–5 years	3
35–39	1	over 5 years	2
40–49	4	unclear	4
50 or over	1		

As with the Brazilian narratives, most Polish interviewees built into their accounts the assumption that work prospects and earning opportunities were extremely limited in their home country ('a disaster' – Krystyna, p. 4) and that experience of working in London would be helpful rather than damaging for their longer-term prospects. However, fewer of them gave accounts in which travel or learning played a significant part in shaping their migration stories. Although travel, tourism and sightseeing were mentioned by 8 of the 25, either as reasons for paying a first brief visit to the UK before coming to work, or as secondary motives for their journeys from Poland, in none of these is this sustained beyond the first page of the interview transcript, except where one woman took 'time out' from undocumented work to do some sightseeing with her mother, who visited London for a holiday. All the rest gave straightforward *workers' accounts*, in which it was taken for granted that the UK offered wages and employment that were absent in Poland, and gave little detail about previous work there, or what precipitated their decisions to migrate. The only specific triggers mentioned were redundancy in a Polish factory (Zofia), failure to get a place at a chosen University (Janusz) and – in the case of the Romany man – political persecution (Marek). Most common were laconic statements such as:

> Many people were going to England, we talked about it quite often, so I came as well (Teresa, p. 1).

> Barbara went to England and I thought it could be fun, that I would go to the West and everyone would envy me … (Natalia, p. 1).

> We are not in a hurry to go back to Poland because there is nothing we can do in Poland (Jerzy, p. 12).

> I had never worked in Poland. … After finishing the mechanical trade school I claimed an unemployment benefit and then I did my military service (Jerzy, p. 12).

It was clear that there was a strong culture of working abroad to earn and save, and that it was sustained by networks of practical assistance and moral support among friends and families. One young woman was offered a job and accommodation by a friend who was already in London.

> Everyone was telling me to go so I decided to go (Natalia, p. 2).

A man aged 40, who came along on a tour bus to meet a neighbour's partner in London, but failed to make the *rendezvous*, commented:

... if I left [to return to Poland], I would have been a laughing stock. ... Everyone back home expected me to come back much later with the money (Zbigniew, p. 2).

It is clear from several of the accounts that the interviewee was recruited for undocumented work by family or friends working in England. One, who was made redundant by her employer, was effectively transferred to a job in England.

My boss offered me a trip to England to work. They were the ones who would arrange everything (Zofia, p. 1).

Most interviewees had contacts (either family or friends) to advise and ease their entry to the UK – the only exceptions were Margareta, Ivona, Zbigniew, Marek (the Romany asylum seeker) and Teresa. One respondent had himself become a recruiter for his employer (Stanislaw). Freedom and labour-market opportunities were mentioned as reasons for choosing the UK, rather than Germany, the destination for the largest number of migrating Poles.

Because you can feel free and be free here. Not like Germany (Zbigniew, p. 1).

It is clear from these accounts that – like the Brazilians – Polish migrants knew (from the direct accounts of their friends and family who were in England, or had been there) that the lack of internal regulation made it easy for them to get work, and to evade the internal immigration authorities once they got past the port (or airport). The 'freedom' of which they spoke – and they gave examples of the easy-going attitude of UK authorities as well as the indifference of citizens – was a direct reflection of the political and economic culture of liberal individualism, quite different from the more tightly regulated societies of the Continent, and especially from German society. Two respondents gave examples of British people working for the regulatory authorities (a policeman and a Home Office official, but not a member of the Immigration and Nationality Directorate) who had employed them, knowing full well that they were in breach of their immigration status.

This shared knowledge of shadow labour markets, earning opportunities and the ease of evading detection was clearest in the case of skilled building workers, men who came to London to work on renovating old houses, usually for Polish subcontractors. They knew before they came that they could earn decent wages (£3.50–£4 per hour, much more than they could get in Poland) from the moment they arrived, and had the contacts to do so. They tended to be older (in their late 30s or early 40s), and several had worked abroad before, but saw the UK as their best option.

It is a paradise here for my profession (Daniel, p. 5).

Among younger men and women, the decision to choose the UK as their destination was influenced by a desire to travel and have new experiences, as well as to earn and save.

I wanted adventure. I was young. I gave up college and came here to see England and have some fun (Olga, p. 1).

Desire to learn English, and the fact that they already knew some English, were subsidiary reasons for choosing the UK, mentioned by three respondents (Irena, Ivona and Dariusz). One student was actually invited to the UK by someone who had taught her English in Poland.

Because we all studied at the College of English Language (Irena, p. 1).

However, for these younger interviewees, as well as the older, better qualified ones (the building workers and the dressmaking teacher), the primary attraction was the earning opportunities.

England is a country where you can earn money. People talk in Poland how and how much you can earn here (Renata, p. 2).

TURKISH AND KURDISH MIGRANTS

Of the 25 interviewees from Turkey, 18 had applied for asylum, and 13 were of Kurdish origin. In all, 16 were men and 9 women; it proved more difficult to recruit women respondents than men. It was necessary to employ a female interviewer to increase the number of women recruits, as very few were willing to speak to Thomas Stapke, the original interviewer. As we show in Chapter 5, the differences between male and female versions of migration experiences were much stronger among interviewees from Turkey than from either Brazil or Poland.

The decision to include asylum seekers in a study of irregular migration was controversial. Many commentators – including some representatives of refugee support agencies quoted in Chapter 6 – would argue that asylum is a separate issue from economic migration, and from irregular economic activity. However, the UK government was, at the time of our research study, claiming that most asylum seeking was a disguised form of economic migration (see pp. 82–3). Furthermore, there was evidence from other countries of an extensive shadow economy of Turkish entrepreneurs and workers in several European cities (see Chapter 3, pp. 63–4). Hence, it seemed important to compare the accounts of migrants from Turkey, including asylum seekers, with those of irregular migrants from the other two countries.

The qualification for being included in our recruitment of interviewees was simply having engaged economic activity in breach of immigration status. By this criterion, those from Turkey were involved in just the same irregularities as those from Brazil and Poland. They had all worked in the shadow economy, either before being given permission to work (after six months or more) as asylum seekers, or as overstayers when their asylum applications had been refused, or when in some other status. Furthermore, and unlike the other nationalities, they had also done undocumented work which was undeclared to the tax and benefit authorities while they were asylum seekers with permission to work, which was obviously also against the rules. Finally, the profile of their work activities (as we show in Chapter 5) was remarkably similar to that of the Polish irregular migrants, and in many cases they were working side by side in the same workplaces. Seen purely from the perspective of their economic activities, there were more similarities than differences between the three groups of interviewees.

However, as we show, the migration histories of interviewees from Turkey were much more complex than those from the other two countries, and involved more changes of immigration status. We recruited people who had come as tourists, *au pairs* and students as well as those who had entered the UK as asylum seekers. We also aimed to see whether those who were active members of political groups or cultural associations gave different accounts of their economic motivations and activities from those who did not participate in these, and whether those with Turkish ethnicity described their experiences differently from those of Kurdish origin.

In order to try to allow for these possibilities, and answer these questions, we recruited interviewees by a variety of methods, and from a number of sources. Networking key persons in the community and chain referral are appropriate methods to employ when the target population is small and/or the research is sensitive, as in this case (Biernacki and Waldorf, 1981). Each of seven major Turkish and Kurdish advice centres, community centres and cultural centres, spanning four different boroughs, was approached about the research. Two (identified with PKK politics) refused point-blank. Four of those who took part were associated with political parties; one was not. They supplied two gatekeepers; the other gatekeepers were two interpreters and a health advocate, two of whom themselves became interviewees, and they helped to recruit another 11 respondents, five of whom were interviewed in political centres in the narrower sense. All the rest were met through family or friendship networks, or were users of health advocacy services.

Table 4.3   Interviewees from Turkey

Education and previous employment	
University graduates	4
University or college students	4
Accountants	3
Engineers	2
Teachers	2
Architect	1
Geographer	1
Chemist	1
Craft workers	2
Manual workers	2
Clerical workers	2
No educational or work qualifications	1

Interviewees from Turkey – age and time in UK			
Age		*Time spent in UK*	
20–24	5	Less than 2 years	7
25–29	6	More than 5 years	8
30–39	10	Ten years or more	9
40 and over	2	Unclear	1
Unclear	2		

If anything, the Turkish and Kurdish respondents had even higher educational and work qualifications than those from the other two groups. There were fewer skilled craftsmen than among the Poles (Table 4.3). These migrants had on average spent longer in the UK than either of the other two groups, and were slightly older.

Migration stories tended to be complex. Nine interviewees had undertaken internal migrations in Turkey (mainly from rural to urban locations); and 10 of the 25 mentioned stays or passing through other countries. Of these, three had stayed in Greece, and three in Germany, from where one had been deported. Some had not intended to come to the UK for long.

I wanted to stay here for a year, learning English, and then go to America (Abdulla, p. 1).

> I thought about going to Canada, but it is very difficult to go there directly. ...
> With falsified documents I came to England ... but to travel to Canada there is a
> special immigration desk; I was caught, ... arrested at the airport and had to apply
> for asylum, otherwise I would have been sent back (Halit, pp. 2–3).

Others did not know they were coming to the UK; five were smuggled here:

> I came here in '94, ... with the help of smugglers. ... Then it did not matter where
> to go, ... the smugglers decided where I would be brought to, ... you did not
> choose, ... it could have been any country (Metin, pp. 3–4).

> I found a smuggler ... we entered this country (Nazim, p. 3).

In such accounts, the most important decision was to leave Turkey. Once
this had been decided, periods of wandering through the European Union,
experiencing uncertainty and a process of trial and error, were not uncommon. Hence, the accounts consisted of an initial justification of the decision
to leave, followed by an explanation of how they came to choose the UK,
often after trying elsewhere.

In all, 20 interviewees gave political reasons for leaving Turkey (that is
more than the number who had applied for asylum). Two had been arrested
and tortured.

> My family always give everything to politics ... They searched for my cousin, and
> when he wasn't there they took me to the police station, they beat me, tortured me
> (Metin, pp. 2, 8).

However, most either heard that they were being sought by police, or fled
when other family members were arrested.

> I was involved in student activities and was being sought ... (Sirin, p. 2).
> I came as a student and after three months I learned that I was sought [by police]
> and only then I applied for asylum (Mehmet, p. 9).
> I would have been imprisoned ... (Ali, p. 3).
> My brother is in and out of prison, they wanted to get me too (Kadir, p. 1).
> My brother's life was in danger, he was forced to escape, afterwards I left too
> (Baran, p. 2).

Another reason was being conscripted into the armed forces to fight in
Kurdistan – four respondents gave this as the precipitating event, along with
political concerns. But overall there were few differences between the accounts given by Turkish and Kurdish interviewees. Clandestine entries were
all among the latter, more of whom had relatives in the UK, fewer gave
educational reasons for coming, and fewer spoke English, but all these differences were small.

The choice of the UK revealed a secondary process of reasoning once the decision to leave Turkey had been made. Language was frequently a factor – respondents either spoke English, or wanted to learn it.

The most important reason was to find an English-speaking country, ... I did know some English (Kadir, p. 3)

Why did we come to England? My wife spoke English, we wanted to go somewhere where it would be some use (Osman, p. 2).

One woman who mentioned political and family reasons for leaving Turkey, chose the UK for the chance to study and live on her own.

I worked in a textile factory as an accountant, to get on I would have to speak another language quite well. There were English people working there: I thought that if I could speak proper English I could do a better job ... I decided to come here, to learn the language (Idil, p. 1).

Several men who had spent time in other countries had informed themselves about the situation of asylum seekers in the UK; but what influenced their choice was political and personal freedom, not the economic situation or the availability of benefits.

In those days England seemed to be best because Germany and France had restricted their asylum procedures (Timur, p. 7).
Asylum conditions are better here, ... in Germany there aren't these opportunities. Furthermore, we had learned that in England human rights are more acknowledged (Mustafa, p. 3).
After I learned about England I thought about applying for asylum. After I came here, I applied (Ahmet, p. 2).

In all, 11 of the 25 mentioned language (either existing ability or desire to learn English) as a reason for choosing the UK; the same number gave the fact that they had relatives or friends there (three linked these two reasons).

In Turkey I was under pressure, ... I had relatives here and because of democracy I chose this country [and] applied for asylum (Mehmet, pp. 2, 6).
Four of my brothers and sisters [are here] (Metin, p. 2).
When my friends were coming here, I wanted to come as well (Halide, p. 1).
... because my wife's father lives here (Nazim, p. 4).

Only two of the 25 interviewees gave economic reasons for leaving Turkey, one in 1988, the other in 1993.

'I support my family, when I came here the situation [there] wasn't really good, ... that was why I came here, to support them' (Faruk, p. 2).
'The financial situation forced me to leave Turkey and go to Europe' (Timur, p. 1).

Thus Turkish/Kurdish undocumented workers' migration narratives generally started from a quest for political freedom, and explained their shadow activities in the context of life in the UK.

'The main reason was that I was disgusted by the political situation in Turkey, ... I was lucky not to be imprisoned, ... I am not an asylum seeker, ... I wanted to get away from Turkey' (Ali, pp. 1–3).

But – as we show – the interviewees also described problematic and changing immigration status, and their economic behaviour must be understood as related to these issues also.

CONCLUSIONS

The choice of migrants from Brazil, Poland and Turkey reflected the 'new migrations' (from the further continents, from the former communist bloc and from the near East) that began in the 1990s (Castles and Miller, 1993). We deliberately chose groups for whom there were no strong post-colonial links, although in the case of Turkey, the Turkish Cypriot community in North-east London, and in Hackney in particular, provided a base for chain migration. The aim was to see how 'economic migration' and asylum were related, and how an immigration control system designed primarily to regulate migration from the New Commonwealth coped with the challenge of new arrivals from other countries, coming with different strategies, plans, links and motives.

These groups did not fit the model put forward by Sassen (1988) either, since none of the countries of origin was a particular focus for the investment of UK capital. Direct investment by UK companies in Brazil, Poland and Turkey did increase in the 1970s and 1980s, but in none of them was the UK a leading presence, compared with Germany and the USA. Hence, we are required to seek other explanations for the migrants' choice of London as a destination; they were not simply following the economic logic of investment flows and trade.

The second part of Sassen's (1991) explanation of such migratory flows is more relevant. London is certainly a 'global city', and these migrants were – as shown in Chapter 5 – drawn into the service infrastructure of the city, as part of a cosmopolitan mixture of such workers. However, as we demonstrate, there were particular niches that they occupied, and some unexpected interactions between them.

Yet although the common outcome for all these migrants was irregular work within the shadow labour market of the city, their ways of making sense of their decisions to come, and their strategies for staying, were extremely varied. Our research methods aimed to reveal the ways in which these interpretations of the migration experience fitted with their orientations to the UK immigration rules, labour-market regulations and welfare systems, and how these, in turn, were sustained by their cultural resources and support systems.

Immigration rules and policies are ostensibly designed to facilitate advantageous economic transactions between citizens of different states, and provide humanitarian protection for those in fear of persecution. But the existence of a shadow market for foreign labour in London drew these individuals to the city. For Brazilians, this was framed within an account of their responses to the limited opportunities for educated people within their society, and as part of an exploration of the global range of openings for alternatives elsewhere. For Poles, it was a more focused project for improving their economic situation, treating the UK as one of the options for increasing their earnings through willingness to take the risk of travelling. Both of these groups entered through the channels open for tourism, study and business, while having other economic purposes.

The case of migrants from Turkey was far more complex. The constraints on political freedom in the country, and the existence of movements resisting these oppressions, supplied the cultural resources for leaving their homeland, and seeking new lives elsewhere. However, even if asylum seeking had no economic motives, it certainly had economic consequences. The rules surrounding this immigration status involved interviewees from Turkey with the UK authorities, including public services, far more than their counterparts from Brazil and Poland. Hence, they were required to account for their irregular economic activity both within a narrative of their search for political freedom, and as part of an account of their continued engagement with the immigration control and welfare systems. In the next chapter, we consider how these different orientations affected the three groups' strategies for survival and security in London.

5. How they survive

There are two factors that make the lives of irregular migrants – those without proper immigration status, either to be present, or to be working – more difficult than those of citizens or legal entrants. The first is that they have to remain invisible to the immigration authorities and (presumably) to other officials concerned with law enforcement, and to citizens and legal residents who might perceive them as harmful in some way to their interests. The second is that they have to live without the support of those institutions designed to sustain the lives of lawful members of that society, including welfare systems, regulatory bodies and agencies for the protection of persons and property.

That they do in fact survive, in some cases for long periods, and that a few prosper, is therefore of more than passing interest, from the standpoint of economics, law, sociology and social policy. It also links our research with the interdisciplinary study of transitional communities (Vertovec and Cohen, 1999). The question of how they remain undetected by the enforcement authorities is dealt with only briefly in this chapter; it is treated far more fully in Chapter 7. How they survive without legal membership or official support is the central issue for this chapter. We show that they do so partly because they adopt well-tried strategies, based on cultural resources available within their communities; partly because they assimilate to other groups of citizens and legal immigrants, who live on the margins of the economy and society, and who use somewhat similar strategies for survival; but mainly because they make themselves inconspicuously useful, and are broadly welcomed for what they can offer, being largely indistinguishable from other hardworking and hard-pressed members of minority groups in cities, and especially in London.

The economics and sociology of irregular migration are contested territory, and raise complex issues. Broadly speaking, economic theory suggests that irregular migration from a poorer country to a richer one will occur when the difference in potential earnings between the two is greater than the wage in the poorer *plus* the likely costs associated with breaching the barriers to migration – including travel costs, accommodation, job search, language skill acquisition and (above all) the chances of being caught and sent home. Thus, although in the long run wage differentials will tend to be reduced both by trade and by movement of capital (see Chapter 1, pp. 19–20), the existence of immigration restrictions will prolong the disequilibrium in labour markets, and irregular migration is a response to this situation (Chiswick, 1999, p. 4).

As we have seen (pp. 75–6), the presence of irregular migrants may have a number of different economic and social impacts, and may affect some groups adversely, and others advantageously. This helps explain why – as in the UK in the period under study in our research – some groups (such as Roma and Kurdish asylum seekers, many of whom were attacked by UK citizens, and one of whom was murdered in August 2001) were treated with extreme hostility, both in the media and by some of their neighbours, while others remained unnoticed and unmolested. In this case, those evoking hostility were legal entrants, but perceived as 'bogus' applicants for asylum, whereas all our interviewees were or had been living in breach of immigration rules, yet none reported experiencing hostility from UK citizens.

The obvious causes of rivalry between citizens and irregular migrants are competition for accommodation, jobs and welfare benefits. Campaigns (by newspapers and by racist political groups) against asylum seekers in 1999–2000 emphasised that they occupied social housing, and that they were paid benefit rates well in excess of those going to citizens. In fact, of course, the high rate of payments went to their landlords (local authorities, housing associations or commercial companies) and to supermarket chains, and almost not at all to the asylum seekers themselves. The accommodation they occupied was often either virtually unfit for habitation, or had been impossible to let to citizens. But the perception among disadvantaged white citizens remained that asylum seekers were getting more than they were – reflecting the neglect of exactly these communities by successive governments since the late 1970s (Jordan, 1998, ch. 5). Rivalry was the result of the exclusion and deprivation suffered by these citizens, and largely the product of government policies.

On the other hand, the work activities of our interviewees may have damaged the interests of low-skilled UK citizens, albeit indirectly. Their shadow work may have contributed to the fall in wages of such workers, and the increased insecurity and casualisation of their employment (see Chapter 3, pp. 59–64; Chiswick, 1999, p. 7). In particular, they may have been in direct competition for work with some members of UK minority ethnic groups – and this may partly explain the fact that, according to Home Office enforcement staff, some 70 per cent of phone calls from UK citizens denouncing 'illegal immigrants' come from members of such minorities (see pp. 178–9).

However, the fact also remains that none of the interviewees were aware of having been denounced by a UK citizen, and both Brazilians and Poles were far more concerned about denunciations by their fellow nationals (see pp. 178–81). This contrasts with Brazilians in Berlin, who had been denounced by Germans, and who knew others who had been. In the UK, despite the government's efforts to encourage anonymous denunciations of neighbours (for example, on benefit fraud), this is not culturally approved (Jordan *et al.*, 1992, ch. 7). But equal relevance is the fact that irregular migrants, even as they were contributing to falling wages and casualisation of employment, were proving advantageous for high earners, for entrepreneurs and for the owners of land and capital – groups with far more political power than those whose interests they might have been damaging (Chiswick, 1999, p. 7).

Turning to the question of how they orientate themselves to the host society, and make their ways within it, this raises important questions about the role of institutions in social life, and the ways in which both formal and informal institutions structure action. If social actors steer their lives by reference to rules (both formal laws and regulations, and informal norms and codes), how can people whose scanty knowledge of the former consists of having a strategy for breaking them, and without any familiarity with the latter, manage to survive within the host society?

Our study certainly casts some light on these issues. In the first place money, markets and exchange provide a kind of universal language for all kinds of transactions in the age of globalisation. Brazilians and Poles were both adept at finding commercial suppliers of information, accommodation, National Insurance numbers and other important items, as well as employment. With the help of a few trusted friends from their own countries, and a small initial sum to pay for their induction into UK society, they could find their way through the shadowy reaches of London's economy, without needing to understand the subtleties of UK law, politics, culture or even the welfare system. What is interesting is to discover how self-sufficient this shadow world of undocumented commercial exchanges is in London, and how little need its participants have for the official world of recorded, taxed transactions, registered workers, recognised citizens and legal entitlements. What is also important is to note how, in the absence of the taken-for-granted infrastructure of public goods, such actors became victims of each other's exploitation, mistrust and domination.

All this is also in significant contrast with more regulated societies such as Germany (Jordan and Vogel, 1997a), or Holland (Kloosterman, Van der Leun and Rath, 1999; Rath, 1999), where irregular migrants both need legal entrants or citizens to sponsor their entry into the economy and society, and require a better knowledge of how the world of official transactions works, to survive. For instance, it was ironic that most Brazilians wanted to learn English as part of their motivation for choosing London; yet their counterparts in Berlin were more likely to succeed in learning German (because they needed it to survive), even though this was not one of their goals in selecting Berlin as their destination.

For the Turkish and Kurdish interviewees, rather different factors came into consideration. Not only were there larger numbers of their fellow country people in north and east London; they were also far more organised, both in terms of large, formal associations and in terms of smaller, informal community groups and kinship networks. In Hackney in particular, these played a full part in local politics, in the structures of community health and social services, and in civil society. Furthermore, unlike Brazilians – who lacked organisations, other than churches and some informal cultural groupings – or Poles, among whom there was hostility between organised, legal, long-term residents, and new undocumented arrivals, Turkish and Kurdish communities welcomed and included the interviewees, organised in defence of their interests, and offered them support (see pp. 161–3).

At a theoretical level, this indicates that the influential distinction between *institutions* and *organisations* (North, 1990, p. 4) is largely misleading. In the 'new institutional economics', institutions (both formal and informal) are 'perfectly analogous to the rules of the game in a competitive team sport', whereas organisations can be compared to the teams that play that sport, since they mobilise individuals strategically for interactions within those laws and norms. But Turkish and Kurdish groups and associations could act as institutions at one level of social exchanges (ordering and structuring relationships), and as organisations at another level (mobilising members to participate as interest groups in the local politics of a London borough). A collective body is both an institution that guides its members' actions through rules and norms, and an organisation that activates them for competition with other organisations, within rules set by institutions at a higher level (Jordan, 1996, p. 59).

The great majority of Turkish and Kurdish interviewees oriented themselves strongly towards the particular networks of associations, cultural and political groups with which they had had links in their own country, or towards groups of friends and kin, or both. From their point of view, these provided a set of institutions, through which they achieved a kind of 'embeddedness' in the host society (Mahler, 1995; Portes, 1995; Jahn and Straubhaar, 1998). They also oriented their economic activities towards entrepreneurs who were fellow nationals, and with whom they often shared some of these other links (Kloosterman, Van der Leun and Rath, 1999; Van der Leun, 1999). This meant that they had only gradually to learn to understand and respond to UK institutional systems. They had a ready-made set of structures, which provided a degree of support, both psychological and material, and a bridge into life in London (Böcker, 1994). But in the long run, this form of transition had costs. The particular segment of London society into which they gained this access had its own power relations and economic systems, which contained their own oppressions and exploitations – different from the 'law of the jungle' that applied to most Poles and many Brazilians, but no less real.

Furthermore, in the 'pecking order' of north-east London social structures, their position was largely analogous to that of the poorest UK citizens, to whose economic and cultural practices they rapidly assimilated. Thus, although they were more 'embedded' than either Brazilians or Poles, their stories contain more accounts of unemployment and poverty, and less of 'upward mobility', than either of those other groups. London Brazilians became relatively 'British' in their behaviour, just as Berlin Brazilians became relatively 'German'. Poles carved out for themselves a kind of ruthless economic niche, in which they could get higher rewards the longer they stayed. Turks and Kurds stayed rather Turkish and Kurdish, and rather poor.

ENTRY

Because the UK implements immigration control primarily through embassies (visa countries) and checks at the point of entry, those arriving in the country faced the moment of maximum jeopardy for their plans to migrate to London when they reached the border. The great majority of them were prepared for this moment, had rehearsed the story they would tell immigration officials, and had made sure that their luggage and personal effects were consistent with it.

Many of the *Brazilians*, entering as tourists, came after spending time in other European countries, either to try them out, or to make their stories sound more convincing.

> I went to Portugal first, because I thought it would be easier to get in ... . I didn't make any money in Portugal. Portugal is an underdeveloped country, like Brazil. ... I wanted to go somewhere else to have better chances. ... Sterling is a powerful currency, I thought it was my best choice (Rob, pp. 1–2).

> My friend told me I wouldn't get in with three children. ... I flew to Brussels and came by boat. They asked one all sorts of questions at immigration control. ... I said I was visiting some friends and gave an address and telephone number. ... I said that I just wanted to stay here for two weeks. They kept me for 20 minutes (Rita, p. 2).

> I went to France with a tourist visa ... I used to go to Holland and Spain. ... I decided to come to England to study ... At that time things were much easier (Rico, p. 1).

And to come to the UK, we came as part of a tourist group, we were together with many Spanish people, just the two of us were Brazilians. We didn't have any problem. They asked for our passports as if we were tourists (Carmen, p. 1).

Others, who came directly from Brazil, were well prepared.

They asked me how much money I had, and asked me to show them the money, and where I was going to stay. I had £1,500 with me. They said it wasn't enough money to see Europe. I answered back, I don't want to see the whole of Europe. They let me go only when I showed my business card, and gave me a tourist visa. ... They gave me a hard time. Asked why I had so many bags, etc. I was prepared for that, people told me it would be that way (Bete, p. 2).

I brought $1000. I bought the ticket with this friend of mine. They prepared me to come. I had all sorts of tricks. I didn't have anything that could show I was going to stay. No addresses, nothing. ... When I arrived, nothing happened. Nobody asked me a thing (Flavia, p. 2).

We planned well. They asked us at immigration control how much money we had. Altogether we had $7000. It was a lot of money in 1990 for three blokes, and they didn't give us any trouble (Angelo, p. 2).

One man, who was not prepared, was coming on a train from France, and got last-minute advice.

It was funny because I was in this train, and I met a Brazilian. I had two big suitcases, and he told me 'With those two you are not going to get into the UK'. I opened one of the suitcases, took some stuff out of there that I needed, and threw the suitcase out of the window. ... I said I had come for the weekend. They didn't ask me anything (Rico, p. 1).

Toni, a musician, had a letter from an English colleague to cover his arrival.

Alan said that it was difficult for Brazilians to get into the country, especially if you didn't have money. He sent me a fax in English, asking me to bring from Brazil his percussion instruments, his bass and his *cavaquinho*, which were mine. ... The officer asked me what were these instruments for, saying I came here to work. I said 'No, no, I am on holiday', and showed him the fax. ... They did everything they could to keep me there, they tried to find drugs on me. ... Always very polite, but ... (Toni, pp. 2–3).

Luisa, who had overstayed on a previous tourist visa, returned to the UK with a new passport, claiming she was visiting for the first time.

They found an English coin in my luggage, and a necklace from an English shop. They kept me for hours, investigating my life. ... I had taken all the shop labels from my clothes, but of course I had clothes from here. ... She [immigration officer] was upset, but could not prove that I had been there before (Luisa, p. 2).

Migrants from *Poland* all tended to use the same route – the bus – but had two strategies. The most reliable was an invitation from someone in the UK. Of those who entered by invitation, five had letters from a family member (three were to be carers), and five more from friends.

We had no problems with entering the country because we were invited by the family, my girlfriend's sister (Daniel, p. 1).

I talked, using my poor English, showed him my passport and letter inviting me, and I smiled at the Immigration Officer and showed them my small travel bag and said that was all I had with me. Finally I got my passport stamped and I had a six-month visa (Janusz, p. 1).

When I cam here the first time I came with a tourist trip. The other two times I came with invitation letters and had no problems entering the country (Teresa, p. 2).

Some had been invited by a friend, recruiting for a particular factory or workplace.

It was all well arranged; she wrote an invitation letter for me, she arranged it all. I wasn't scared at all. I didn't even know then that I should have been worried that I might be sent back to Poland from the port. It is only now that I hear about the problems people have entering the country (Stanislaw, p. 2).

Among those who came without letters of invitation, there were detailed accounts of interrogations and searches.

The Immigration Officer picked on me; I could see he was nasty and he didn't want to allow me to enter this country. ... Then he asked me to get my cases from the coach. They looked through all my things, cases, handbag, everything, how much money I had. ... I remember them asking what my job was, I told them I was a dressmaker. I don't know what the interpreter said to them, because I seemed to cause some problems. Anyway in the end I was allowed to pack my stuff and join the rest on the coach (Zofia, p. 2).

I was asked how long I was coming for, what I was doing in Poland, how much I earned and who invited me here, who paid for the journey, and where I would stay. Typical questions; he didn't interview me for a long time (Natalia, p. 2).

She (a friend) also gave us some instructions what to say to the Immigration Officer at the port of entry; that we were students, that we were coming to see some interesting places in England, and we had about £300 to show at the port of entry, so we were prepared (Anna, p. 1).

Some complained that they had been questioned intensively.

> When I came here for the first time they interrogated me like some bandit, literally. I was nervous. They asked me thousands of questions. ... They took me to some special room and asked me why my uncle had a Scottish name. I didn't know about it then. How could I know? I had never seen him. ... I tried to explain it all but they wouldn't understand anything; it lasted for about two hours (Karel, pp. 5–6).

> When our coach arrived in Dover it was only seven out of 50 people who were allowed to enter the UK (Zbigniew, p. 1).

The most complex and strategic account of entry and re-entry concerned a woman who originally came to join her husband, claiming to be the sister of her father-in-law, who was living in England. After six months she returned to Poland to have a baby, being joined there by her husband. After he returned to England, she again joined him, but went back to Poland to be with her child. She returned a third time, posing as her father-in-law's second wife's friend, accompanied by her baby. On this visit she applied for asylum, and claimed income support, but went to work while her mother was visiting (see p. 146). However, when her mother became ill and returned to Poland, she decided to withdraw her application for asylum, in order to visit her. She went to the Home Office. The official who interviewed her was happy to accept her withdrawal, and she enquired about returning to the UK.

> He told me that if I got myself a new passport and weren't checked on the computer I might be lucky and get leave to enter the UK. The guy was all right (Silvia, p. 7).

The fourth time she came to the UK, however, her attempted deceit was spotted, and she was sent back to France. In Calais, she met a man who offered to get her to the UK for £200. She joined a party of French tourists with a borrowed passport, which she returned after getting through immigration control. Her baby returned with her father-in-law, who had a child of much the same age, and had come over to Calais with her husband to help organise her return. She was therefore in the UK with no immigration status, and listed on the computer as refused entry.

None of the other interviewees entered the UK illegally on their first visit though – as we have seen – some did on subsequent visits, by not revealing previous stays, or using others' passports. In the case of interviewees from *Turkey*, the majority (13) entered illegally – either clandestinely (the five who were smuggled), or by deception (with falsified, bought or borrowed passports, obtained from relatives or provided by political comrades or smugglers). Another two indicated that their reasons for coming were not the ones they had declared, though of course this was also true of all the Brazilians and Poles who came as tourists or students, but with the intention of breaching their immigration conditions by working, or working more than they were permitted to do.

All those who entered either clandestinely or by deception gave political reasons for leaving Turkey (see pp. 108–9). The most clear-cut motives for illegal entry were those who could not get Turkish documents, and who were fleeing persecution, or those who could not apply for documents without revealing their intention to flee, or were being sought by the police.

> I was restricted from travelling abroad, it was difficult to get a passport (Osman, p. 1).

Only two of the 13 illegal entrants were caught and detained by the authorities.

> When I arrived – my passport was not in order of course – I was asked for my documents ... and I said that I wanted to apply for asylum. I was detained for three days ... really terrible (Metin, p. 4).

> I was in prison for two months ... because I used a false passport (Halit, p. 2).

At the time of interview, seven of these 13 had managed to gain some kind of secure status. But of the whole group of 25, 14 in all had experienced a period of extralegal stay in the UK, and another four had been in breach of their visa restrictions. In other words, the majority had not only worked illegally, but also stayed illegally for a time.

This reflects the fact that all but two (who entered by deception and immediately applied for asylum) experienced changes of immigration status during their time in the UK, and most had several changes. Indeed, if a complete list of all the statuses held by the 25 is drawn up, no status (14) is the second largest category after asylum applicant (18), and followed by student (9), married to refugee or EU citizen (7), tourist (5), refugee (4), leave to remain (3), *au pair* (3) and seven-years' rule (2). A full list of all the 25 interviews, with their reasons for leaving Turkey and changes of status, is shown below:

1. Persecution – entry by deception – no status – asylum – leave to remain
2. Illegal entry (on tourist visa but intended to study) – no status – marriage
3. Student visa – breach of immigration restrictions – no status – marriage
4. *Au pair* – breach of immigration restrictions – marriage
5. Persecution – tourist – student visa – overstaying – seven-years' rule – marriage

6. Persecution – asylum – refused and appealed – thinking about marriage
7. Persecution – student – asylum
8. Persecution – *au pair* – asylum
9. Persecution – clandestine entry – asylum – refugee
10. Student – bogus marriage – no status – waiting to meet 14-years' rule
11. Persecution – entry by deception – asylum – no status
12. *Au pair* – breach of immigration restrictions
13. Student – overstaying – asylum – no status
14. Persecution – entry by deception – asylum – leave to remain
15. Student – overstaying – asylum – leave to remain
16. Student – breach of immigration restrictions
17. Persecution – entry by deception – no status – asylum – leave to remain
18. Persecution – asylum and deportation from Germany – entry by deception – no status – asylum – no status
19. Persecution – entry by deception – no status – asylum – refusal and appeal – leave to remain
20. Student – breach of immigration restrictions – asylum – no status – bogus marriage
21. Persecution – entry by deception – asylum
22. Army – entry by deception – asylum
23. Entry by deception – asylum – no status – will get married
24. Persecution – entry by deception – asylum – refugee
25. Tourist – asylum

Of those who came in the late 1980s, several stayed for some time before applying for asylum, as a policy decision within their political group.

> Initially we did not intend to apply for asylum … We talked long about it, we had hoped that the situation in Turkey would improve, that we could with some time, learn the language and return. But then things went differently, not as we had hoped … Due to these difficulties we finally applied for asylum (Osman, pp. 3–4).

Others did not apply because of fear that this would limit the possibilities for return to Turkey.

> For four years I did not apply for asylum in order to be able to return to Turkey later … I was illegal and did not want to [apply] but my friends influenced me (Husseyin, pp. 2–4).

Periods without status occur either – as in the above two cases – at the beginning of a stay; or in the middle (as a temporary situation between two statuses); or as a result of a failed asylum process. The middle group was the largest (eight cases), and often followed the breakdown or expiry of a period as an *au pair* or student.

> They (employing family) said to me they would be good, but things did not turn out as anticipated. [The man] started making indecent proposals, ... after I stayed about six months I decided not to be an *au pair* any more and to leave and look for a job elsewhere (Yasemin, pp. 5–6).

> I left the family on the first day, ... they treated me as a servant, it was real exploitation (Sirin, p. 2).

> After my [student's] entry clearance had expired ... I lived here illegally, after four months I was arrested, ... I said I wanted to apply for asylum, they released me (Faruk, p. 15).

> After 6 months it [student visa] expired and I lived here illegally. ... When they arrested me, I applied for asylum (Baran, pp. 2–3).

Those who stayed after exhausting the appeals process insisted that they feared for their lives; one man who was beaten and tortured was refused asylum on appeal, and had been illegally in London for three years.

> I know what I went through but I could not explain, how can I tell someone? A letter came saying they were going to send me back to Turkey, ... but how could I go there?' (Metin, p. 13).

Another had been without status for a similar time.

> My village does not exist any more, ... my brother is in and out of prison ... I was asked why we did not apply in France, therefore they rejected me ... That is three years ago ... I would rather die than go to Turkey (Nazim, pp. 1–4).

Some readers may find it offensive that interviewees from Turkey are referred to in this text as 'irregular migrants', since most were asylum seekers, several had been given leave to remain and two had refugee status. However, the whole point of this research was to study economic activity in breach of immigration rules, and how this related to different immigration statuses. Most interviewees from Turkey had worked while in a status other than asylum seeker (or person granted asylum), and all asylum seekers had worked before getting permission to do so. Hence their 'immigration offences' were the same as those in the two other groups, in relation to economic activity. In this sense they were indeed irregular migrants, in the way this term is used in our research study.

FINDING ACCOMMODATION AND WORK

What characterises both the accommodation market and the labour market in the UK, in comparison with other EU countries, is their unregulated nature; in this sense, the availability of flats and jobs for undocumented immigrants was simply a matter of supply and demand. Once they entered the country, they were not required to carry identity documents, or to register where they were living; in practice, they were not asked to produce work permits or permissions to get work. Furthermore, there were very few internal controls, since the officials who were supposed to enforce the few rules that did apply to these systems were so thin on the ground, and the police were willing to turn a blind eye to their presence and their activities (see Chapter 7).

Most of those arriving in the country spoke very little English. They therefore relied on friends or relatives to get them over the first few days, and put them in touch with the networks on which they subsequently relied. In the case of Brazilians and Poles, these were commercial systems, shadow markets and small informal networks. In the case of migrants from Turkey, they were usually organisations and kinship groups.

For *Brazilians*, the presence of a friend already in the country, or travelling with them, was clearly an important factor in the entry process, but often just for the transitional phase. Most mentioned these processes rather casually, as if the finding of accommodation and work posed very few problems.

> I had a friend here and it was here that I wanted to live. I came and stayed with this friend and soon after I moved to another room (Joana, p. 1).
> I also had friends here and I didn't know anyone in the USA. I talked to my friend, he was helpful to me. We are living together, sharing the same flat. ... My friend came and asked me if I wanted to work (Alex, p. 2).
> I had an address, a friend of a friend, this sort of thing. She helped me to organise my life here at the beginning (Lucia, p. 1).
> It is a house I share with friends. They have their rooms and I have mine (Flavia, p. 2).

> I lived with Brazilians. It was a bed sit. The owner only wanted to rent rooms to Brazilians. I think he liked samba! Or the house had something illegal, God knows. My friend organised this for me. I think most people come with some form of contact, a friend who helps at the beginning (Luisa, p. 2).

Only a few came completely alone, and fended entirely for themselves.

> I came straight to London and started to work in a restaurant [name of global fast-food chain]. Illegal work, they didn't ask me for anything and paid me very little. They offered me a place to live on the second floor. I was working there, earning very little, studying English, all on a tourist visa. I lived and worked there for two months (Rico, p. 2).

Polish interviewees also often travelled with friends, or had friends in London to ease their entry. But some had family there, some even settled since the postwar refugee migration. The accounts of these relationships often contain acrimony and conflict – accusations of exploitation, or even of treachery. In these glimpses of exchanges on or soon after arrival are prefigured other features of the Polish narratives – mistrust, competition, disloyalty and unreliability. Hence the interviewees selected a small number of trusted friends, and avoided others, including kin.

Of the eight who lived with relatives on arrival, most left acrimoniously, usually with arguments over money.

> According to him [father-in-law] we robbed him. We didn't pay for the flat (Silvia, p. 3).

> In the beginning we lived with my uncle. The one who eventually called the police on us. There was a row about it one day (Thomasz, p. 1).

> ... it was my cousin who told me that if I wanted to carry on seeing the uncle I had to move out (Ewa, p. 5).

Similar stories were told by interviewees who were recruited as tenants for 'Polish houses', in which they sublet from fellow-nationals. They resented the control exercised over them, and suspected that they were overpaying rent.

> The owners, a Polish couple staying here illegally, rent a house and then rent the rooms out to other Poles. And this couple – the man worked at a building site and anyone who lived at their house had to work either at a building site with him, or in that textile factory she was in contact with. So that was their way of getting tenants; finding people work as well as guaranteeing that people had money to pay their rent. And they took a lot of money for rent. For example I lived in a room with three other people; four of us together. And we paid £30 each. ... She was looking for people who would tell her everything that was going on in the house so she could know everything about us (Ivona, p. 5).

> You see, she was telling me what to do. She told me to go back to Poland, that she didn't want me to stay there, or to provide for me. But she never provided for me. I paid rent like everyone else in the house (Stanislaw, p. 3).

> We were told that we couldn't have visitors at night, that it would be too loud. She wanted us to keep the windows shut because a black man could come in and steal something. ... She would walk into our room whenever she felt like it and start telling us what to do and what not to do (Anna, p. 6).

However, others described Polish houses, shared with friends, as providing a suitable environment for their lives in London.

I don't mind; I like it here. I go to bed early and wake up at 7 in the morning. I don't disturb anybody and they don't disturb me (Teresa, p. 7).

I pay £35 a week for my room now, plus £10 a month towards bills. ... We fix things we need. ... We don't want any conflicts, because we are happy in this house, despite all of that (Dariusz, p. 8).

All the Polish interviewees found work within a few days of starting to look (most within a few days of arriving). Their means of finding work were as follows (Table 5.1):

Table 5.1   Means of finding work by 25 Polish interviewees

Recruited by friends or employers (when in Poland)	6
Through friends	10
Agency (one Polish)	2
Own search	1
Advertisement in centre or shop	3
Unemployed (Romany asylum seeker)	1
No information	2

Because Polish migrants represented themselves primarily as rational market actors, responding to economic opportunities and price signals, it was no surprise to them to have to pay for information about jobs, for National Insurance numbers and often for the jobs themselves.

So I found a job there through a gypsy man, I had to pay for it of course (Daniel, p. 2).

One of the very few interviewees who got a better paid job with an English firm on arrival (and the only person without manual working skills to do so) replaced a friend, who introduced him for no payment. But the friend himself had 'bought' the job.

He bought the job from some bloke. He had to pay £50 for it. There is a trade like this, and it still exists – selling jobs. But I think that it exists only amongst Polish people, because I saw the ads at the [name of place where Polish people met]: 'I am selling cleaning jobs'. That's the case; Poles don't help one another for free. Poles make money out of each other (Dariusz, p. 2).

(In fact, this practice also occurred among Brazilian migrants – Dina bought one of her cleaning jobs from someone who was returning to Brazil.)

Five Polish respondents had bought National Insurance numbers, and one had paid to borrow one.

Darek for example has a dodgy NIN. He bought it from a gypsy. ... Darek paid £150 or £200 for that NIN, and he gave it to his employer and pays his tax and all (Silvia, p. 10).

... these Polish guys ... said they know a guy who was selling NINs ... I met him and I bought it. I paid £260 for it. I don't know to whom the NIN belongs, I have no guarantees, I only guess it belongs to a gypsy as there is a gypsy name on it (Jerzy, p. 9).

I have two National Insurance numbers just in case, as a form of ID card (Margareta, p. 8).

My friend told me that I had to get myself a National Insurance number so we bought one for £225 (Janusz, p. 4).

We needed NINs to work there. The boss gave it to me. It belonged to some Spanish guy. Naturally I had to pay for it (Daniel, pp. 2–3).

I got it from someone I knew. I paid for it, for borrowing it. ... I paid £80 for borrowing it (Ewa, p. 3).

As we show in Chapter 7, the availability of National Insurance numbers well in excess of the actual workforce is one of the many aspects of the UK labour market which makes it easier for irregular migrants to work here than in other European countries (see p. 183). But what distinguished Polish respondents (and, to a lesser extent, Brazilian ones) from Turkish and Kurdish interviewees was the fact that they took for granted there would be a market in such assets, rather than that they would be lent and borrowed among a network of collaborative kin or political allies.

Indeed, the reliance on helpful networks (rather than on a few trusted friends), sharply distinguished from *mistrusted* other fellow nationals, in the case of Poles and Brazilians) was one marked feature of the accounts by *Turkish* and *Kurdish* migrants (Böcker, 1994). In their narratives of arrival, and the transitional process of finding accommodation and work, family and friends played a prominent part, and financial support (rather than exploitation) was a feature. It is clear that some were supported for many months, while others were part of systems of sharing. There were no stories about quarrels over money or dependence in the Turkish and Kurdish accounts, or of denunciations to the authorities by family members. In all, four mentioned help from relatives, and 12 help from friends.

I have been living in this room you have seen and I get support from my relatives (Mehmet, p. 2).

I used to live with friends and share meals with them (Metin, p. 7).

When I wasn't working, at that time I borrowed from friends. So, from my friends, people I got to know here – later I paid them back (Kerim, p. 4).

When I first came, we slept on the floor of a friend's flat. They were a family of four in a flat with three small bedrooms; so my husband, our son and I slept in the living room on an air mattress. We cooked and ate together (Nermin, p. 2).

I live with my friends. [I don't pay rent], they do. I share a room with one guy (Timur, p. 2).

In all, there were 13 mentions of sharing flats with relatives or friends, under communal living arrangements with living costs shared, and contributions varying according to earnings and circumstances. This is in marked contrast with the more individualistic Poles, who typically had their own rooms in multi-occupied houses. Of the four respondents from Turkey who lived alone in such a room, two men were unhappy and spoke of loneliness (Kerim, Husseyin), and one woman spoke of experiencing violence and abuse (Halide).

Another very clear difference between the Polish and Turkish/Kurdish accounts were that, since almost all the latter started from political reasons for leaving Turkey rather than economic ones, they did not focus on the search for work as a central feature of their migration narratives. Instead, they sought to show how they had to work in the shadow economy in order to survive. Hence finding work was not presented as part of the process of induction into the UK economy and society, since no one – not even Timur, who gave financial reasons as his primary ones for leaving Turkey – said that he or she came to earn and save. In other words, unlike the 'workers' accounts' given by all but one (the Romany, Marek) among the Poles and most Brazilians, work was an almost incidental feature of these narratives, sought only when a place in a network of mutual support had been found, and immigration status attended to.

UNDOCUMENTED WORK

It is therefore important to distinguish between the different contexts in which undocumented work appears in these accounts of migration experiences. Although the actual jobs they did were similar – except that Brazilians, recruited from all over London, were far less likely to work in textile factories or construction than the others, drawn from north and east London – the significance of work for them was quite different, according to the version of the reasons they were giving for being in London.

This is in some way clearest in the case of the Brazilians, since the accounts they gave sometimes varied in midstream, as it were. Starting by describing themselves as *travellers* in search of new experiences and personal growth, some then switched to seeing their visits through the eyes of *learners*, investing in themselves and their future careers, or *workers*, saving up to go home. This is most explicit in the narrative of Farina, an English teacher in her home country, who started out by giving a traveller's account.

> It was very easy at the beginning. For six months I was on holiday, with money and having a good time, I was out of Brazil, everything was very interesting, and I was enjoying myself a lot. I had a part-time job in a shop in Bayswater. It took me some time to come to terms with reality (Farina, p. 1).

At this stage of the narrative, the work she was doing was simply helping to fund her exciting new experiences as a visitor to London. However, she decided to stay on, and switched to a student visa, with the intention of studying English full time. But, in order to finance this, she took a job in a language school, one that brokered visas for its students, even ones who did not attend classes.

> I was feeling a real student, working a lot. I took several courses in literature and English. ... But I was always thinking about improving my skills in English teaching to go back to Brazil and teach (Farina, p. 4).

At this stage, the job was both a necessity (because she had completely run out of money), and part of her investment in herself, as learning through her migration experiences. But here her narrative changed again.

> I started to work more, and new problems appeared. There wasn't enough money, and it was a vicious circle. I could not let my family know about my situation. ... They could not understand why I was here, not even I could understand (Farina, p. 4).

Because she was having problems renewing her student visa, she then married a Portuguese man, purely for the sake of her immigration status. She was currently expecting him to ask for a divorce, as he wanted to marry his real partner, who had his child. Meanwhile, she became a full-time shadow worker.

> For example, at one stage I was desperate for a job, I worked at a café, owned by a Greek woman who never asked me for any documents at all, and of course never paid any tax. She paid me £10 for eight hours of work. And there are many people working like this. I was desperate at that stage. But there are people who are doing this all the time, working for £1.50 an hour (Farina, p. 8).

Some interviewees gave sustained travellers' accounts, and therefore maintained a consistent interpretation of their work as simply funding their personal development, over a longer period. Lucia, aged 27, spent two years in London after graduating as a journalist.

> On the whole, it is almost as if I've given myself time to grow and change. ... I spent the first year doing odd jobs here and there and travelling around. ... I think I came here because I wanted to live in a really foreign culture to me ... I started studying English as well and had my visa extended by one year after the first six months. The English school was not good. Just enough to be engaged in some sort of student life, so that I could get by with the visa. ... I got tired of this English school tale and decided to be here illegally. My boss at the restaurant didn't mind. ... Officially I work as a waitress, but I end up doing all sorts of things for him. ... I play my saxophone now and then as well (Lucia, pp. 1–2).

Other Brazilians sustained learners' accounts, telling how combinations of studies and undocumented work experience had improved their c.v.s, and hence their prospects when they returned to Brazil. Joana, a former manager aged 29, had been in London for five years.

> I will go back to Brazil in the long term, but now I want to enable myself to be more productive here, to develop my c.v., to go back to Brazil (Joana, p. 3).

Angelo, an electronic technician in Brazil, was 25 and had also been in London for five years. He worked in restaurants, first washing dishes, then cooking, then as a barman, and finally as a deputy manager. He had also studied electronic engineering and computing, got married, and supported his wife while she took a degree. After arriving on a tourist visa, he had stayed with no immigration status.

> I could pay an English school just for the sake of the visa. I couldn't attend classes anyway, I was working full time. I decided not to pay and remained illegal. The place I worked didn't mind at all. One day the Home Office turned up there and I had to hide myself in the basement for hours (Angelo, p. 3).

Of all the Brazilians, Angelo was the most obviously successful and upwardly mobile, but he saw all this as an investment in his future.

> I bought a house here. Why should I pay rent to someone who is also paying mortgage with my rent? I am paying the mortgage and when I leave for Brazil I will have all this money back. I will take this money with me to Brazil to help me establish my business there. ... I want to apply my ideas about electronics in Brazil, things I am learning and developing here, they will unfold in Brazil. I want to contribute to Brazil, it can be a better country. ... I have grown so much here. I have found a new world inside myself (Angelo, p. 9).

The fact that more Brazilians than either of the other groups held student visas did not mean that most of them were able to sustain such accounts. In fact, there was no correlation between holding a student visa and pulling off a convincing learner's narrative; most acknowledged that their student status had become, or always was, purely strategic, while some who had invested in their own education and training were staying completely illegally.

The most common type of account was, as with Polish interviewees, a worker's version, based on the attempt to earn and save. Rosa (aged 22), a student in Brazil, explained succinctly:

> I am cleaning people's bathrooms. In Brazil, only poor people do that. ... At least they pay you better at cleaning jobs. It is about £5 an hour, I am making £185 a week. Next week I will earn about £200, because I have another cleaning job. But it is too much work – cleaning and the café. Houses and café. It is from one to the other. Six or seven days a week (Rosa, p. 4).

Others too emphasised the hardship and suffering.

> I am fed up. You make the money here, you make the capital. But life here does not exist. It is too hard, too cemented, no poetry (Rob, p. 4).

> People are living really badly here. They work and work and don't eat to save money. They have never been to Leicester Square, they want to save some money to go back to Brazil with ten thousand pounds. That is all they get from living here, £10 000. They eat the same thing every day to save money (Luisa, p. 6).

These Brazilian interviewees described hard, unskilled physical work in adverse conditions, that bore no relation to their roles (as teachers, technicians or students) at home. Whether or not they came to London to learn, this was the work they were required to do to earn.

> I started by doing cleaning because it is the best way to make money. It is about £5 to 6 per hour. ... I stopped at the café because they pay very little. It is absurd, £2.50 per hour! However, after a month I returned to the café. The cleaning job is very lonesome and limited. You get depressed and lonely. ... I was getting too down and depressed, and only because of that I returned to the café (Bete, p. 4).

These Brazilians contrasted the case with which they were able to get work in cafés, bars and hotels, or as domestic cleaners, with the impossibility of getting work that was in line with their qualifications.

> I worked for two years in a restaurant as a waitress. They knew I was a Brazilian and that I shouldn't work but they don't care. ... Everyone is foreign, very, very few English people working (Luisa, p. 3).

> There are Brazilians working everywhere. Especially at hotels and restaurants. Everyone is illegal (Rosa, p. 5).

Washing up at first, same as everyone else who comes. ... Then I became the cook and afterwards a waiter. ... I have always worked illegally, like many people do (Carlos, p. 2).

I do the washing up. ... It is about £3.50 [per hour], and they deduct tax after that. ... The work tires me out, it is very hard (Alex, pp. 2–3).

However, those with backgrounds in music were able to get work in their field, and to develop their talents.

To live as a musician in Brazil was very difficult. ... My only chance to have a better income was by giving classes. I was a private teacher for middle-class students, playing very little professionally. ... I envisaged the chance to work with music only, at a deeper level. That is what I am doing here. I only survive, but I choose the repertoire and play Brazilian music. I have been composing a lot of music and having the chance to show that (Toni, pp. 1–2).

I decided to come to England to study English and dance. For three years I was in a dance school here. After that I took a postgraduate course and started to work with dance. ... I started to work in a hotel with lambada. I was very good at it, but learned in London (Rico, p. 2).

The only other exceptions were those who were able to acquire Italian citizenship, or who married an EU member state national (see pp. 143–4). For example, Maria got a post with a Brazilian bank when she became legal, and Joana – after several short-term jobs for Brazilian firms – managed to get (undocumented) work with a Brazilian insurance company.

First, like everyone else, I was doing cleaning jobs. I didn't want to work at restaurants because I was scared of the Home Office. ... The cleaning job protects you. ... After I got my passport, I started to look for a job in my area [management]. ... I was so tired of the struggle that I decided to give myself some time working in my area, and having a break from the cleaning (Joana, pp. 2–3).

Joana's account of her own experiences, eventually achieving work experience that developed her business potential, albeit still in the shadow economy (she was simultaneously claiming income support) was in contrast to what she saw among other Brazilians around her.

They don't have a life here. They come to study English and they don't study. They want to make money and they don't make it either. ... People are lost here (Joana, p. 4).

This picture was echoed in Rosa's account.

> I was about to go to university when I left. I can't go back there without anything. I want to go back to Brazil after I have done something here. After I have done some form of schooling. ... I can't go back to Brazil with a cleaning diploma after all these years! (Rosa, p. 4).

This cry of despair was one of the few pieces of migration narrative where the interviewee openly admitted that he or she could not give a convincing account of how their work and sacrifice had achieved their objectives, and made it worth the risks they took. But others (such as Farina and Bete) came close to saying the same things, and others still (like Luisa and Lucia) attributed them to their friends.

Polish interviewees left fewer grounds for disappointment, because their accounts were so narrowly economistic; their aim from the start was to work and save.

> I came here to earn a few pounds. I intend to earn pounds and pounds and pounds. I haven't done it yet. I haven't managed to save anything yet, but I plan to, and then I will go back to Poland (Stanislaw, p. 1).

They told their stories as rational economic actors, responding to price signals, and calculating opportunities and costs. They perceived the institutional landscape around them as designed for such actions and choices, and themselves as responding accordingly (Szreter, 2001). Their versions were individualistic (Durkheim, 1933), and they held themselves accountable for the success of their project to earn and save, even when up against seemingly hopeless odds (Jordan, Redley and James, 1994, ch. 2). For instance, Zbigniew, whose Polish friend failed to meet him when he arrived in London, and who was not able to speak a word of English, went to look for work and accommodation rather than use his return ticket, because he thought that people back home would laugh at him if he came back empty-handed. Visiting what he thought he remembered as being a place where migrants met would-be employers, he found nothing of the kind; and on boarding the tube train to return to his base, he sat and cursed out loud in Polish, such was his despair. At once someone sitting opposite responded in the same language, 'Why are you so upset?' and assisted him to find a job and lodgings – for a price, of course.

Some undocumented immigrants visited for fixed periods, under a virtual contract. Teresa, a seamstress and sewing teacher, had an invitation from an employer for her second and third visits, having come with a tourist party for her first. She explained that she was not seeking to live in the UK, just to work.

> I'm happy in Poland; I'm comfortable. I can't complain; I only wanted to finish off the house we have built. And I want to earn some extra cash, because in

Poland you can't earn any extra money. ... I never came for a long time, only for the summer holidays. [I did] piece work, sewing in Bethnal Green. But this factory doesn't exist any more. It was run by Turkish people. I don't know what happened, if they left or what, but I earned well there. Sometimes even as much as £6 an hour; it depended how many pieces I did ... I used to have £270, £280 a week, I would have had to work for three months in Poland for that then (Teresa, pp. 2–3).

The interviewees had been in the UK for periods of five years to a few months. Adding together all the references made to types of work done in their migration narratives, the following Table 5.2 emerges:

Table 5.2   Work episodes mentioned by 25 Polish interviewees

Textile factory/serving/dressmaking/hatmaking	18
Building/renovation	15
Cleaning – office and private	7
Cleaning (hotel), chambermaid	5
Restaurant/café work	8
Club waitress	2
Fish factory/wholesaler	3
Vegetable picker	1
Taxi driver	1
Dry cleaner	1

Clearly, their work experiences form three clusters – textile factories, cleaning and catering, and building work (with a residue of other service and packing work). The cleaning and catering work was done mainly, but not exclusively, by women, and the building work by men, mostly in the age group 30–40. The factory work was taken by men and women in all age groups. The main difference between the Poles and the other two groups was the number of building work episodes mentioned, and the number of skilled craftsmen among the migrants.

None had a job requiring intellectual skills, despite the fact that around half of them were educated to high school level or above.

But in a coffee shop you think, I'm going to complete my degree soon, and someone like this, nobody is going to tell me what to do, to clean the toilet (Renata, p. 3).

I am a person who graduated from university. I cannot keep hoovering all my life (Dariusz, p. 10).

One man, Stanislaw, who owned his own small sewing business in Poland, but was invited to London by a friend who promised high earnings, found himself sewing in a textile factory for £2.50 an hour.

> But after a week, when I got that £2.50 I asked why, and explained that I could have earned that money in Poland; she said I wasn't suitable for the job and that was it. It was true I couldn't sew. I was running a small textile business in Poland but I couldn't sew well myself. ... I was shocked, well, shocked, very unpleasantly surprised (Stanislaw, pp. 2–3).

Others found the situation they had been expecting. Ewa (aged 18) was encouraged and paid for by her family, and had been in England for two months, on a trip before going to university. In Poland she had been earning £90 a month. She was studying with her cousin, who invited her. On arriving, she found a job straight away as a chambermaid in an hotel.

> It's hard because you have to clean up to 20 rooms sometimes. But it's very pleasant there. People are nice. ... There are a few Polish girls. But the majority are Russian, Lithuanian. The place has become Russian, so you hear Russian all day long, nothing else. ... Russian people are asylum seekers so they have work permits. ... they know we work illegally here. ... You have to have a National Insurance number; not yours of course, because you cannot get one, just some false one (Ewa, pp. 2–3).

One striking aspect of the work experiences recounted was the number of jobs in minority ethnic businesses – not just the textile factories, but the cafes, restaurants and bars also.

> Three years ago you had only a few coffee shops, somewhere in back streets, and now they are everywhere. In [name of district] there are 15 of them and a Polish girl in each. These coffee shops just multiply (Renata, p. 4).

Many Polish interviewees were shocked by the working conditions they encountered, especially in factories.

> It was terrible to have to stay in the factory in this cold, to sit, to work and move your hands. It was warmer outside than in the factory; we went out during the breaks to warm up a bit. When you walked into the building in the morning the ceiling would leak as the snow on the roof melted (Natalia, p. 5).

> You had to stay and work till that late – 8 or 9 p.m. ... Nobody works so many hours in Poland. But we had to stay till 8 p.m. if we wanted to keep our jobs (Zofia, p. 5).

One man who had done agricultural work complained:

... we had to work 14, 16 hours a day. ... The soil was still frozen, everything was frozen. ... The supervisor would watch you all the time and you would never work fast enough according to him. ... We lived in a caravan, four of us there. There was no heating, no toilet, bathroom or cooking facilities (Zbigniew, p. 3).

Men with a background in building work (and some without) were mainly employed by Polish subcontractors, on construction sites, or renovating houses. Their main complaint was not about working conditions, but about the unreliability and exploitation of their Polish bosses (see pp. 124–5). In other ways, the deregulated conditions of the UK construction industry provided them with opportunities to thrive.

I was lucky because I worked for English people. Anyway, it wasn't so much [£4 per hour] but it was good comparing with Polish reality. ... You see, when I came here from communist Poland I felt free here until I tried to legalise my stay. ... No, that's the good thing about England, because in Germany it's terrible. When you work in Germany, I know because we were nicked once. It's not too bad when you work indoors, but working outdoors is terrible. There is a German couple walking, for example (that's what happened to us) and they can hear Polish language and they phone the police (Karel, pp. 2–3, 8).

I work with pleasure. I didn't work with such pleasure, even in Poland. And I found this job accidentally. We were sitting in a pub with friends, talking about our jobs and so on. I told them about my mad boss and they gave me a phone number of someone who needed a worker with my new English qualifications. He liked my work, he thought I worked well, the way he liked it, and we work together since then (Andrej, p. 4).

I'm happy because the English blokes always provide jobs so we are never out of work. I have been working for him for about a year and there wasn't a single week that I didn't have a job (Janusz, p. 4).

I worked there for that English man for a year. Very good, nice job. He even gave me a rise. I got £3.50 an hour in the end (Daniel, p. 4).

Later this man found an even better job, earning £300 per week, working for an unusually fair Polish subcontractor.

Since that day, living and working in London is a paradise for me. People like my work. They like it so much that they ask me, or their friends do, to do up their houses (Daniel, p. 9).

This story indicates how Polish migrants were generally able to improve their position over time. Those who stayed for a year or more increased their earnings. Speaking of their experiences between 1993 and 1998, interviewees told of starting salaries of around £90–£120 per week, or £1.50 to £2.50 an hour when they arrived in the country. The only exceptions were the three with building qualifications (for example carpenter, bricklayer) who got £3–4 per hour; one young man who went straight into a long-term job for an English employer as a cleaner, earning £35 a day; and Teresa, the seamstress/teacher who worked in a Turkish textile factory for about £6 an hour.

But most of those who stayed were able to increase their earnings, by changing jobs or by being promoted. For example, Jerzy who started working in a textile factory for £2 an hour in 1994 was by 1998 working as a bricklayer's assistant for £58 a day. Irena, who started on £1.50 an hour in a fish factory in 1994 was by 1998 earning £3.50 an hour working for a fish wholesaler. Stanislaw, who started sewing in a factory for £2.50 an hour was earning £6 an hour in another textile factory less than two years later. Renata, who started as a chambermaid in an Indian-owned hotel earning £120 per week only a few months before being interviewed earned £120 a night in a Turkish taverna (including tips), plus free food.

These stories were not found among the migrants from *Turkey*. Not only did they very seldom increase their earnings; their narratives also contained more incidents of unemployment, psychological distress and poverty. This was despite the fact that the majority, as asylum seekers, had eventually gained permission to work legally. It seemed that, although they had the support of their communities and organisations, their positions in UK society, and in those communities, trapped them in disadvantage, in comparison to more mobile (and, perhaps most important, white European) Poles.

The Turkish and Kurdish interviewees had been in the UK far longer on average than those from Poland or Brazil, and were slightly older also (see pp. 107–8). However, there was less sign of 'upward mobility' in their work

Table 5.3   Work episodes mentioned by 25 Turkish/Kurdish interviewees

Textile factory	21
Kebab outlet/pizza/burger bar	7
Restaurant/café/coffee shop	11
Cleaning	7
Au pair	5
Agricultural work	1
Construction/renovation	4
Delivery driving	1
Shop worker	2
Pizza delivery	1
Musician	1
Own business	1
Teaching/interpreting (Turkish/Kurdish associations)	3

records, except for those who got employment in Turkish or Kurdish associations (Table 5.3).

By far the most common forms of work, for both men and women, were textile factories and various forms of café, restaurant or fast food outlet – most had worked in one or both of these occupations at some time. Two women had worked as secretaries in textile factories. On the other hand, although no Polish interviewees mentioned training, four from Turkey did – two who had been trained at government expense as asylum seekers, one as a secretary and the other as a forklift driver (Nermin and Hasan); and two at their own expense, as a chef, and on an unspecified course (Selen and Abdulla). Ten interviewees mentioned periods of unemployment, and eight periods of part-time work when they would have preferred to be working full time (often lay-offs or underemployment as a result of low demand for textile products).

> Work in our factory is seasonal, for eight months there is a lot to do. Then the complete factory is closed, two months, three months. ... You cannot get unemployment benefits, so you are forced to put some money aside (Faruk, p. 11).

They also emphasised the insecurity of their work situations.

> They [employers] know it is illegal work and that we cannot join the trade union. They can sack us any time; they can do what they want. ... You don't have any rights (Mustafa, p. 4).

However, it was not only the experiences of the undocumented workers from Turkey that were rather different from those from Brazil and Poland; their accounts were framed in other terms, and drew on other repertoires. Initially describing their decisions to leave Turkey in terms of political freedom – either flight from persecution (mainly men) or from oppressive family power structures (mainly women), they went on to describe work as often reproducing their former experiences of oppression or constraint. They brought a political perspective – sometimes specifically a socialist or Marxist one – to their accounts of work in London, and saw resistance to it in terms of collective action (usually blocked) through trade unions. In some ways this was ironic, since their background was far from proletarian; most had been academics, professionals or managers, and very few had experience of manual work in Turkey. But whereas no Polish migrant (who had grown up under communism, and known of the trade union movement Solidarity in the 1980s) spoke of trade unions, and only one had acted as a 'workers' representative' (Stanislaw, the most entrepreneurial Pole), Turkish interviewees frequently interpreted their experiences as class-based economic exploitation or patriarchal domination. This was despite the fact that these migrants all tended to occupy the same or similar work places.

It is mainly employers who suggest illegal working, they always have an excuse, it is working 'on trial'. I find it wrong to blame the workers (Hasan, p. 8).

Foreigners should come together with the English ... those who are against these laws, for example the working class. Only then can you achieve something (Mustafa, p. 6).

We have often talked to the employers and explained that they are exploiting the workers. They let them work for 10 to 13 hours standing on their feet and pay them only £1 or £2 per hour. But our talks were not very successful. The employers did as they wanted (Timur, p. 6).

These (British) unions must at least show an interest. ... On the one side, we as foreigners must take more interest in claiming our rights, in getting our rights; on the other side, the others – the groups who struggle – should co-operate more in this work. We must come together, this is one part. The second part is that we must really change the policy of the state (Kadir, p. 12).

I've got a lot of English friends who have the same problems as me. ... This friend was working there and he just took me there. It was on a building site. My English friend was also working illegally (Hasan, p. 7).

I left the family [where placed as an *au pair*] on the first day ... they treated me as a servant, it was real exploitation. ... The bad thing is that you are exploited. You have to work 12, 13 hours and get one third of what a normal worker gets [in factory work] (Sirin, pp. 2–3).

In these quotations, what is glimpsed is a kind of social movement, or at least collective consciousness, which is class-based and transnational. It is reminiscent of a kind of action advocated by Pierre Bourdieu, to counter the Third Way politics of the late 1990s. As he wrote:

Such renewed trade unions need activists who genuinely think internationally, who can break away from national tradition and barriers. It would be better to draw on a kind of *Internationale* of immigrants of all countries, in order jointly with indigenous workers to fight a common struggle (Bourdieu, 1999, pp. 2–3).

Emphasising 'the second and third generation of ethnic-minority youth engaged in Peasant Revolt-style suburban riots', Bourdieu postulated a self-organisation among migrants which was conspicuously missing among Polish and Brazilian interviewees, and is not mentioned in studies of Turkish irregular migrants in cities such as Amsterdam (Rath, 1999).

However, many of the interviewees were well aware of the obstacles to such self-organisation and collective action. In line with Rath's analysis and that of Van der Leun (1999) and others, one interviewee in particular, Kadir, indicated how the dynamic of Turkish enterprise in the textile industry, together with that of migration, held back the claims of migrant workers.

> Of course there are organisations that look after [undocumented workers] ... for example, in the textile industry there are two organisations, and they went on strike one day, for about 15 to 20 days, but a lot of people who worked there did not take part in the strike, and there were only about five to 10 people who did (Kadir, p. 16).

One reason for lack of solidarity was clearly the mixture of statuses of workers from Turkey (some legal, some illegal). Another was the mixture of nationalities of those without proper status – many workers in the same factory would have been Polish, and lacking in collective consciousness or willingness to protest, as we have seen from their accounts, even though they too resented the conditions. But another factor was the system of recruitment.

> One of the problems is that the people working here are mainly relatives from the same village or near surroundings, so they cannot do things against each other, they cannot withdraw from each other, because they are either neighbours or relatives. ... For example, you come from Turkey and you own a factory, you come from Kayseri, from the village of Abbas ... and you have a contact with the mafia, and for example you need a workforce, and you send a message to the village that you need new people to work here, and then they bring these new people, and they start to work there, and instead of receiving maybe £30 they receive say £15, ... and they are grateful, and they cannot complain about this. Maybe later, when they realise how the situation really is ..., but then their relatives [back home] will think they are disloyal, so although they earn [so little] they have to be thankful for that, so that's the way the system works. ... This is the way how it goes in the textile industry. ... In factory A, you earn £5 per hour, but our people get only £3.50, so we are really exploited, and there are really bad conditions. ... And when they want to complain about the situation ... because the owner of the factory comes from their village, he is in fact their relative, he can write to the village and say look, your Kadir, whom you have sent here, he is an anarchist, he destroys our factory, and your relatives say, 'Oh Kadir ... why are you so ungrateful?', so that's why in the end people do nothing about it (Kadir, p. 12).

The other radical perspective that came through in the accounts by interviews from Turkey was a critique of UK government policy over minimum wages, the regulation of the labour market, social benefits and their relation to wage levels. This stemmed from their experiences of the relative rewards from formal and informal employment. Even when they received permission to work (usually after working for some time in the shadow economy) they insisted that they could not survive on the wages available, taking account of their housing costs. They saw the selective benefits system – both income support for those outside formal employment, and family credit (as it then was) for the working poor – as inducements for employers to pay low wages, and for those with low earning power to work 'on the side' while claiming.

For this reason, Turkish and Kurdish migrants often did not distinguish between the work they did as clandestine entrants, or those without proper status to work, and their shadow employment after they got permission to work as asylum seekers (that is undeclared work while claiming). It was also why their earnings from work did not go up when they remained in London for many years. Their income did in fact rise, but this was because they combined benefits claims – at that time still available to them from the moment they claimed asylum – with undeclared earnings, as Rath (1999) and others found was the pattern in Amsterdam (see pp. 63–4). And this, in turn, related to their accommodation; many more interviewees from Turkey had flats, and were paying higher rents (up to £90) than Poles, most of whom shared or occupied rooms in multi-occupied 'Polish houses' (Table 5.4 and 5.5).

Table 5.4   Accommodation mentioned by Turkish and Kurdish interviewees

Own flat (council)	5
Own flat (private)	8
Room (alone)	5
Room (shared)	3
Shared flat/house	13
Hotel/hostel	4
Squat	1
Au pair family	5

Table 5.5   Rents paid (where mentioned) by Turkish and Kurdish interviewees

Council flats	£56
Private flats	£50, £85, £90
Rooms	£40–60
Sharing rooms/flats	£35–60

Part of the reason for this was that more of the Turkish and Kurdish interviewees were whole families – but this was offset by the fact that several Polish women had had children since being in the UK (see pp. 146 and 204). It seems that those from Turkey had adopted the strategy and cultural practices of UK claimants (Jordan *et al.*, 1992; MacDonald, 1994; Evason and Woods, 1995; Jordan, 1995) in combining income support with shadow economic activity as a way of breaking the poverty trap. But – with their collective consciousness and trade union perspective on the labour market – they criticised the UK for creating this trap, employers for taking advantage of it and even themselves for adopting the strategy.

> Illegal work is good for some people, for some employers. They have cheap human labour, and achieve competition between workers (Mustafa, p. 8).

> You are forced to work illegally by the circumstances. The rent is very high. On the other hand, if you work legally, it's not enough for living. ... Now when you subtract the tax and rent, it's really not worth it. ... I don't know whether I'm right or wrong, but I think that among the English a lot of people do have the same problems we have (Hasan, p. 7).

> Illegal work is organised by the British government. ... And there is something in it, since students are clearly a cheap labour force. Here comes the employer. ... British or living in Britain ... and employers give that impression, and for the illegal workers, the illegal employers and the government give them reasons for that impression. There's a consensus that it's like that (Kerim, pp. 5–6).

> It's not right for the state to criminalise people. These people work and the state needs them as cheap labour. The people give their labour power and the state needs them just ... they're really cheap. Most of these people have a high work motivation, OK, so they need to earn money. These people have done this country big favours. ... So for the state to criminalise them makes no sense (Aysen, p. 24).

It might be thought that this view was confined to interviewees who were recruited through Turkish and Kurdish political associations. But in fact there was no correlation between membership of such associations and these accounts of collusion between employers and the UK – those recruited through snowballing and other contacts were just as likely to put forward such criticisms, based on a politicised perspective.

However, women were more inclined to criticise other aspects of UK society, in line with their motivation to seek personal freedom, and particularly freedom from oppression in the family. Several gave accounts of harassment by employers or landlords, some of whom were Turkish. This was specially the case for *au pairs*.

> ... after a week, things started to change. Every day they were checking up on me. What I ate, what I drank. They started to give me extra housework. They wanted me to hoover every day, to dust every day, to wash the clothes. ... When things like that started, I became very uneasy (Yasemin, p. 4).

> In the first family the house owner said the very first day that we would sleep together in one room because there were no free rooms in the house. I left the family immediately the next day (Sirin, p. 2).

> So, during the night I was alone at home with the children and the father. … He
> started to make indecent proposals to me. Will you sleep with me? … When I
> understood that, I could not stay with this family … (Yasemin, p. 6).

But most women also shared the men's critique of exploitation at work,
and the UK government's collusion in this, even though they were not members of trade unions.

> People like me, who are well educated to university level, who have a profession
> and so on, should not be discarded and forced to work in odd jobs with terrible
> conditions just because of their English. At the beginning they should have classes
> to improve their English, then maybe something like training in their own area of
> work. It is the system that forces you into illegality; you are forced to work
> illegally in these horrible, dirty conditions (Selen, p. 13).

> … people try to make ends meet. But more often than not they cannot, and so they
> work under illegal and very bad conditions (Emine, p. 8).

IMMIGRATION STATUS, STRATEGY AND STAYING

There were significant differences between the three groups in how they acted
strategically to prolong their stays in the UK, by changing their immigration
status over time. Most Brazilians came as tourists, and then applied for student
visas, under the auspices of language schools. Many of them genuinely wanted
to improve their English or take other courses and some did; others drifted
away from classes into full-time work; and others still enrolled in schools that
were little more than visa brokers, with no intention of attending. Finally,
several sought and gained Italian passports, which enabled them to get social
benefits and services, and changed their survival strategies; and a few women
married EU citizens. All the Poles (except the Romany man) arrived as tourists
and only two others applied (strategically) for asylum. A few women married
EU citizens and claimed benefits and services; but most Poles, if they were
detected and removed, simply got new passports and returned. Finally, migrants from Turkey arrived in a wide variety of immigration statuses (see
pp. 120–21), about three-quarters of them applied for asylum at some stage,
but they had frequent changes of status, and living without any status was
something that most experienced at some stage of their stay.

Among *Brazilians*, study was – as we have shown (pp. 101–2) – an important part of their migration motivation, and several, such as Angelo and
Flavia, managed eventually to undertake further education courses, after
prolonged period of shadow work. But these were the exceptions. Farina,
who worked in a language school that had accepted both genuine students
and those seeking student visas, commented:

A lot of people came to study. But it is not possible to live here without working. It is expensive to live here. Students became demotivated soon. The school did not have a structure. I saw students going through this cycle (Farina, p. 11).

Several interviewees explained that they could pay a reduced fee at their schools if they had no intention of attending language classes; the school simply put them on a list for visas from the Home Office, knowing that this was the real reason that they had enrolled:

I was never totally illegal. I was always under the protection of an 'English school'. I went to learn English at the beginning. After some time I just paid the fee so that I could have the visa, like many people do. There are schools that seem to specialise in that – visas. That is all they do (Carlos, p. 6).

Here I've learned an 'old trick'. I applied as a student a couple of days before my visa expired … it is an English school, but I don't go to school. … It is £400 per year. … The letter to the Home Office says that I pay much more, £700 or £1,000, I don't remember. It also says I am a full-time student, that is that I go there for three hours, three times a week. I haven't been there at all in both years (Toni, p. 7).

Of the 21 Brazilians, only three had lived in the UK for periods without any immigration status. In all, seven had passports of an EU state, of which six were Italian. At the time, Italy granted passports to those who could prove that they had a grandparent (formerly a great-grandparent) who had been born in the country. Several interviewees gave accounts of how they spent considerable time and energy establishing their claims (see also p. 131 for effects on employment).

This strategy was closely linked with use of welfare services in the accounts. In all the other narratives, social services were avoided, and seen both as too risky to use, and the prerogative of UK citizens (indeed, what allowed them to avoid unpleasant work, and hence created a niche for foreigners' labour). Those who got Italian passports saw these as giving them access to benefits and services.

I also want to apply for my husband's Italian papers. His grandmother was Italian and we have the right to Italian passports. I brought all the necessary documents to apply for the Italian passport from here. … After that I can even ask for welfare support, I think they can pay some rent for you. It will be easier for the children to go to school as well. You can have income support as well, as a European citizen (Rita, p. 6).

I got hold of an Italian passport. Because of that we are also planning to get housing benefit, asking for help to pay the rent. It has been an advantage to have this passport, it is a real pass for a lot here (Dina, p. 2).

In this past seven years it is the first time I've asked for anything. I've asked for housing benefit. ... People from the welfare agency came to see the flat, and asked how many people lived there, and measured it. Two months after, they started to give me £30 a week towards the rent (Marcos, p. 2).

At this stage, I found that I could get hold of an Italian passport. ... That changed my situation here totally. It helped me a lot – after that I went to university here. I suddenly became part of the EC I had the right to go to university with a grant (Angelo, pp. 5–6).

The topic of marriage was a sensitive one; it was difficult to ask an interviewee whether his or her marriage was strategic, for visa purposes, if this information was not volunteered. For instance Fred, a musician.

I am married to my wife, I love her, and she is French (Fred, p. 2).

After speaking at length about the problems in her marriage to an Iranian with residence in the UK, Rosa acknowledged that there was a strategic element in the decision to marry.

It was half and half. Half because of the visa, half because I liked him and he insisted that we should get married. He was different at that time (Rosa, p. 6).

But two others were clear that their decisions to marry were strategic.

I was living with my girlfriend in the second year of the college. She wanted to help me and we decided to marry. She is English. What happened then was after a year, when you have to renew the papers, we were not together any more, and my papers got held back. ... Now my ex-girlfriend decided to help me with the visa. She said that she would agree to saying that we are together. I have just sent my papers to the Home Office now to renew my visa as a married person. She is helping me to lie (Rico, p. 2).

I had a friend that had a friend. She said he was rather a nice fellow, good-hearted. She asked him and he said he would do it for me. He did not want anything, not money or nothing. Only that, as soon as I get over it, all the problems sorted, we'll get divorced (Farina, p. 5).

For all Brazilians who stayed in London for a period of two years or more, the questions of an Italian passport or marriage arose, as possible strategies. It seemed that these were necessary conditions for a longer stay, either because of increased security of status, or for the sake of welfare benefits and services.

For interviewees from *Poland*, returning home for a period, and starting again – often with a new passport – were the main strategies described. Several said that they had come for three or four trips (see pp. 118–9).

I also considered going back to Poland and coming here again with a brand new visa. That's what most people do. When your visa expires, or just before that, you leave England, they don't stamp your visa when you leave the country any more, so nobody knows when you left Britain. When you come back in a week or maybe in a month's time and say at the border that you were in England about a year ago for a week, and now you are coming for a week again to visit your friends or family, whomever. And then you know enough people to find someone who would agree to write you an invitation or confirm over the phone that they are waiting for you if the Immigration Officer has any doubts (Olga, p. 5).

The only one who applied for asylum on entry was the Romany man, who came with his family.

... the most important reason is that we are persecuted in Poland. They really pick on us. ... it is the truth that they burn our houses, beat us in the streets. ... If you report incidents to the police, they will write statements but will not do anything about it, anything at all. ... [England] is the only country without racism, like in America. You can feel free here, you can do what you want, and say what you want as well (Marek, p. 2).

Although he seemed to be conducting some flourishing informal economic activity, he was the only Polish interviewee who was not in employment. He received income support (this was 1998), and insisted that it was too risky to take paid work.

No, I have never tried, because I'm scared. Because I have heard that if you receive benefits and you are caught working illegally you are sent back to Poland immediately ... I try to avoid work for as long as I can because I don't want to be deporte (Marek, p. 3).

Three others applied for asylum after being in the country for a time, and made it clear that they did so for strategic reasons. In one case, a woman and her husband applied after being arrested during a Home Office raid on their house.

You see, before we didn't know what asylum was ... that I could apply for it. ... So after that incident, Tadeusz, my friend's cousin, told us that he had applied for asylum. ... So he took us to a solicitor's office and she took our case from there. ... And it has been two years in January since we applied. So we waited for interview for two years (Agniesza, pp. 4–5).

Jozef, who started as a building worker, said that his wife was the only Polish worker in a Turkish textile factory, where she bought (for £150) information about asylum. They claimed that as communists they had been persecuted in Poland. Their claim was refused. After this he applied for a business visa. His application stated that he was running a culturally sensitive funeral service for Polish war veterans. He did not need any capital, as he had hired the services of UK funeral directors, and had merely provided translations and a Polish flag. In fact he had not carried out any funeral services, and was working as a minicab driver, earning about £300 per week.

Finally, Silvia, who had been four times to the UK in various guises (p. 119), and was currently living without immigration status, had applied for asylum, but later withdrew her application.

> I think Darek had known about asylum for some time, but that evening he somehow realised that it would help us financially. You see it was difficult to make ends meet at that time. He said that way we could rent a flat and have it paid and get some money to spend as well (Silvia, p. 6).

Only one Polish woman was married to an EU citizen, in her case an Englishman, whom she had met in a fish warehouse where she was working. She was a former dentistry student, and had come to London with several friends four years previously. While staying with other friends, they were offered jobs at that workplace, as undocumented workers, eventually paid £1 an hour. Although she regretted it, she stayed on, working at a Turkish café and a burger outlet, eventually supporting her husband.

> Steve never contributed towards anything. I don't know – stupid, thoughtless, English man. He had money. He bought other kinds of things, things like television, music station, etc. ... I wasn't happy with Steve at all. ... Because it was only work, work, work and the house, and that was all (Irena, p. 7).

However, she got pregnant, and at that time her husband was sent to prison for fraud. A year after her marriage, she received her visa and work permission. She had a job in an office at the time of interview, still in the shadow economy, for £3.25 per hour. Her husband claimed income support for himself and the child, as she had no access to public funds. She planned to return to Poland for her son's education.

We have already noted the changes of immigration status among interviewees from *Turkey* (see pp. 120–21). It is more difficult to assess the extent to which these were strategic. The fact that several, who gave accounts of reasons for leaving Turkey based on persecution, did not apply for asylum on entry, required explanation. For example Mehmet, who said that his cousin was killed and he would have been next (because of his connections with a political organisation), was asked why he did not apply for asylum at the port.

> Actually there was no real reason for me to do so. The murder of my cousin had consequences for me. A couple of friends of mine were arrested and they searched

for me at my parents' house. ... I came as a student, and after three months I found that they were searching for me, and only then I applied for asylum (Mehmet, p. 2).

Similarly, Ahmet had already decided to apply for asylum when he entered the UK, but did not do so immediately.

No, no, I came here with a tourist visa. I never planned to stay in Germany. I'd already planned to go to England, and after I found out about England, I thought about applying for asylum. To go to school, to learn the language, to find refuge and so on. ... So after I came here, two weeks later I applied for asylum ... (Ahmet, p. 2).

Osman made a decision to apply for asylum quite a long time after entering the country in another status in 1988. But this was not a strategic but a political decision, taken after long debates within his political association (see p. 121).

Halit had decided to seek asylum in Canada, but he was arrested in London and imprisoned for using a false passport, so he applied then. His reason for leaving Turkey was being drafted (as a Kurd) into the army fighting in Kurdistan against his people. Of the women, Sirin said that her change from *au pair* to asylum seeker was not planned, but she should have applied for asylum on arrival.

... I was not sure, because I didn't know anything about it. I was scared and insecure. ... It was my fault that I didn't apply at the border, but I thought I wouldn't stay for long, and I was hoping the situation would improve so quickly, and thus I applied for asylum because my life [as a student activist] was in danger in Turkey (Sirin, p. 3).

Of the other women, one had applied for asylum on entry, and four had married in the UK. Of these, Leila came as a student and married a Kurdish refugee she met at work. There was no evidence of strategic motivation in the accounts of the other three, though Selen and Emine give no details of their decisions (to marry Turkish men). Yasemin says she fell in love.

As I went to school, I got to know a young Turkish man. And our friendship developed. After I stayed for about six months with his family, I decided not to be an *au pair* any more, and to leave and look for a job elsewhere. ... Through these friends we hired a room and I started living with my boyfriend. ... My boyfriend was working, so I started working as well, in a clothing factory (Yasemin, p. 6).

Finally, two women gave complex accounts of long periods in the UK (eight and six years) in which it was unclear whether their changes of status were planned and strategic, or merely responding to circumstances. Aysen had entered as a student (but worked as an *au pair*), then prolonged her student visa (but worked most of the time) and finally applied for asylum. She barely commented on this, saying simply:

> Then, on the advice of a friend, I applied for asylum. I explained that I could not live in Turkey any longer ... (Aysen, p. 9).

Halide, aged 61, summarised her life in London since 1992 as follows, without explaining her change of status from tourist to asylum seeker, having worked in a large number of different jobs during her time there.

> I just wanted a better life. That was all I expected. ... I came here as a tourist. I didn't have any problems at immigration when I arrived. They were hospitable and kind. I am waiting for my 'right to stay here'. I have signed the necessary documents. Thanks to the English state, which I now think of as my own govern-ment because I live here. I thank them for giving me the right to stay here; they found me eligible and worthy to stay here ... (Halide, p. 2).

CONCLUSIONS

In this chapter we have dealt with the main themes of these migrants' survival activities in their accounts, and especially their work experiences. Other aspects are dealt with in subsequent chapters. In particular, their encounters with the police and immigration enforcement authorities are analysed in Chapter 7 as well as the important topic of trust between fellow nationals in the immigrant groups.

Although one of our most important findings in the research was the centrality of undocumented work in their reasons for coming to the UK, and the relative ease with which they survived in the shadow economy, both Brazilians and Polish migrants lived in fear of denunciation by fellow nation-als. This meant that, although the deregulated labour market provided much better opportunities than they would have found in Continental Europe, unre-strained competition for this work, and a rampant culture of competitive individualism, made the same environment full of risks for them. Every other Brazilian or Pole they encountered, with the exception of their closest friends, was a potential threat. This contrasted with the accounts given by Brazilians in Berlin (see pp. 114–6).

Interviewees from Turkey presented a rather different picture. It appears that coming to the UK as asylum seekers, or at least for broadly political reasons, influenced their self-perceptions, and their perceptions of others from their country. However, the economic dynamic of migration, and their relations with their employers from Turkey, put them at disadvantages that this collective consciousness could not overcome. Hence, although they helped each other more, and acted in their common interests, their situation in UK society was in many ways worse than the other two groups, and the costs to them – in terms of physical illness and mental suffering – were higher.

These differences between the social relations of irregular migration in the three groups contribute to the burgeoning literature of 'transnationalism' and the diversity of transnational communities (Vertovec, 2001). In particular, our research shows how economic migration from Poland was sustained by continuing family and friendship links with that country, and return visits, allowing migrants to use their earnings in the UK as part of individual and household projects, and longer-term income strategies, to be pursued back home. For migrants from Turkey, however, asylum claims implied longer-term settlement, despite their strong dependence on employment by mobile, transnational Turkish entrepreneurs, especially in the textile industry, echoing some aspects of economic relations in Latin America and the USA (Portes, 1996). These aspects, and their interactions with settled communities from their countries in the UK, are further discussed in the next chapter.

6.   The role of support organisations

As we have seen in Chapters 4 and 5, irregular migrants relied heavily on fellow nationals already in the country for support, especially during the early parts of their stays. They often received help finding their first accommodation and employment, and – in the case of migrants from Turkey – sustenance over longer periods when they met adversity. This corresponds with theories of 'network' (Boyd, 1989), 'chain' (Böcker, 1994; Wegge, 1998) and 'secondary' migration, all of which imply that flows of migrants to a particular country are related to the stocks of immigrants from specific countries of origin already settled there (Bauer and Zimmermann, 1997), through transnational links.

Many of these networks are concerned with informal facilitation of migration (Banerjee, 1983; Fawcett, 1989), and form part of emerging transnational communities and social spaces (Glick-Schiller, Basch and Blanc-Szanton, 1992; Smith, 1994; Pries, 1996). They act as two-way communication channels between emigration countries, migrants and the host society, providing information about the migration process safety nets for newcomers, knowledge about the host society and options for settlement strategies.

For migrants arriving in the UK in the 1990s, there already existed an organised infrastructure of campaigning and support groups and agencies in London, dating from earlier waves of immigration, originally from the New Commonwealth countries. These organisations were primarily concerned with responding to legislation restricting further immigration flows, and addressing the disadvantages experienced by immigrants in the UK by lobbying for equal rights (Sivanandan, 1982; Ramdin, 1987; Rex, Joly and Wilpert, 1992). This chapter analyses the relationship between irregular migration and these support groups – both those more formal organisations which had become long-standing features of the UK social infrastructure, and the more recent and often more informal ones of the past decade. Our research project conducted interviews with policy officers and front-line staff in 25 organisations across this range.

Grass-roots and self-help organisations, including those made up of immigrants and ethnic minority groups, are a distinctive feature of UK civil society (Seligman, 1992; Hall, 1995). What we seek to explore in this chapter is how they oriented themselves to issues of immigration and asylum, how they responded to individual 'cases' and why they did not recognise irregular migration as an issue for mobilisation, campaigns or clients' problems. We argue that this can be understood in terms of the earlier emergence of racism as the dominant theme for opposition and resistance, and of asylum as the main focus for the defence of individuals through casework. This formed part of the taboo on research and debate about irregular migration (see pp. 81–2), and led to puzzlement when representatives were asked to reflect on policies and practices in relation to this topic.

Organisations for immigrants and ethnic minority groups emerged, as part of broader social movements of the late 1960s and 1970s, and when UK society was mobilising around previously unrecognised issues among previously unorganised people. In that political climate, the theme of challenging racism allowed diverse new groupings to come together, both in opposition to new immigration restrictions, and to combat discrimination and lobby for equal rights (Sivanandan, 1982). As a consequence of the inner-city riots of the early 1980s, such organisations and networks were granted funding by central and local governments (Solomos, 1986; Eade, 1989), and their agendas became part of the cultures of the public services (see Chapter 8).

At the same time, under the Conservative administrations of 1979–97, public policy was bearing down on the lowest income groups in UK society, worsening their relative (and in some cases absolute) position. Pressure was exerted on public services and local authorities to reduce expenditure, and new structures and rules reinforced these policies. Hence, the focus of new support groups and organisations was often resistance to welfare retrenchment, as well as provision for the special needs of black and Asian communities. It was into this political culture that new immigrants – both asylum seekers and irregular migrants – arrived in the late 1980s and the 1990s, and within this culture that they formed their own support groups and campaigning organisations.

By the mid-1990s, a Home Office study found that all national and ethnic groups had their own local community groups (Carey-Wood *et al.*, 1995), while it was also acknowledged that refugee agencies and the refugee community played a key role in the reception and settlement of refugees in the UK (Refugee Council, 1997b), providing for both crises and a diversity of needs (Bloch, 1996). Most of these were based in London, where by the late 1990s 85 per cent of refugees and two-thirds of asylum seekers were living (Haringey Strategic Planning, 1997), and represented spontaneous action by these groups on their own behalf, organised around their specific needs, interests and concerns (Bloch, 1994; Policy Studies Institute, 1993; Refugee Advice Centre, 1996).

As we show in this chapter, the diversity and distinctiveness of these organisations, and their contribution to every aspect of immigrants' and asylum seekers' lives, must be understood within the overall culture of UK civil society, its structures and its mobilising themes. The older and more established agencies, including the umbrella organisations for immigrants and refugees, which were more grounded in the earlier period and its political culture, defined the central themes as being racial equality and combating discrimination on the one hand, and access to welfare rights on the other. Hence, there was no real debate within these organisations over the question of irregular migration and its impact on their members or the host society. While recognising that it occurred, and dealing with its consequences, they did not take a position on the issue, or attempt to identify the special needs of those without proper immigration status as an interest group, other than as potential victims of racism and discrimination, or individuals denied access to welfare benefits and services.

However, as restrictions on immigration, and access to benefits and services for asylum seekers tightened in the late 1990s, new support and advice groups at the local level found themselves dealing with increasing numbers of people without proper immigration status, with no means of support. Many of them were surviving by working in the shadow economy. Hence, practitioners were, by default, dealing in issues of irregular migration.

Furthermore, the UK legal system encouraged or required them, either directly or indirectly, to enter into a mass of detailed determination over both immigration and welfare issues. The common law tradition in decision-making channelled activity into the defence of individuals in terms of the exceptionality and particularity of their claims. This, in turn, promoted the growth of legal practice and unqualified advisory services around asylum, as the obvious focus for such casework. It represented practitioners' 'best response' to the restrictions that had been put on other channels of immigration, but it consumed vast amounts of these organisations' time and resources, to the exclusion of broader issues and activities.

Among the themes largely excluded by these approaches was the position of immigrants and asylum seekers in the labour market, and the effects of their presence on wage levels and conditions. Although practitioners were aware that many of their members and clients engaged in documented work, most were not concerned directly with their rights as workers, or their relationship with employers and UK labour-market organisations.

In broad terms, it is possible to distinguish between three sets of actors in the field of immigrant and refugee support, and who are represented in our interview research. The first were national non-government organisations (NGOs), including those concerned exclusively with immigration and refugee issues (like the Refugee Council and the Joint Council for the Welfare of Immigrants) and others which include these issues in their remit (like the Commission for Racial Equality and Shelter). The second were specific legal advice services, including commercial legal practices. The third were community organisations and groups, of which we focused on those concerned with migrants from Central and Eastern Europe and from Turkey (for the latter, those in north-east London).

However, no such neat distinction is in reality possible, since most of these organisations undertook both campaigning and casework activities to some extent. Hence, we analyse their responses to the issues around immigration and asylum, rather than by type of organisation. In this, we seek to explain the paradox that they were giving an enormous amount of detailed help to irregular migrants while largely denying the significance of the phenomenon in their policy statements.

THE EVOLUTION OF SUPPORT ORGANISATIONS

One question for our research study was why there has not emerged in the UK a social movement for irregular migrants, to parallel those in several Continental European countries. Despite the emergence of vast numbers of advice, support and campaigning groups, none have organised overtly for those without proper immigration status in the UK. By contrast, a range of initiatives have appeared in other EU member states. In France, the *Sans Papiers* movement for irregulars emerged in 1996 (IM Media, 1997), and almost simultaneously the Italian alliance *Il 3 Febbraio* was established in Italy, to organise clandestine immigrants, refugees and antiracist organisations lobbying for regularisation (Il 3 Febbraio, 2001). In Germany in 1997 the support network *No-one Is Illegal* was set up by human rights activists, journalists, churches, trade unionists, social workers, artists and migrants. Its manifesto called for support for medical care, education, accommodation and the means for survival (Cross the Border, 1999). In Spain in 2000 and 2001 *Sin Papeles* (Without Papers) organised nationwide protests (No-one Is Illegal, 2000), and in Switzerland in the summer of 2001, several collectives of irregular migrants occupied churches to draw attention to their plight (*Schaffhauser Nachrichten*, 22nd August 2001).

The answers to this question emerged from the accounts given of their organisations and activities by the representatives of support agencies, sometimes more by way of omission and denial than by direct explanation. First, the longest established organisations, the Joint Council for the Welfare of Immigrants (founded in 1967), and the British Refugee Council (founded in 1984, and funded partly by the Home Office), reflected the main preoccupations of the immigration policy community in that earlier period.

... the standpoint that we have is basically to call for a non-racist immigration policy; we do believe that as it's presently constituted British immigration law does operate in a highly discriminatory fashion with people from Africa, the Caribbean and the Indian Sub-continent facing the brunt of immigration laws and policy (project worker, national NGO, p. 2).

While this represents a good summary of the basis of UK immigration policy, and it is clear that race has been the main theme of immigration restrictions since the early 1960s (Dummett, 2001), it seems to underestimate the recent shift towards exclusions based on economic criteria, and the influence of the notion that it is global economic factors that now fuel migratory pressures (Home Office, 1998, paras 1.3–1.7). The commitment to anti-racist perspectives, the determination to 'campaign and develop policy around refugee issues', combine to justify playing down irregular migration and unauthorised economic activity by migrants as a focus for their organisations' tasks.

We are of the view that irregular or undocumented migration is not a major problem (project worker, national NGO, p. 3).

We do try to separate refugee work from illegal and undocumented work because there are so many people who would say they are the same thing. So we would on balance distance ourselves ... from becoming too involved in that issue (development worker, national NGO, p. 2).

The difficulty in sustaining these positions in practice has been that, as immigration restrictions and welfare rights for asylum seekers have been tightened, more and more people have been stranded, either without proper status, or without means of support. Consequently, a growing proportion of migrants have found themselves in the position of becoming irregulars, through changes in immigration rules, or because they have resorted to undocumented work. This has happened at the same time as new groups were arriving from Central and Eastern Europe, such as those from Poland discussed in Chapters 4 and 5, whose primary motive has been to work and earn.

Most of the smaller, local support agencies in north-east London were established in the late 1980s and early 1990s, when asylum applications began to rise. Almost all of them had the word 'refugee' in their titles, and defined their work in terms of support for people seeking humanitarian protection.

... we were founded in January 1992, and the type of work which we are doing is mainly on asylum and immigration (chair of refugee advice centre, p. 1).
... the Commission for Racial Equality ... recommended that a centre for refugees should be set up. Finances were identified and this place was also identified and refurbished in 1994 (senior officer, refugee centre, p. 1).

... this project was set up about 1989 when we had a lot of refugees and asylum seekers, Turkish and Kurdish immigrants coming into [borough] (staff member, community refugee network, p. 1).

... we were founded in '91, our main aim is to help the refugees, specially Kurdish refugees in the United Kingdom, advice, information, housing, health, education, training, and that kind of work ... (advice centre worker, p. 1).

However, practitioners quickly acknowledged that much of their work concerned people without proper status, either at risk of deportation or removal, or without means of support. One advice worker spoke of Kurdish migrants who came to London before visa restrictions were introduced.

Many people when they come before that restriction they become illegal and some of them they applied for political asylum, some of them working in factory or some shops as illegal immigrants, eh, in my experience I know some, I knew some people who was in that position, but later they applied for political asylum and some of them have been catched by immigration and sending back to Turkey or Kurdistan. ... Well, because we are giving advice as a centre and some people they come someday openly, they say I am without passport, without documents, I'm illegal in this country ... (advice worker, advice centre, p. 2).

Another practitioner outlined the problems succinctly.

... most of the individuals who come, ... we'll find most of them will be working, ehm, undocumented ... most of the people who've come to me with problems of overstaying and so-called illegal entry you'll find because they won't have access to any of the benefits. You'll find most of them will have jobs of some description; but to supplement their income ... with the ever tightening of the immigration rules, [they] don't fit into the immigration rules, ... a number of cases who are people who don't understand the immigration rules and fall through them ... from a refugee point of view, the majority of my cases are not refugees, they are people with immigration, day-to-day immigration problems (aid worker, aid centre, pp. 2–5).

Several factors combined to ensure that these groups and centres retained their refugee focus, rather than mobilising and campaigning around irregular migration – amnesties, regularisation or employment conditions for undocumented workers. One of these has been that funding was tied to issues of asylum and the settlement of refugees.

... this post here in [borough] is specifically funded by the local council for campaigning on anti-deportation and immigration issues (practitioner, law centre, p. 1).

But the main reason was that asylum offered the obvious channel for action to protect the interests of those in crisis, as a result of threatened removal or destitution. Casework around asylum applications and appeals, negotiation over access to benefits and services, and eventually provision of support related to asylum claims, all provided a rationale for these agencies, and allowed expertise to develop among staff. The causes and consequences of these developments are discussed in the next section.

THE ACTIVITIES OF SUPPORT GROUPS

Our second research question was whether the activities of support groups were successful in representing and advancing the interests of migrants, including those without proper status. Given the fact that front-line staff in these agencies acknowledged that irregular migration was a widespread issue – if only because of tightening of the immigration rules and welfare entitlements of migrants – did their strategies and tactics effectively protect their constituencies, and combat the adversities that they faced?

It is important to bear in mind that these centres and agencies were mainly staffed by members of minority ethnic groups, often themselves refugees (Escribano, 1997). Some of those who gave interviews to us had moved from positions as volunteers to ones as paid staff (see also Carey-Wood *et al.*, 1995), and a few had lived in the UK without proper immigration status. Most of the organisations were direct responses to the needs of migrants, and were controlled by membership with current experiences of immigration issues.

However, those representing immigrants and asylum seekers were under two kinds of criticism at the time when we were conducting our research. On the one hand, the Home Office was criticising 'unscrupulous advisers' for exploiting the asylum system.

> There is no doubt that the asylum system is being abused by those seeking to migrate for purely economic reasons. Many claims are simply a tissue of lies. Some of these are made on advice from unscrupulous 'advisers' simply as a means of evading control or prolonging a stay in the UK without good reasons (Home Office, 1998, para 1.14).

From the perspective of irregular migrants, this might mean that 'advisers' – both staff of centres and support groups, and specialist solicitors – were using the only channels available to pursue their interests, and protect their vulnerabilities. It could indicate that they were acting effectively on their behalf, and that the great mass of casework that they undertook was the best use of their expertise and time. However, senior managers in the Home Office Immigration Service Enforcement Directorate also indicated that many asylum seekers whose appeals had been unsuccessful, and who could therefore legally be removed immediately from the country, were reporting to their offices, rather than absconding. In their opinion, this indicated that they were being badly advised (see p. 177).

In explaining the heavy load of casework undertaken by these agencies, the principle that the Home Secretary should use his discretion to take account of individual circumstances was seen as a specific feature of UK law, providing opportunities for advisers and solicitors to 'curb the worst excesses that the government might seek to pursue'.

> So, there actually is a framework of law, and if the Secretary of State is not seen to be taking into account all the relevant circumstances of an individual's situation then potentially you could go to court in order to, in an action which is called a judicial review, in order to have a judge ... form an opinion of whether the Secretary of State has exercised the discretion which has been granted him by parliament in accordance with the law (project worker, national NGO, p. 5).

Solicitors and law centre staff argued that the Home Office changed its policies without giving public reasons for doing so, and leaving practitioners with no alternative but to argue each case of a negative decision on individual, compassionate grounds. An example was the decision in 1993 to stop granting exceptional leave to remain as an alternative to asylum for Turkish Kurds, resulting in much higher refusal rates, and a growth in asylum appeals. One solicitor interviewed was handling about 500 of these cases. Another practitioner, in a law centre, explained why such work was so detailed and took so long.

> ... it is really a case of sitting down with someone and going through their entire life, in a way, their motivation for coming here, their experiences here, their reasons for wanting to remain, and why they don't want to be sent back. ... basically, on discretion, begging the Home Office to let them stay ... you have to argue that it is compassionate and exceptional, which is quite a difficult thing to do (law centre worker, p. 15).

The volumes of work undertaken by these agencies was enormous, matching the backlogs of asylum cases mounting up in Home Office files. For example, Newham Refugee centre had 5476 visits in 1995; Waltham Forest Refugee Advice Centre 1500 enquiries and 403 live cases in 1995–6 (Refugee Advice Centre, 1996); Asylum Aid dealt with 924 cases, of which 193 were continuously represented (Asylum Aid, 1997); Hackney Community Law Centre handled 327 immigration cases and seven precedent campaign cases (Hackney Community Law Centre, 1998). Drop-in centres and daily advice sessions were in constant demand.

In addition to liaison with the Home Office and solicitors, front-line staff in these agencies were unendingly engaged in other negotiations and conflicts with local authorities and public services over welfare needs. At the time of our first research interviews, dispersal policies had not come into force, and social services departments were still responsible (under the National Assistance Act) for providing accommodation for asylum seekers. Practitioners were heavily involved in making representations for applicants denied accommodation, on the grounds that they were not destitute or homeless (see pp. 207–8). But, at the same time as they were referring clients for these needs, and pressing their claims, they were also receiving referrals back from social services and other public agencies, for practical and material assistance, special needs and other forms of support.

> Social Services, they make referrals to our day centres, … they give them the vouchers, they give them accommodation, and then they refer them to us, so that we can help them with other things, like blankets, pillows. … We do help the people with shopping because some don't speak English (senior officer, Community Refugee Network, p. 10).

Other agencies organised for single homeless migrants, or those denied accommodation, to stay with families in their houses, sometimes for a night at a time.

> … we're building up a list of what we call a hosting scheme, of people who've got an empty room or are willing to take in a refugee (aid centre worker, p. 4).

As restrictions on welfare entitlements tightened, support organisations were increasingly drawn into both adversarial advocacy on behalf of applicants, and the provision of very basic material assistance and psychological support. The problem with the strategy of focusing on arguing for asylum claims, and providing for those needs not met by public services, was that these agencies have been caught up in a downward spiral of deteriorating standards, with ever more basic, crisis or destitution services. Instead of being able to advocate for better, more generous standards for their clientele, they have found themselves on the defensive, playing for time in appeal cases, or providing the bare minimum for people facing homelessness and hunger.

INTERACTIONS WITH MIGRANTS

Although the emphasis on asylum casework and practical support over welfare issues consumed the great bulk of staff time, and formed the main activity of these agencies, there was evidence from the interviews of the emergence of other issues around irregular migration, and the possibility of proactive campaigns and lobbying around economic issues, rather than defensive strategies that relied on asylum processes. Some of these emerged through top-down policy initiatives; others came from grass-roots recognition of new problems, leading to new responses to migrants' needs. It was also interesting to compare the accounts given by representatives of support organisations with those given by irregular migrants themselves, and to see the different emphases they placed on the role of these agencies in their lives.

The development worker from the national NGO mentioned both amnesties for migrants involved in long-standing cases, and the issue of permissions to work for other family members of asylum seekers. The latter issue arose because:

> ... the person, the principal applicant gets the permission to work, but the wife doesn't get permission to work. They might be waiting four years for the asylum application, meanwhile the son becomes 18, 19, 20, an independent person but dependent on them, he won't get permission to work (development worker, national NGO, p. 15).

Exactly this issue was identified by practitioners in support agencies, as a factor leading to breaches of the immigration rules, and hence jeopardising the security of asylum seekers.

> ... only the applicant, the main applicant, is entitled for a work permit, and that's only after six months, and if they have a big family, ... wages are obviously not enough to live on, and also ... welfare benefit is not enough to live on, that's a well-known fact. So, eh, most of the women do work, and they don't have a work permit. I don't think they are even aware of the fact that they don't have a work permit, ... they provided very cheap labour in sweatshops and clothing factories, they still carry on working like that without a work permit (women's group worker, p. 4).

This led her support group to try to take action on this issue, and become involved in applications to regularise women's and young people's work and immigration status. In her other role, as an interpreter for a firm of solicitors, she reported that:

> ... we have many people [come] to regularise their work situation. There are some women, yes, wanting to apply for work permit who are refused, or other dependants. ... The only thing is just to pressurise the Home Office to change their decision, but ... the individual, we have to advise them to work illegally, otherwise they will starve to death (women's group worker, p. 5).

This was confirmed by a solicitor, who was experiencing an increase in cases involving permissions to work, both from asylum seekers and students.

The largest category was asylum seekers waiting for appeals, without access to benefits or work permission.

> And it was a very serious, difficult situation, because as soon as your asylum claim is refused, you cannot get any benefit plus you cannot work. And obviously these people were forced to do illegal activities, including taking employment illegally, or in robbing, becoming robbers (laughs), that kind of stuff. But there was a High Court case in July or August, and the court decided that all those whose asylum claims were refused should be given permission to work (solicitor, pp. 2–3).

Another group, which was formed specifically to protect the interests of overseas domestic workers, was also involved in a regularisation programme. Such workers were admitted to the UK under a special status, when they came to the country as servants to rich foreign employers; many of them fled as a result of abuse or maltreatment, and remained in the country without proper status. As a result of regularisation programme announced in 1998, the organisation was now helping those who came forward to take advantage of this opportunity to stay legally in the country.

> ... some of these girls have been here 11 years. ... You can only apply for this concession if you're working as a domestic, you've got to prove you are working as a domestic. They will give you a visa indefinitely if you prove that you are working for four years consecutively as a domestic. ... We are going to process all the papers for a year (rights worker, support group, pp. 8–10).

In addition to these groups, we also interviewed a representative of a trade union in the textile industry, concerned with issues of exploitation of Turkish undocumented workers in north-east London. He explained that his union was attempting to include undocumented immigrant workers to advise them, and where possible to represent them in disputes with employers. But he said that it was unrealistic to expect them to take formal employment, because of the low pay and insecurity of work in the industry. He largely endorsed the arguments put forward by the Turkish and Kurdish undocumented workers (see pp. 137–9).

> Wages were really low ... And in these circumstances it was quite impossible to ask a worker to work formally. ... We knew the situation was not going to be stable (trade union officer, p. 7).

Furthermore, even the representatives of those organisations who were not acting on economic issues spoke very knowledgeably about the conditions faced by migrants in the shadow labour market, and around combining shadow work with claiming. In particular, the staff of Kurdish and Turkish refugee associations were well aware of the economic factors affecting the lives of their constituencies.

> ... usually they work for the catering industry, building work and some factories like tailoring, ... because [there is] maximum exploitation, because they ... can't be part of a union, they don't have any legal rights and they are afraid they will be expelled and arrested ...' (resource centre worker, p. 5).

> in one area ... it was nearly 1,700 factories, just textile factories over there, and more than 50 per cent of that factories [employed] illegal workers, and many times ... the tax office, VAT, ... they came in, some of them run away; I remember one lady, she tried to jump from window to downstairs, and she broke her leg, because she was working illegal, she didn't want to catch by police, and then she went to hospital for two month, something like this (advice centre worker, p. 3).

These interviews showed that the support group staff largely shared the perception of the UK government's motives put forward by the irregular migrants themselves.

> An immigration authority, also this government, they know there are many illegal people in this country, many refugees, immigrants, and I think in many cases they are happy, because they are cheap workers, you know, they are working in very low wages, and they're affecting British economy positively, that's the other side (advice centre worker, p. 3).

> Because of this situation, and because people get little social assistance, because of the high living costs, there is a high incentive to work illegally. So I think because of this a lot of people work illegally. There are serious faults in the system. ... It is a state system (advice centre worker, pp. 2–3).

It was not surprising to find this shared interpretation of the dynamics of undocumented work, because irregular migrants from Turkey were so much involved with their local cultural associations, centres and advice groups. This was part of a pattern in which they received far more support from, and were much more active participants in, the community organisations of their ethnic group in London. The positive side of this was that these associations helped sustain their identities, and their sense of membership of networks of solidarity, mutual aid and collective action. The negative side was the amount of time and energy consumed in struggles to achieve refugee or legal resident status, or access to various welfare benefits and services.

By contrast, irregular migrants from Brazil and Poland had very few contacts with such groups and organisations. Although they were therefore much more isolated, and vulnerable to the intense competition among undocumented workers (see pp. 124–5), they were also not involved in those demanding activities over negotiating their immigration status and welfare entitlements. In this sense, both for them and the host country, the transaction costs of their irregular migration were lower for the Brazilian and Polish migrants than those for immigrants from Turkey.

Most Turkish and Kurdish interviewees were involved in local associations and groups, and spoke of the assistance they received from them. For some, especially the women, it was the cultural aspects that were emphasised.

> Personally I attended folk dance classes there and generally took part in all sorts of cultural activities within the community – we used to go to exhibitions, to the cinema, together with friends, whenever there were plays, cultural activities, concerts, social events, yes, whenever such things happened (Selen, p. 12).

> I used to go to community centres more often in the past when I was trying to get used to life here. These days I only try to go to some of the activities they organise, like concerts (Emine, p. 10).

> When there is a theatre performance or something like this. Especially when there is a guest theatre group from Turkey. Then we do. We attend such activities regularly (Yasemin, p. 13).

Many of the men remained involved in the political commitments of their organisations, concerned with Kurdish struggles and class conflicts in Turkey. Some criticised their own associations or others for being too preoccupied with these issues. But most also relied on them for advice over their legal status, and especially over asylum claims.

> The community centre gives me advice and legal help (Mustafa, p. 5).

> My friends from the association have a lot of ideas. They know for example how to get a flat from the council. They help us with filling in the applications (Hasan, p. 6).

> It was the [advice centre]. They were very nice to me, and they helped me because they sent their solicitors to the company where I was working (Abdulla, p. 5).

> They started to establish organisations. ... They started to explain to others how to apply for asylum. ... Without this organisation you were alone before (Osman, p. 8).

In addition to being represented by associations and advice centres, interviewees from Turkey almost all had solicitors, and were involved in long-standing, complex, asylum cases.

> In the court, the solicitor said it would last 10 minutes. But it took over three hours (Ali, p. 6).

I had a solicitor who went [to court] with me. I had to explain everything again, and I was again afraid of being sent back home. But how to explain the main points? ... I couldn't explain to them how my party works. ... There were too many questions, and they couldn't be properly answered, so some things were left out, though I didn't lie, and I was refused [asylum]. ... But my solicitor went to the High Court. ... After my second refusal, I talked to the solicitor and he told me that he would make an end to the whole case ... (Metin, p. 8).

The amount of involvement of advisers, representatives and lawyers in the lives of interviewees from Turkey was all the more striking, because of the absence of such figures in all but a very few of the accounts by irregular migrants from Brazil and Poland. This was clearly because so many of the Turkish and Kurdish migrants were asylum seekers, and hence became embroiled both with the legal system and the various welfare agencies. Since the strategies of the other two groups relied mainly on avoiding all contact with the law and public authority, their need for advice and representation arose only when they were caught for breaches of the rules, or when they decided to try to settle in the UK.

The only support organisation referred to by Brazilians was a church, mentioned in two interviews.

I have always been linked with a spiritual church. The church has an appeal to me. ... I feel it has helped me a lot. The priest is a very nice and a strong person. ... The priest motivates everyone to help everyone else (Joana, p. 4).

This same priest commented on the Brazilians who came to her church.

They are frightened and jumpy. They are always concerned with immigration problems. ... I tell them that the Bible says that people must obey laws. ... It is not a good thing to marry someone as a business, to live illegally is wrong. ... Once they can't pay the school, they are not managing well here, it is time to go home. They have a country and a home to go to. They don't have the necessity to live illegally (Dulce, p. 2).

She saw her role as attempting to maintain morale, morality and solidarity among Brazilians – for instance by preaching against informing for the sake of getting another's job (see p. 178) – rather than advocating with the authorities on their behalf. This was a very different interpretation of the kind of support needed by migrants.

Among the Polish interviewees, the two who had applied for asylum for instrumental reasons (see p. 145), and the one who had been involved with the police through criminal proceedings (see p. 185), mentioned seeing solicitors. The only one who was involved in a protracted asylum case was the Romany man, Marek.

I was refused asylum. And then some friends told me to get myself a solicitor, that I had to have a solicitor. The solicitor said he would get me out of this mess. I hadn't known about solicitors; I didn't have the money for a solicitor. But they told me it was the Home Office who provides a solicitor for you. Or maybe it's the DSS who does that, I'm not sure. So I was told that it wasn't enough to be a gypsy, to have your house burnt, to be beaten, to be granted asylum. But I'm not involved in politics; I'm a persecuted gypsy (Marek, p. 4).

This pattern was in line with our research on support organisations for migrants from Poland. Only two of these identified themselves as working with recent migrants, and were willing to be interviewed. One was a small advice centre, the other a refugee network. Both highlighted Roma asylum seekers, as a major client group, especially the latter.

All my clients are asylum seekers, they're not entitled to any kind of social benefits ... so basically I'm trying to tell them where to go and get free or very cheap clothes, ... where to apply for schools, ... to find them GPs, dentists, just really basic service provider' (volunteer, refugee network, pp. 1–3).

Although, as we have seen, groups of friends supplied important support and assistance to each other, no formal organisation was mentioned in the other interviews with Brazilian or Polish migrants. A small centre functioned as an unofficial exchange for information on undocumented opportunities and accommodation among these networks. Typical of the responses of Polish migrants were the following comments.

If I am caught, it doesn't matter if I have a visa or not. ... I don't think I could be caught on the street; it's true it happens sometimes, but I'm an optimist. ... You see, it's my choice to work illegally and everyone knows what it means to work illegally. Anyway, I think I have done quite well for a person who is here illegally (Stanislaw, p. 8).

To be honest, I haven't had any problems to seek advice about. You talk to people at work. Everyone talks about themselves and their cases, and that's how you hear things, and later if needed take advantage of them (Tomasz, p. 7).

CONCLUSIONS

These very different patterns of interaction within the immigrant communities illustrate how transnational networks are shaped by the laws and public institutions of the host society, as well as by the cultures of their countries of origin. In the case of the UK, what these irregular migrants had in common was that they were all working in similar occupations, and often side by side in the same workplaces. All were occupying niches in the shadow economy, and hence taking advantage of the relatively unregulated nature of the UK labour market, and all were doing so in breach of either their immigration status conditions, or the benefits regulations, or both. In this sense, their shared experiences as irregular migrants seemed significant, and we might have expected them to have been supported and sustained by rather similar organisations.

In fact, as we have shown, the type of support they received, and the likelihood of their belonging to an organisation, related as much to their immigration status as to their nationality. It is true that the interviewees from Turkey were far more likely to speak of having been involved in political, trade union or cultural activities in their home countries than those from Brazil or Poland. But – as the example of the Polish Romany man indicates – even those who were not politically active, but who applied for asylum, needed support and advocacy to sustain their claims, and became involved with UK welfare agencies. In the nature of the asylum process, and the institutional systems that surrounded it, support organisations focused on these migrants' legal cases and their rights to public services, rather than on their economic activities, and their position in the labour market.

Furthermore, even their undocumented work took on a different significance if they were asylum seekers receiving benefits, as many at that time still were. It became work that was undeclared for benefit assessment purposes, rather than work that was in breach of immigration status conditions. And yet in practice interviewees from Turkey found it difficult to distinguish between the work they did before (as asylum seekers) they received permissions to work, the work they did as overstayers if their applications were refused and the work they did without declaring it to the benefit authorities. In fact, it was usually the same work, often for the same employers.

In the UK political discourse has been shifting towards a more positive interpretation of economic migration (Roche, 2000, 2001). As a leader in *The Guardian* put it:

> ... behind the scenes, David Blunkett's department is engaged in a welcome rethink of Britain's immigration rules. Last week, the Home Office minister, Lord Rooker, outlined the government's plans to increase legitimate migration to deal with skills shortages. For too long, the debate has been based on the false premise that there is something wrong with economic migration, resulting in the demonisation of people who have simply decided to take Lord Tebbit's advice to 'get on their bikes and look for work' (*The Guardian*, 11 December 2001, p. 15).

On this analysis, economic migration across borders is identical with desirable forms of labour mobility, in a globalised environment. Not only does spontaneous economic migration provide a mechanism for establishing equilibrium in labour markets; it is also the mechanism that involves lowest transaction costs. This becomes obvious when it is compared with the processes by which those seeking humanitarian protection are screened for access to labour markets through asylum procedures. Even where an applicant is successful in gaining refugee status, the costs to the host society (in public expenditure) are extremely high, and these are paralleled in the costs that fall upon the asylum seeker's own community, through its support organisations.

It seems as if the UK government, in recognising this, is also acknowledging that the easing of restrictions on economic migration might also involve a greater tolerance of irregular entry, or at least of entries that require regularisation for migrants as workers at a later stage of the process. There are economic arguments for such policies; the costs of combating irregular migration may be more efficiently allocated to other uses (Entorf, 2000).

However, there are at least two difficulties inherent in this approach. The first is that the UK government's strongly restrictive policies on asylum seeking in the 1990s encouraged populist campaigning against foreigners, and the perception that they were motivated by the desire to live at taxpayers' expense. In this way, new forms of xenophobia flourished in UK society, and opposition to asylum seeking came to be a proxy for the racism that had fuelled earlier anti-immigrant opinion (Fekete, 2000). Although it would save an enormous amount of government expenditure to allow those now entering as asylum seekers instead to come as economic migrants, this would risk a backlash precisely because the government has pandered to xenoracism during the previous decade.

Second, it is not clear that the migration of foreign workers to do unskilled jobs in the UK is an unequivocal blessing. This is because it potentially plays into existing distortions in the labour market, including the shadow labour market of undocumented and informal work. As a result of the fact that labour markets are not like markets for products, and have been managed in ways that try to influence income distributions, participation rates, family formations and communal relationships, immigration does not necessarily impact upon it as the optimistic economic model suggests.

It seems invidious to point to the relative advantages of Brazilian and Polish irregular migrants compared with those from Turkey. After all, the latter were mostly asylum seekers who were seeking political freedom, if not all fleeing individual persecution, and they had often suffered grievously, both in their own country and in the UK. It also seems to belittle the enormous efforts made on their behalf, not only by individuals and organisations in their own communities, but also by many working in the public services in the UK (see Chapter 8). We have no intention of suggesting that these factors are not important, which is why we have devoted considerable space to recording them in this part of the book. Our point is that, by insisting that migrants from Turkey choose between illegality and asylum seeking, and then restricting the rights and opportunities of asylum seekers in the way it did, the UK government *both* pushed them into a cycle of immiseration and perpetual legal struggle, *and* drove them towards activities which were outside the law.

In many ways, a dispassionate observer looking at our data might advise a migrant wishing to enter the UK for any reason to avoid the status of asylum seeker if this was in any way feasible for him or her and opt instead for complete illegality. In spite of the vast amounts of advice, assistance and representation being provided for asylum applicants, and considerable sums of public spending (very little of which reached them as individuals), their situation was extremely unenviable. All these aspects are further discussed in Part III of this book, and in the conclusion.

PART III

The Response of the Receiving Society

7. Internal controls and enforcement: immigration authorities and the police

Border checks and internal controls reflect states' fears about the potential ill effects of irregular migration. However, as we saw in Part II, irregular migrants who did undocumented work in London were readily accepted by employers, and lived largely without friction among the wider population. In this part of the book, we turn to the responses of the official agencies of the state, and consider how the UK in particular dealt with the issues raised by irregular migration. In this chapter we look at internal enforcement practices.

Our research was conducted at a time of transition in immigration policy, both in the UK and in the European Union (EU). Between 1970 and 2000 immigration policy in the UK responded primarily to considerations of 'race', restricting immigration from the New Commonwealth countries, on the grounds that this was necessary for 'good race relations' and 'racial equality'. This argument was still used up to 1998, as a justification for 'fair, fast and firm immigration control', especially in relation to asylum claims (Home Office, 1998, para 2.3). From 2000 economic considerations became far more significant, as was signalled by ministerial speeches and Home Office reports (see pp. 79–80). Not only was recruitment abroad expanded (see Chapter 9), but other forms of migration came to be assessed from the standpoint of their potential economic advantages.

This change was not easy for the Home Office Immigration and Nationality Directorate to handle, because it was in crisis over the computerisation of its work. Hence, the change in focus from restrictions based on fears of 'swamping' and 'conflict' through uncontrolled black and Asian immigration, to assessment of the costs and benefits of economic migration, was beyond its scope. Although we did this part of our research in 1998–9, it was clear then that labour market controls and the investigation of undocumented work by immigrants were low priorities, and the attempt to rationalise the asylum system has remained its main preoccupation since then. The White Paper of 2002 projects more focus on 'illegal work' (Home Office, 2002, Chapter 5).

The very thin cover of internal controls, especially in relation to the labour market, is certainly a feature of the UK. The Immigration and Nationality Directorate of the Home Office had most of its administrative staff at a site in Croydon, others in Liverpool, and its main front-line deployment at the ports of entry. In terms of internal controls, almost all IND's Immigration Service Enforcement Directorate (ISED) staff were based in London in the period of our research. They could not possibly check for immigration offences among the whole population of the capital – there were some 500 staff, including clerical workers, to cover a city of eight million people. Although many Brazilian, Polish and Turkish interviewees had had direct experience of raids on workplaces and houses, these seemed to be the result of denunciations, either by members of the former two nationalities, or by minority ethnic British citizens, and to stem from economic competition or personal quarrels. By comparison, several Brazilians in Berlin had experienced checks of their immigration status after being stopped for minor infractions (such as not paying for a tram ticket).

Hence it was not surprising that Brazilian and Polish migrants contrasted the UK (a 'free country') with their experiences of, for instance, Germany and Switzerland ('police states'), and found their lives relatively relaxed by contrast. They also spoke of the implementation practices of immigration officers and police as, for the most part, easy-going or even lax. And although several interviewees from Turkey had experienced harshness from the authorities, they could not forebear to comment that this scarcely compared with their previous experiences in their home country.

Our second (ESRC-funded) research project allowed us to interview senior staff, middle managers and front-line officers in one ISED base in London, that covered the boroughs where the interviewees lived. As far as we are aware, this was the first academic research project to investigate this service, and our study also involved observing four workplace raids. Some of the ethical issues of this research have been discussed above (pp. 93–5). The ISED was merged with the Ports Directorate in late 2000, and over 500 officers now do work that combines entry control and enforcement functions, but the numbers in enforcement offices remain much the same.

What was especially valuable was to compare the accounts given by ISED staff with those of irregular migrants. The strategic orientation of the ISED was known to irregular migrants, and the ISED staff knew of all but one of the migrants' strategies that we uncovered. The ISED's priorities at the time were concerned with removing failed asylum overstayers, and detecting marriage abuse. Among the Turkish and Kurdish interviewees, there were a few overstayers, and one who admitted having made a bogus marriage (Abdulla, see below, pp. 185–6). As we will show, there was a possibility that they might have been traced through their workplaces being raided, but this was rather unlikely. The ISED had very limited resources for workplace-related enforcement, and the raids observed yielded a poor harvest of arrests, and no immediate removals. Issues of co-operation with the police and the Benefits Agency Benefits Fraud Investigation Service (BABFIS) are discussed at some length in this chapter, since they held the key to the success or failure (usually, from our observation, the latter) of these operations, and subsequent research interviews with the BABFIS revealed that they had been abandoned, at least in that form.

What was particularly fascinating was to find that the account given by one undocumented worker of an illegal practice in a textile factory tallied with the researcher's observations during one of these raids. This may or may not have been the same factory; the practice may have been quite widespread. For ethical reasons, the country of origin of both the interviewee and the factory owner are not given in our descriptions of this coincidence.

For migrants, the risk of detection and removal was part of their calculation of the costs and benefits of entering and working without proper status. For the host society, the costs of detecting and removing irregular migrants has to be set against other possible uses of the public funds (Entorf, 2000). In other EU member states, with higher rates of unemployment, higher social insurance contributions and more regulated labour markets, the policing and enforcement of internal immigration restrictions could be combined with that of the labour market and the benefit rules, without greatly increasing costs. Even so, the employment of irregular migrants is widespread in certain industries and in agriculture, because of employers' demands for flexibility and mobility (Garson, 2000), and an incentive to save social insurance costs (Tapinos, 2000).

In the UK, the priorities and practices of the ISED must be understood in the context of its liberal tradition, in which employers in particular have been little regulated, and rules have been lightly enforced. They must also be viewed in the light of the situation in the Home Office at the time.

INTERNAL CONTROLS

As a background to the study that we conducted, it is important to emphasise that the Immigration and Nationality Directorate (IND) of the Home Office was in a state of administrative crisis, not only during the period in question (1998–9), but in the subsequent years. In mid-September 2001, at the height of concerns over national security and asylum seekers trying to board trains or walk through the Channel Tunnel, the Home Secretary acknowledged 'cumulative running errors' in the counting of asylum applications to the UK. These went back to the change from manual to computerised counting and processing methods in 1998, and emergency measures were being introduced, including returning to manual methods. The numbers of applicants awaiting decisions had been recalculated at 43 130, rather than the previous published figure of 23 580 (*The Independent*, 20 September 2001). This admission gave some indication of the scale of the problems afflicting the service throughout the period of study, as staff struggled to come to terms with new methods that made some of their previous skills redundant, and with systems that were ill-designed to cope with their tasks.

Furthermore, problems were not confined to the processing of claims. New systems for dispersing asylum seekers to peripheral areas were heavily criticised, both for administrative errors and for their social consequences, and the Home Secretary has announced reforms of the dispersal system, and the abolition of the voucher scheme. Finally, a decision by the High Court on 7 September 2001 ruled that the secure Home Office 'Reception Centre' at Oakington, Cambridgeshire, was in fact a detention centre, and contravened the human rights of those asylum seekers held there. The Home Office argued that it was holding them merely to 'fast track' these asylum hearings, not because there was a risk to national security or because they might abscond. However, the court found that conditions were consistent with detention, not reception, and some 11 000 former inmates were likely to claim compensation, subject to the result of the Home Office's appeal against the decision (*The Guardian*, 9 September 2001). This decision has since been reversed on appeal, but will be further appealed, to the House of Lords. This will be of key importance, as the Home Secretary's reforms focus on the extension of the system of reception centres to include most or all applicants for asylum.

The IND was particularly unfortunate that the New Labour government's reforms of the public services, in line with its general principles of modernisation, efficiency, responsiveness and user-friendliness, came at a time of external pressures. The programme was summarised by Tony Blair as one for 'national renewal'.

> Reform is a vital part of rediscovering a true national purpose, part of a bigger picture in which our country is a model of the 21st century developed nation (Blair, 1998, p. iii).

Within this broader picture the reform of the immigration and asylum systems, to make them 'fairer, faster and firmer', included more efficient methods of enforcement.

> Enforcement of the Immigration Rules is a key part of a fair and firm system. In fairness to those who have followed the rules and to deter others who might consider abusing the system, we must be able to identify and deal appropriately with those in the UK without authority (Home Office, 1998, para 2.1).

At the time of our study, the Immigration Service Ports Directorate was far larger than the ISED (over 2000 staff still specialised in entry work). This reflects the fact that most of the UK's system of immigration control implementation is focused on the point of arrival in the country (or before that, in the tasks of consular staff abroad, concerned with the issue of visas). The ISED's task was to detect and remove immigration offenders of all kinds, including those breaking their entry requirements, or overstaying their visas. In 1998, when our study was carried out, the Directorate had only 564 staff in ten offices.

Both the size and the structure of the Immigration Service are distinctive, and different both from internal immigration control systems in other European countries, and from other public services in the UK. In Germany, for example, *Ausländerbehörden* (immigration authorities) are administrative units integrated with general local authorities. They make decisions about whether someone is legally or illegally in the country and decide about deportation. However, other authorities, such as the Federal Employment Office, customs officers or the police, may detect undocumented immigrants during their work, and have them arrested. It is only since 1999 that immigration officers in the UK have had the power to enter premises and search for an offender, or seize evidence. At the time of our research they depended on the police for these functions. But above all, the ISED was far smaller than its continental counterparts; in a London borough with high concentrations of immigrants, staffing is far lower than in an average German city, where there would also be a full-time interagency team specialising in labour-market investigations.

Our interviews and observations were conducted in the office of the ISED that covered north and east London, where Polish and Turkish respondents were recruited. Although the structure of the office and development of staff were explained to us by managers at different levels and front-line officers, the terminology ('teams', 'divisions', 'sections') was confusing, and it was difficult to understand the relationship between the units (Asylum, Deportation, Administrative, Intelligence and Marriage Abuse). In addition, staff were allocated to 'sectors', corresponding to Metropolitan Police Authority districts, and each officer had links with a 'patch', in which they were encouraged to liaise with police and other agencies. There was also a 'duty' system (comprising a Chief Immigration Officer and an Immigration Officer) to make 'rapid assessments' of incoming information. An Immigration Inspector commented:

> ... we keep track of the number of pieces of work for each division and if we find that we have too many then we ask for another, for further officers to be put in there, or if we find we're not getting enough we can release officers to go to help somebody (Immigration Inspector, 1998).

A front-line officer was *both* a marriage abuse specialist *and* responsible for liaising with police in a key borough. She herself said that she did 'kind

of dabble in other things too, but just to get a break from the marriage work',
while among her colleagues, 'most do [routine] marriage visits' (p. 12).

Both in describing their work, and in observed action, ISED staff displayed
a strong commitment to catching and removing 'immigration offenders',
notably asylum overstayers. This reflected government ministers' priorities
and targets.

> ... the removal of failed asylum seekers is the main priority, as ministers have
> been saying recently ...' (Immigration Inspector, 1998, p. 3).

> ... our government ministers have told us that we have got to prioritise our
> resources on failed asylum seekers (Chief Immigration Officer, 1998, p. 5).

The organisation and administration of the office was therefore driven by
the imperative of meeting targets for 'removals' (that is, deportations of those
who had broken the terms of leave to remain, and – more commonly – return
of illegal entrants).

> ... as long as we are improving our removal stats. This is what ministers want
> (Chief Immigration Officer, 1998, p. 6).

At the front line, officers spoke of their work in a manner typical of those
involved in enforcement – for instance, the police (Bittner, 1965) – using
quite a lot of jargon, abbreviations and acronyms, and a tough, laconic style.
Interviewed immediately after a raid on a factory, a Chief Immigration Officer explained:

> Yeah, I mean the decision will be taken on each one [held] tonight, in as much as
> whether we can detain them, and whether we can issue them with various papers
> ... the casework section here ... would look at dealing with four people, we'll
> then be looking toward hopefully removing them ... and one of them has been in
> the country a long, long time ... if he's not an illegal entrant he's a deportee that's
> gonna have to go to the deports group, didn't he? (Chief Immigration Officer,
> 1998, p. 5).

Such work involves considerable discretion, and the use of judgement by
front-line staff (Lipsky, 1980; Baldwin, 2000). Street-level bureaucrats develop codes of their own for interpreting rules and policies that are necessarily
imprecise.

> We have very little written down about how we should do our job, or what
> guidelines we work within, and these are commonsense kind of guidelines. ... But
> there's no written guidelines, no. ... I can think of one interview we did, and with
> each of them [marriage partners] took about three quarters of an hour, and the
> only discrepancy we'd get was who'd baby sat the previous Saturday night. One

of them said her mother and the other said someone else had. ... And it, I mean it wasn't enough to knock the marriage down, but it was to make me doubt (Immigration Officer, 1998, pp. 14, 21).

Managers and officers took pride in the fact that they were bound by rules that, while constraining the scope of their enforcement actions, also ensured that they operated fairly, and that civil liberties and minority rights were protected. They emphasised that, in relation to workplace raids, they were not allowed to conduct 'fishing expeditions', but had to target specific immigration offenders (usually overstayers), who were likely to be working at this employment. This involved time-consuming preparation of files, documenting evidence against these 'targets'. On the other hand, of course, other offenders might be revealed (for instance, when they ran away during a raid), and could then be questioned. But in general terms, and like others involved in enforcement, they relished the idea of a 'hunt', conducted under known rules, for which they were publicly accountable (see also pp. 190–91). Although they resented the intervention of representatives who were seen as opportunistic and obstructive, they said that they respected the practice of the best immigration lawyers. The former were seen as 'unscrupulous advisers' (Home Office, 1998, para 1.14).

> ... they're making a living out of trying to make life difficult for us, and they will try to frustrate our attempts to remove people. ... There are people making a good living out of this ... simply constituting abuse of the system (Immigration Inspector, 1998, p. 24).

However, these obstructive representatives were contrasted with effective practitioners who 'made sure that procedures are followed, good practice is adopted' (Chief Immigration Officer, 1998, p. 11). The officers of ISED got little job satisfaction from removing overstayers who, as it were, 'fell into their laps' because they had not been given the most obvious advice about how to avoid being picked up.

> ... the majority of those we detain are coming through either by catching them signing on when they reach the end of the line [i.e. the appeal process], or by police assistance – the police did 16 for us in May. They are either detained at the police station when they sign on there, or they are arrested for criminal activity, or absconders are identified on the PNC [Police National Computer] ... I am always surprised when they [asylum seekers] continue to report when they reach a certain stage in the process, because they must know once they have had their reason for refusal letters, but still they come in. If it was me, I would not come near the office, but they do. ... If I was a rep and I was looking after someone's interests, I would say to them, you realise you have got this letter, so if you want to stay, do not go near that office, abscond (Chief Immigration Officer, 1998, pp. 6, 8).

As well as acknowledging their debt to the police for information, and for detention of overstayers, ISED staff recognised that they depended heavily on denunciations.

> … quite frankly, we get far more in the way of denunciatory information than we can possibly handle (Immigration Inspector, p. 4).

One Chief Immigration Officer estimated that 70 per cent of denunciations came from members of minority ethnic populations. Clearly, neither they nor we could discover how many of these came from irregular migrants who were denouncing others in the same situation, and how many from UK citizens or accepted refugees, resentful of irregulars taking their jobs, or damaging their interests in some other way. What we had was massive evidence from both Brazilians and Poles that denunciation was part of a culture of unrestrained competition among both groups. Without any prompting by the interviewer, many respondents spoke of fearing denunciation, knowing others who had been denounced, or directly experiencing being denounced (in the case of some Poles, even by family members).

Among all the Brazilians who mentioned this, these comments are typical:

> Every time you meet a Brazilian they have this kind of news to give you, that so and so was deported. The Brazilian community here is very messed up. … One of my friends here was denounced by a Brazilian as well, because of gossip and arguments (Carmen, p. 3).

> People in the 'black' are highly competitive. … I started to hear about people being caught and sent back because of betrayal and accusation (Farina, p. 16).

> … there is a lot of grassing (informing) around. People do grass! … It happens a lot. It is dangerous to let others know. Brazilians betray others (Cris, p. 4).

> I think most people come here to work, and think about money only. They don't develop good relationships with Brazilians here – with exceptions, of course, but they are rare. The want to get your job, they threaten people, I heard a lot about it. I don't want to be close to Brazilians (Alex, p. 3).

> I am lucky because at the hotel I used to work at the Home Office turned up because of someone grassing. They caught a Brazilian who was deported after. … That was because they had a fight at the hotel and someone called the Home Office (Rosa, p. 5).

Polish interviewees were less specific about denunciations in the workplace, but made it clear that their levels of trust were equally low, because of unrestrained competition.

Too many people looking for work. And everyone is scared. ... A stranger comes, it's all illegal, you know, they are scared (Ewa, p. 5).

Poles envy you for having something, for having a good job and so on (Jerzy, p. 11).

Polish interviewees emphasised that their fellow nationals exploited each other.

Poles don't help one another for free. Poles make money out of each other (Dariusz, p. 2).

He (employer) makes promises but I don't even listen because I know he's not going to keep them (Stanislaw, p. 7).

It's terrible that Poles are like that to one another (Krystyna, p. 10).

... I came across so much antagonism of Polish people ... especially the ones who have been here for a while (Renata, p. 4).

... a Pole knows what your situation is here and tries to use it against you as much as he can (Jerzy, p. 8).

It's only Poles asking questions all the time; where do you work, how much do you earn, you know what Poles are like (Silvia, p. 9).

This lack of trust among Brazilians and Poles, which seemed to be the chief cause of their fear of detection as irregular immigrants, and the ISED's main weapon in its efforts to curb offences relating to undocumented work, requires explanation. Research on social capital has shown that Brazilians are among the least trusting people in the world in relation to their fellow citizens, and that Poles are among the least trusting in Europe. However, Turkey is another country in which trust is very low, near the same level as Brazil (Rothstein and Stolle, 2001). Hence, it was very surprising to find that Turkish and Kurdish interviewees did not mention denunciation or fear of denunciation, in their narratives of undocumented work, or of life in London. Furthermore, Brazilians in Berlin feared denunciation by Germans (two had in fact been so denounced), but not by other Brazilians.

In part, this might have been for legal reasons. In the UK, someone who is denouced is likely to be removed quickly. In Germany, such action by the authorities is less likely to happen at all, or it will take a few weeks to be implemented (Jordan and Vogel, 1997a, p. 12), so the informer may be identified. In London, too, the denunciation causes an immediate vacancy, because the undocumented worker is removed, but the employer is very unlikely to be prosecuted. In Berlin, the employer is far more likely to be prosecuted, and hence far less likely to take on another undocumented worker immediately (Cyrus and Vogel, 2001). But perhaps a stronger reason is that Brazilians in Germany depended much more on networks (of Germans and setled migrants) to find work and accommodation, and to protect them from detection. Hence, it was the market competition among Brazilians (and Poles) in London that explained the differences from the social relations of their counterparts in Germany.

The case was rather different for irregular migrants from Turkey. As we saw in Chapter 5 (pp. 126–7) they were much more likely to receive help from wider networks of kin and friends, and to belong to cultural and political associations. It seemed as if the relations of solidarity between members of such networks and associations acted as a strong restraint on competitive behaviour, including disloyalty and denunciation (but not economic exploitation by employers from the same networks or associations). Because there was no discussion of informing in the Turkish and Kurdish communities, we cannot tell whether this was an explicit or implicit rule of such networks and associations. But in one case, an interviewee was asked whether undocumented workers ever informed on each other, and he replied, 'No, because we are all in the same situation' (Timur, p. 13).

On the face of it, this seems to confirm the view of social capital theorists, such as Putnam (2001), that associationalism and the experience of membership organisations develops trust and reciprocity. But this may be an incorrect inference. We do not know that these interviewees were not members of associations in Turkey – in fact, many of them said they were. What was different about London was the overall context. Turks and Kurds did not attempt to oppress each other, or struggle against each other; what they had in common as asylum seekers and refugees was stronger than what had divided them. They had both fought against the authoritarianism and oppression of the Turkish state. Mistrust in Turkey seemed to reflect more about the overall political culture of the regime, and the actions of the police and security services, than about associationalism or its absence in Turkish society. Democracy and respect for civil rights in the UK were enough to reduce the lack of trust that was endemic in Turkey. By contrast, Brazilians and Poles, almost none of whom were in the UK for political reasons, became *more* mistrustful, because of intensified economic competition, absence of regulatory restraints *and* the lack of an associational context. Brazilians in Germany became apparently *more* trusting of each other, despite their irregular status.

As far as the ISED were concerned, unrestrained competition and denunciations among Brazilians and Poles meant that they could target individual immigration offenders quite effectively; and it led to generalised anxiety and caution among the population of irregular migrants from these countries. Conversely, the kinship, cultural and political solidarity of Turks and Kurds protected them from internal controls, and the fact that their association was active in local politics meant that neither ISED nor police forces were keen to take actions against these communities which might be seen to be provocative (Espinosa and Massey, 1997).

However, the ISED had no more proactive plan or policy to counter the strategies of those engaged in undocumented work (the chief means of economic migration). For instance, in relation to the fact that many language schools were simply acting as visa brokers for Brazilian students, Farina, who worked in one such school, said:

> The Home Office has a black list of schools, especially the cheap ones. … It seems that there is some kind of agreement. There are schools that have a lot of students and [only] three classrooms, but there must be a sort of agreement because nothing happens to them! … Almost every week there is some sort of enquiry, and they write more than they ring. … And some people are checked always. Others have been here for three years and have never been checked (Farina, pp. 11–12).

The Immigration Inspector's line on this was consistent with Farina's view, saying they seldom investigated the schools themselves, only following up individual students.

> … we have conducted visits to language schools … to verify information that someone has given us about attendance at the school … it is possible during the course of our investigations we come to some conclusions about the reliability or *bona fides* of the school itself. … There are some language schools that, ehm, are pretty disreputable … but there is probably quite a large number of schools that simply don't ask questions (Immigration Inspector, 1998, pp. 5, 13).

CO-OPERATION

Because of its very small staff and limited powers, the ISED relied heavily on the co-operation of other public agencies to carry out its control functions effectively. At the time, ISED staff had powers of arrest for some immigration offences, but it was policy not to use these in practice, and they required the police for entry and search. There was clearly some disagreement between the staff interviewed about the wisdom of this policy, because this meant that they depended too much on the police for apprehending offenders. The police have a very different functional and regional structure from the ISED, and considerable local autonomy; they are also accountable to local interests, including ethnic minority groups (such as Turkish and Kurdish associations in Hackney) through community policing institutions.

... certain police forces who'd put a lot of effort into increasing their community policing, they are a little bit reluctant to get involved in certain aspects of immigration work, especially enforcement work. ... it very much depends on the chief constable in the area ... how he views immigration work (Chief Immigration Officer, 1998, p. 17).

One ISED front-line officer described how she used tact and diplomacy to gain police support, but acknowledged that they willingly participated when they could see someone arrested and removed very quickly – 'they find that quite attractive' (Immigration Officer, 1998, p. 2).

As shown in Chapter 8 (pp. 202–3), for the other public agencies, especially those concerned with education, health and social services, the ISED was both functionally and organisationally distant. It was seen as a somewhat secretive and unaccountable service, with a quite distinctive culture of control and enforcement. When interactions were required, in order that they should do their own jobs effectively, they found the Home Office generally slow and inefficient, and this caused additional resentment and frustration. Hence, there were few incentives for these services to co-operate with the ISED (see p. 211).

However, there were two exceptions to this rule. A small caucus of London Registrars of Births, Deaths and Marriages had instigated proactive collaboration with the ISED, to denounce suspected bogus marriages to a newly-established ISED Marriage Abuse Section, which then sometimes conducted raids on the civil weddings in question. (Formal arrangements now exist allowing registrars to pass information about suspected 'sham' marriages to the Immigration Service.)

> Dununs, eh, well registrars aren't officially allowed to talk to us. They have to go through general registrar office. But we talk to them quite often, because we get statements from them. We get denuns through ... (Immigration Officer, 1998, p. 20).

At the time of our study, the Marriage Abuse Section seemed to be much the most proactive, geared-up and effective of the teams in the office we investigated. The Chief Immigration Officer in charge of it was young, brisk, purposeful and zealous, someone whose sense of mission was in some contrast with the relative world-weariness (almost resignation) of other staff, who brought a sense of irony to their recognition of the impossibility of their tasks. The head of the Marriage Abuse Section explained the strategic decision to set up his unit.

> It was too big a loophole. ... there was a perception on the streets of London, if you want to earn a few pounds all you have to do is to go through a 'deaf' marriage ... and we were getting information from registrars who were saying

they couldn't remember the last time they'd married ... genuine, two British people together ... they estimated that over 90 per cent of the marriages they conducted were sham. ... So in the context of that we decided we ought to form some sort of team of dedicated officers, just to look at marriage and divorce. ... to look at trying to prosecute people ... and prosecute fixers and racketeers. ... (Chief Immigration Officer, 1998, pp. 2–4).

He, unlike his colleagues in other teams, offered accounts of systematic attempts to catch marriage brokers as well as individual offenders, through co-operation with these registrars.

The other agency that co-operated actively with the ISED was the Benefits Agency Benefit Fraud Investigation Service (BABFIS). Alone among the public services approach by the ISED, it had signed a 'Memorandum of Understanding' over co-operation. The policy origins of this were described in very different terms by two Immigration Inspectors. The first claimed that the ISED was responding to an initiative by the BABFIS, and by its presence at workplace raids (see pp. 186–92) aimed to protect immigrants from exploitation by racketeers. When BABFIS planned such raids

... if they ask us to accompany them, or if they tell us that, you know, there are large [numbers] of foreign workers there then, you know, if we have grounds to suppose that we are going to find offenders there we will go. But, I mean, very often we are able to sort of eliminate people from our inquiries fairly quickly. ... So I mean ... although obviously there's a sense in which in those operations we are bearing down on some individuals, there's also a sense in which, eh, you know, we are establishing very quickly the innocence of others ... (Immigration Inspector, 1998, p. 8).

The other Immigration Inspector saw the sanction against employers (section 8 of the Asylum and Immigration Act, 1996) as concerned with the 'vast problem' of 'illegal employment' among immigrants, which caused displacement of (mainly minority ethnic) legally employed British workers. It was he who reported that 70 per cent of denunciations came from members of ethnic minorities (and he assumed these to be citizens). He argued that the ISED and BABFIS had a common interest in this field – the protection of British workers.

... there is a problem with National Insurance numbers; the key to employment is a National Insurance number issued by the Benefits Agency, and they've lost control over that, there are a vast number of these numbers in the system that are unlawfully issued. ... it's such a big problem that the Benefits Agency have difficulty coping with it. And that's why the Benefits Agency are now keen to getting to facts, questioning people, eh, and we're going with them as often as possible to try to see the immigration side of things, they will cover the benefit side, so it's a two-way agency approach, and it does work, it does work (Immigration Inspector, 1998, p. 7).

As we shall show (pp. 190–92), it seems that two years later the BABFIS did not share this assessment of the effectiveness of their joint operations. But the general orientation of the second Immigration Inspector to the purpose of enforcement action at workplaces was given endorsement by senior policy officers of the IND at that later stage. In relation to the work permit system, the other arm of immigration policy, allowing legal channels for economic migration, the two policy officers interviewed subscribed to the view that '... the work permit system exists primarily to safeguard the interests of the UK workforce, so it's ... subject to labour-market tests' (IND Policy Officer, 2000, p. 6). This seemed to reflect an overall Home Office point of view on economic migration.

> ... the reason these people come here is to work really, they are economic refugees, aren't they? ... and there's no doubt there's a huge problem, because they are displacing others who could be doing the same work who live here ... (Chief Immigration Officer, 1998, pp. 7–8).

It was interesting to compare these accounts of joint operations and co-operation with those given by irregular migrants themselves. All three groups contained individuals who had been directly involved in actions against workplaces; several Polish and Turkish respondents had come into contact with the police, either as being suspected of criminal offences, or as witnesses or victims of crime. We analysed these accounts to see how they tallied with the ones given by ISED staff.

The first point is that irregular migrants made a sharp distinction between workplace raids (or raids on houses), which they saw as conducted by 'the Home Office', and criminal investigation, which was a police matter. Of course, as the ISED emphasised, the success of their work depended on co-operation, but the interviewees perceived that immigration enforcement and criminal justice work were actually quite separate in the UK, and that co-operation was tenuous. This was one reason why they had been able to escape during ISED raids; the police presence was not adequate for the task.

> The Home Office only came when they were told something about a place, that is, there was a grassing, someone told them that there were illegal workers somewhere. They came straight away and caught whoever they could. ... Then I ran away from them, I still don't know how I managed, I ran downstairs, I hid myself almost in the freezer. ... I didn't want to go back to Brazil at that stage (Angelo, p. 4).

> There were seven of us Poles working there. Someone must have informed them; maybe we talked Polish too much and too loud. And me and another lad were working in the garden, building a patio. We could see the police, so we jumped over the fence to a neighbour's garden. It later turned out that everyone was detained ... including the boss, who didn't have a work permit (Daniel, p. 3).

Once the [national fast food chain outlet] where I was working was raided by the police, trying to catch unauthorised workers. We were smuggled out through the back door. ... the manager helped us because otherwise they would be fined. ... I heard of many similar raids, especially on clothing factories, especially those where Turkish people worked. ... my only precaution was to continuously watch the front door for any policemen or immigration officers (Silvia (3), p. 10).

Conversely, when interviewees were picked up by the police for suspected criminal offences, Home Office responses were usually less than dynamic or decisive. One Polish man had been arrested when walking down the street, holding a piece of glass he had found in a nearby garden. He had dirty hands and was carrying the tools of his (building) trade, both indications that he could be either a burglar (the original reason for arresting him) or an undocumented worker. Having no further evidence to support the former suspicion, the police held him at the station while they tried to check his (manifestly irregular) immigration status. In his account of the interview that followed:

I said ... that I had lost my Home Office paper, and that I had tried to go to the Home Office to get a replacement ... I told them a different name as well ... She [policewoman] said that she would check it, and she told [wife] that she would come back at midnight to see the passports. An officer came in and asked who that criminal was, pointing at me, and she said, 'Polish glazier'. They really had a laugh at my expense. And she also said that I didn't have any papers, couldn't speak any English, so all I deserved was to be sent back to Poland. And I said nothing at all. And finally she told me I could go home and I should go to the Home Office to get a new paper, and that they would come to check up on me after Christmas. And nobody has turned up ever since (Karel, p. 7).

Although it may be that the police did not bother to ring the Home Office in this case, it seems more likely that they did, supplying them with Karel's false name and real address, and that there was no response at the time or subsequently. One Turkish man, Abdulla, who had a criminal record in Albania and Turkey, had three brushes with the police. He was more proactive in exploiting the potential for non-co-operation between the police and Home Office, going on the offensive on both occasions. The first time, he was (quite illegally) running a small business in Hackney, and was picked up for an unspecified offence and taken to the police station. At the time he had a student visa, and was restricted as to work, but this was not initially checked. His account continues:

It was a young racist policeman and he was very strict with me. He told me directly that he would expel me from the country. I showed him my visa and told him he couldn't do that. I denied that I was working, because they couldn't prove it. I was detained there for six to seven hours, and they wanted to bring someone from the Immigration Centre. Before they released me I told the policeman what I thought. In the presence of the Chief Inspector and five or six other policemen I asked him how would he feel, if I came back to my country and treated an Englishman just the same way as he treated me. He went red, and the Chief Inspector apologised and told me not to work any more (Abdulla, pp. 2–3).

Again, it is unclear whether Abdulla was released because the Home Office were slow to respond to police enquiries and the latter lost patience, or because he called the police's bluff, and exposed their lack of expertise over immigration offences (or some combination of the two). Either way, co-operation was ineffective, even though he was probably guilty of a crime, and certainly of at least one immigration offence. With growing panache, he then used the same technique when arrested for driving at 100 m.p.h. on the motorway, and being stopped by the police. He was asked about his flat, his job and his salary, and given a spot fine, then allowed to go without showing his passport. He thought this was because he was not on the police computer. Finally, he was questioned by a policeman over trespassing on private property, and was asked where he came from.

> ... I told him that, since he wasn't from the Immigration Office he mustn't ask me that. He apologised and left. Although I stay illegally here, I live in peace. I've also got a dog. This wouldn't be possible in Turkey. I feel good here (Abdulla, p. 3).

In general terms, the interviewees regarded the UK police as fair, and were aware how low in their priorities immigration offences fell. One Polish man contrasted this with Germany, where he had been denounced by a German citizen.

> No, that's the good thing about England, because in Germany it's terrible. When you work in Germany, I know because I was nicked once. There is a German couple walking, for example (that's what happened to us) and they can hear Polish language and they phone the police. And here I was working, building a wall, two policemen were walking [by], I got worried, and they just started chatting to me, very friendly; English police are fine, no problems. I have to admit that ... I even worked for a guy who worked for the Home Office. Really. He told me not to worry, he said unless someone denounces, they do nothing (Karel, p. 10).

WORKPLACE RAIDS

Part of our research study in 1998–9 was observation of workplace raids in which the staff of the ISED office we were researching took part. This was the aspect of the research that raised the greatest ethical difficulties. On the one hand, it felt very uncomfortable to be taking part in actions against the kind of people who had helped our study by giving interviews about their activities as irregular migrants. On the other, we were observing practices by the ISED which were shrouded in secrecy, and where there could be security issues at stake. The strategies of both sides were aimed to thwart each other, and we were becoming privy to both. Finally, there were times when we seemed to recognise that something described by the irregular migrants was being missed by the authorities, as we show below.

Interviews with ISED senior managers claimed that co-operation on these raids was effective – 'it does work' (Immigration Inspector, p. 7). However, there was evidence that success was limited, even before our observation. In the first place, despite the fact that this was over a year after the sanction against employers taking on undocumented immigrant workers without proper checks (section 8, Asylum and Immigration Act, 1996) had been implemented, there had still been no case of an employer being prosecuted. This was at odds with the Immigration Inspector's claim that the main aim of enforcement in the workplace was against 'organised immigration abuse', 'unscrupulous employers' and 'the exploiters themselves' (Immigration Inspector, pp. 2–4). When asked why it was the undocumented immigrant workers who were targeted, rather than the employers, despite these declared aims, he gave a number of reasons why such prosecutions had proved too difficult to implement.

> ... we envisage some difficulty in identifying who the employer actually is. For example, the government is very concerned about the activity of illegal gangmasters ... in the agricultural area ... in general a farmer will employ people, ... a workforce, which is supplied to him by a gangmaster, and the farmer is going to say, 'Well, I'm not the employer, the gangmaster is the employer', and we envisage the gangmaster is going to say, 'Well, although I supplied this particular gang, ... I got them from someone who is subcontracting to me', ... and we envisage that might be quite a difficult matter to establish. ... prosecutions will not be easy, because you might be taking statements from, ehm, a Russian ... (Immigration Inspector, 1998, p. 5).

This reluctance to prosecute employers, or at least the low priority given to such prosecutions at that time, can be contrasted with enforcement practice in both Germany and the USA. In Germany, the enforcement units of the employment authorities and some customs units go on workplace raids to check both workers and employers for social security contribution evasion, benefit fraud and the employment of unauthorised foreign workers, all in the same operation. In practice, they tend to focus on construction sites, and use informal discretion to select those sites where evidently 'foreign' (that is brown or black) workers have been observed (Cyrus and Vogel, 2001, p. 14). Although the statistics about such raids are far from perfectly transparent, it is clear that many employers are subsequently prosecuted and heavily fined, and that the main focus of enforcement is on Germans rather than foreigners, most of whom are simply passed to the local aliens' authorities for decisions over removal. (In our research on Brazilians in Berlin, one had been caught and removed as a result of a raid.) Table 7.1 shows the statistics for Labour Office sanctions against foreign employees and employers in the Federal Republic of Germany in 1998 and 1999 (Cyrus and Vogel, 2001, p. 16).

In the USA investigating units of the Immigration and Nationality Service (INS) are responsible for workplace raids. They prepare a case and take out a warrant to search a worksite, where they suspect that undocumented immigrants are working. In 1994 there were only 245 federal worksite investigations in the whole of the USA (*Migration News*, 1995), though resources were increased after 1996. This makes the intensity of such specialised regulation and enforcement nearer to the UK's (500 plus non-specialist staff for a population about a quarter of the size) than Germany's. Labour inspectors and tax inspectors do not check employees' individual papers, or use sanctions against them; instead they collect evidence to prosecute employers' violation of labour regulations and tax laws (Vogel, 2000). There were 804 investigators who conducted about 60 000 worksite visits in 1995 (US Commission on Immigration Reform, 1996, p. 94), so Department of Labour (DoL) is a more significant regulator and enforcer than the INS. Qualitatively, their focus on employers makes them more like the German authorities, but quantitatively, the combined effect of DoL and INS is more like the UK than the German in its impact.

In what follows, we describe three of the four raids observed, one not being reported for ethical reasons. In all of these, the intention was to combine BABFIS and ISED operations, supported by the police to make arrests. ISED staff had prepared in advance, and identified 'targets' in each case, one senior officer being especially keen to apprehend a particular offender himself. In the event, ISED took part only in the first raid, for the reasons given below.

In the first raid, the workplace targeted was a foodstuffs' factory. Through intelligence work – checking workplace files supplied by the 'co-operative' employer in advance against Home Office files – five employees were identified as suspected immigration offenders. The operation started with a rendezvous at the district police station, to muster the joint team and agree tactics. However, on the evening in question only five cells were available at the police station for all purposes, and the police expressed concern that more serious criminal offenders might require this accommodation. The subsequent operation was characterised by a precise division of tasks rather than *joint* action. Police officers sealed off the area, executed the search warrant and carried out the arrests. The ISED staff conducted the inquiry and the interviews. What had appeared in the files to be clear-cut cases turned out to be far more complex. The identities established through Home Office file

Table 7.1   Statistics for Labour Office sanctions against foreign employees and employers (FRG, 1998 and 1999)

	Employee				Employer			
	Total suspected	% forwarded for prosecution	% of admin fines	Average fine (DM)	Total suspected companies	% forwarded for prosecution	% of admin fines	Average fine (DM)
1998	34 356	13.2	23.5	237	39 728	11.9	44.3	2 698
1999	34 923	13.9	29.3	300	40 906	11.3	45.9	3 221

checks did not fit the individuals interviewed. These turned out to be three legal asylum seekers working in false identities; one lacking any status, who then applied for asylum; and one who seemed to have lived for 13 years in the UK without documentation. In the last-named case, the person was subject to some immigration policy concessions, and therefore secure against immediate deportation or removal (the ISED staff's goal in all five cases), as he was entitled to appeal. Balked in their objectives, the ISED officers' mood was low at the end of this operation.

Raids 2 and 3 were initiated by the BABFIS, who invited the ISED to accompany them. However, on this occasion the visit to the local police station revealed that no police cells were available. The ISED officers immediately withdrew from the operation, explaining that 'if we cannot bang them up, it's not worth going in there'. This left the BABFIS team to check two textile factories, both owned by members of ethnic minorities, on their own.

The first factory was exceptionally clean, and apparently very efficiently managed. The operation by the BABFIS concentrated on computer-assisted checks of National Insurance numbers, contributions and claims. It was carried out in a professional, correct and polite manner, while factory staff – almost all of whom had the relevant social security documentation to hand – remained calm and apparently unconcerned, continuing their work and answering questions readily. Although some details were noted down for further checks, no obvious irregularities were detected.

However, when the wages book of the factory owner was examined, the researcher could not help noticing that all the staff (including those working in the office) were paid the same wage (£120 per week). This seemed strange, and somewhat suspicious, although BABFIS officers appeared to make nothing of it at the time. It was not until the transcriptions of the interviews with undocumented workers were re-examined that the following account came to light (for ethical reasons, neither the pseudonym of the interviewee, nor his or her nationality, is given here).

> ... normally it is 40 hours [per week], then you earn £240. ... Now, in the factory, things are totally different due to these things with the tax. So, when I earn £240, the factory owner is only declaring half of it. From this £120, tax is deducted, very little. I don't pay tax for the whole amount of £240. ... when I get £6 an hour, usually, then only £3 is declared to the state. The other money I get in cash.

There are various possible explanations of this coincidence. It may be that this was not the same factory; or that the sum of £120 was the same one used by various employers to cover the same irregularity; or that the BABFIS officers did notice this, and report it to the tax authorities, who carry out separate inspections. Or it may be that this interviewee, who admitted various other dubious practices, and was contemplating a bogus marriage, was simply making this up. However, it does indicate that the raid observed may have missed a significant breach of regulations, which included the fact that this interviewee was in fact working in breach of immigration rules. It is noteworthy that the interviewee said that the authorities had checked the factory four times, including doing computerised checks of National Insurance numbers, and that 'nothing was done' after they had assured themselves that employees were paying some tax and National Insurance contributions.

The third raid targeted an Asian-owned textile factory, where conditions came close to those associated with a 'sweatshop'. It had a much smaller, ethnically mixed workforce of Asian, African, white and black British workers. Several of the employees did not produce any papers and refused any co-operation; they stared in front of them without saying a word, not even giving their names and addresses, and seeming not to understand what was happening. The BABFIS staff's reaction was completely different from their behaviour in the previous raid; they took no further interest in the benefit fraud, but shifted completely to focusing on immigration offences. The same officers were quite rude, aggressive and tough; they were shouting and even tugging at employees. Repeated telephone requests to the ISED asking for support were refused, due to staff shortages, causing some anger among BABFIS officers. The police officers present on the periphery of this scene appeared completely unaffected by it, aware that they could not in any case make arrests. In the end, the only realistic course was to insist that five people suspected of immigration offences leave the workplace immediately, which is what happened.

These observations revealed the fragility of co-operation between the agencies which shared an enforcement ethos, but lacked a common set of priorities, and the resources to act on each other's main concerns. The police prioritise serious crime and threats to public order (such as football-related incidents, the reason why no cells were available during the second raid). The ISED are required to focus on removing identified immigration offenders; the BABFIS seek to prosecute those who commit benefit fraud. It is typical of the implementation dilemmas facing the New Labour government that – despite its efforts to 'join up' approaches of public services on all these issues (6 *et al*, 1999), and to promote a shared enforcement ethos (Jordan and Jordan, 2000) – co-operation actually broke down.

Furthermore, although we did not have access to the ISED in our 2000 study, it was evident from our interviews with the BABFIS that the policy of joint raids on workplaces had been abandoned, for reasons of efficiency. The manager of the BABFIS in one of the boroughs in question told the researcher:

> ... since you were at [name of district] ... the Programme Protection came in, in April last year ... and our style of work changed. At that time ... we did very, very

similar work, and we could quickly get results from going out, doing raids on factories, and claiming at that time what we call weekly benefit savings, WBS. That is no longer the way we work. We now work and concentrate on achieving a quality investigation. ... But the days of raiding factories, really we haven't done this for a year at all. ... What it was leading to was fairly unsatisfactory types of investigations, and the more quality type of investigation suffered as a result. We didn't get so many people to court (BABFIS manager, interview 13, 2000, pp. 8–9).

REGULATION, DAILY LIFE AND UK SOCIETY

As might be expected, these irregular migrants were conscious of the need to make themselves invisible, to avoid drawing the authorities' attention to them and to be careful not to infringe against minor rules. However, no one group was in general more afraid of the UK authorities than any other – the main difference lay between those from Turkey who trusted their fellow nationals, and those from Brazil and Poland who feared denunciations. Apart from this, variation was between individuals within groups over how wary they were of the authorities, and this depended on their temperaments, length of time in the UK and previous experiences in London. They exercised prudence, rather than hiding themselves, or seeing either UK citizens or the police as hostile to them, and some clearly regarded the social environment as a rather benign one. Among the Brazilians, several spoke of the lack of checks and harassment.

> ... I am very calm, I never had any problems. Some people stay for years without any passport. Totally illegal (Rosa, p. 5).

> I think the work that immigrants do doesn't threaten English society. We work in an end of the market that [English] people are not interested in. Society needs us to do these jobs. I have never been discriminated against here. No complaints about that. I know it exists. I have seldom seen Brazilians complaining about it. I think Brazilians work hard, don't speak English, and manage to get by (Rob, p. 3).

> I am not fearful. I am too laid back. I think everything will be alright. I don't have to live here the rest of my life (Toni, p. 9).

> I would like to go and visit Brazil, not to live, life is too difficult there. I want to die there, it is my country, I miss it. But for the moment I want to stay here. What could I do there? To be a teacher? It doesn't really appeal to me. My parents always give me a hard time because I work in bars here, I am a barman while I could be a teacher in Brazil. But they respect me here. It is alright (Marcos, p. 2).

> I love it here. With the cold weather and the fog. I like it here. I think it is beautiful. I don't like the darkness in winter. That really annoys me! But other

than that I am fine here! ... People ask me when I am going back to Brazil. I say only when the Queen takes me home and sends me back. ... It is an adventure to live here, my day-to-day life (Cris, p. 6).

I don't want to go back to Brazil. I like big cities. I like to have a lot to do. I like the busy, messy, city life. ... Everyone says that English people are cold. They are quieter and shy, they are more reserved. ... But it is alright, just more difficult to establish relationships (Julia, p. 2).

Others were slightly more guarded and ambivalent. Fred was asked about discrimination on grounds of colour.

Well ... yes. I think there is always a difference. And the black community [here] has the defence of being English. I am black and not English and I feel the difference (Fred, p. 3).

There is very little intimacy in this culture. Nothing much is shared. English people are too reserved. ... [Brazilians are] doing jobs that English people don't do. ... It is such a slave life! ... In this First World, immigrants are an island of poverty (Lucia, p. 3).

I am quite shocked, yet pleased to be here. Every Brazilian I know here has such a hard life. Everyone works such long hours. ... They forget pleasure, enjoyment, art and culture (Flavia, p. 1).

We live under very poor conditions here. Life is hard in Brazil, but we live much better (Bete, p. 1).

Similarly, Polish interviewees were either blithely relaxed or nervous, more by temperament and in general response to the environment than from specific information.

I didn't think about it at all. I don't know if I'm so stupid, but I never thought about it. Because I thought no immigration people would get as far as [outer London borough]. So that wasn't a problem at all until the moment when a policeman walked into [name of burger outlet]. When I saw him for the first time my heart stopped, I didn't know why he was there. A policeman. But my boss was smiling and started talking to him, very friendly. And he introduced me as a new worker. And then we became friends. He was a laugh. So it was a stress that passed very quickly (Irena, p. 7).

Rafal [husband] is careful, when he goes to work. ... After work he comes straight home. He doesn't go anywhere, to any pubs. We don't go out in the evenings. ... We avoid situations, places, where we might be asked for documents (Krystyna, p. 7).

The Home Office might come here to look for somebody else and find us as well. You don't know what other tenants do. The police might be after them if they come and look around. We might be found out like this (Silvia, p. 11).

I am worried I might be stopped by the police and that the first question might be where I am from and if I have a visa. Apart from this, I am not worried at all. Because wherever I go, to any office for example, nobody asks this kind of question (Jerzy, p. 11).

In fact, as other Polish interviewees were aware (see p. 164), the possibility of being stopped in the street was negligible in London. This was explained to the researcher by the ISED Immigration Inspector:

… we are not allowed to go and stop people on the streets and say, 'Excuse me, are you an illegal entrant?' or whatever it is; we can only act on research and act on specific information. The government will not let us, eh, stop people in the street and ask for papers, I think in the continental system they can do that, because they have internal controls, people should have identity cards with some numbers … (Immigration Inspector, 1998, pp. 2–3).

Turkish and Kurdish interviewees had had most, and most varied, contacts with the police (see pp. 185–6), partly because they had been in London the longest on average. However, their attitudes towards being visible to the authorities were somewhat ambivalent. Since most were asylum seekers, they had less to fear from being in contact, so long as it was not for criminal offences or undocumented work. The most inconsistent in his account was Mehmet, who said that he had already been arrested for unauthorised work. It had reminded him of his experiences of prison and torture in Turkey, and 'nobody can prove it is different here' (p. 4). On the other hand, he threatened to report the Home Office to the police if they lost his papers (p. 3). Sirin commented:

… a lot of my friends do [have trouble with the police]. … For example, arrest. … Yes, I am afraid of being caught through my illegal work. I think it would have negative consequences for my asylum application, or it would lead to my arrest (Sirin, p. 5).

However, Osman, a Kurdish man who had been in London since 1988, took a more relaxed view.

Well, there are many people working illegally, but I think the state doesn't care much about this. Because if the state cared, all the workers would get a proper wage. … That's why there are no controls. … Well, I wasn't afraid … Because according to my logic, if they caught me, I would immediately apply for asylum, and I was also a student. … But since we had problems with the language, we were afraid to get in contact with the police. … When my car was stolen, I told the police about that, and they asked me how and where it was stolen, and where do I come from (Osman, p. 4).

Faruk had had several contacts with the police.

After four months, I was arrested by the police. ... I told them that I want to apply for asylum and they released me. ... From '94 I lived illegal again. ... after I got my deportation order I moved house, I changed my workplace, and afterwards I didn't hear anything. It might be that they carried out a check, but I removed everything. ... No, they behaved fine. I've been in the old police station, they were fine (Faruk, pp. 4, 9).

Mustafa had had good experiences of police in the workplace, intervening on behalf of strikers (see p. 139), but a bad experience of being threatened with arrest on another occasion – 'they treated me as if they wanted to beat me' (p. 8).

CONCLUSIONS

Our study was conducted before the shift in policy on 'economic migration', at a time when immigration control and enforcement in the UK reflected the government's obsession with deterring asylum seeking. This, in turn, was an updated version of UK administrations' long-term policy of limiting black and Asian immigration, the aim of legislation and implementation in the previous 30 years. As Michael Dummett has put it:

> The term 'immigration' came by itself to mean 'coloured immigration' – the immigration of people from the Caribbean and the Indian sub-continent; it was not applied to the immigration of white people from Australia and elsewhere. It was a code-word. The people who demanded an end to immigration were not concerned with migration as such, even though they often talked of 'this crowded little island'. If they had been, they would have been relieved by the fact that, throughout the 1960s and 1970s, Britain was a country of net emigration: more people left than arrived (Dummett, 2001, p. 96).

In the 1990s both Home Office policy and the practice of the ISED were still shaped by these considerations, though redirected towards the new issues of asylum claims and 'marriage abuse', both of which were more likely to concern migrants from the Middle and Far East and from Africa. In so far as economic migration entered this frame, it was as an explanation of why they wanted to come to the UK. Hence, the immigration control system was still seen as related to the skin colour of these 'economic migrants', rather than their potential contributions or costs to the UK economy.

> Britain's immigration policy is deeply guided by race, ... it is designed to keep out black and brown people and let in white people. But it dare not do that explicitly. So it maintains a charade of non-racist controls behind which lurks a deeply racist practice (Commission for Racial Equality, interview 1998).

ISED managers and staff frequently indicated that working without proper immigration status was not, in itself, seen by them as a very serious immigration offence. This could be justified in policy terms, given the government's apparent lack of concern about those irregular migrants arriving as business-people, students and tourists, but actually involved in unauthorised economic activities. They accepted that, with their numbers, and given the extent of this activity, the best they could do was 'let people know they were about', and hope that a certain amount of mythology about their effectiveness, together with denunciation and betrayal, would keep irregular migrants on their toes. Several officers, at all levels, indicated off tape that they did not regard work in breach of immigration status conditions as a serious infraction, and all confirmed that it was not high in their priorities for enforcement work. This may change if the focus shifts to 'illegal work' (Home Office, 2002, ch. 5).

In fact, we have seen in this chapter that most of those irregular migrants whose main objective was to improve their long-term economic position were quite realistic about their chances of being caught, and had strategies about how to respond if they were. Furthermore, migrants from Turkey (who were working in the shadow economy, but whose motives for coming were political) had an ideological view of the UK government's policy purposes in allowing the shadow economy to burgeon, and believed that it was part of its cynical attempt to develop a specially exploitative type of capitalism.

From the standpoint of the ISED, the underlying racial element in these policies was well disguised. As far as they were concerned, they were trained in anti-racist and anti-discriminatory approaches; several of their officers were from ethnic minorities; and they took a pride in acting with fairness and impartiality. One Immigration Inspector emphasised that staff were mostly graduates, and understood about the cultures of the immigrants they dealt with. But he also claimed:

> I think most of them [immigrant communities] do perceive ... firm immigration controls being in the best interest of race relations ... most people in immigrant communities as well as the indigenous population ... (Immigration Inspector, 1998, p. 19).

However, the fact of the matter was that, in giving priority to the removal of those groups most likely to be black and Asian, policies fed into deeply ingrained assumptions and stereotypes held by ISED staff.

> ... and of course Turks, Indians, Pakistanis, whole range, but West Africa is definitely our biggest problem in this particular office (Immigration Inspector, interview 3, 1998, p. 5).

The crisis and administrative chaos over computerisation and the reforms of the asylum system meant that these priorities and preoccupations were to continue during the whole period of the first New Labour administration. The events of 11 September 2001 added a security dimension to the tasks of immigration control. But from 2000 onwards, economic arguments were pointing towards new criteria for entry, new immigration channels and new directions for policy.

One problem for the UK will be how to combine existing immigration control and enforcement services with the newly developed agencies for recruitment from abroad. After all, the IND has had a 30–year history of implementing policies directed against non-white immigrants; its critics argue that its bias has now become unconscious and institutionalised (Dummett, 2001, p. 62). As we shall see in Chapter 9, there is considerable tension between the organisation for granting work permits and its constituency (the UK business community) and the IND.

8. Irregular migration and the public services

After the UK general election of 2001, a remarkable consensus among the political parties emerged about a crisis in the country's public services. Not only was the Labour government committed to a large increase in spending on the public infrastructure as an investment for the future; the Conservative opposition too announced that it saw public service regeneration as more important than cuts in taxation. The Liberal Democrats had been campaigning during the previous two elections for priority to be given to improving public services.

This chapter investigates the impact of irregular migration upon these services, and the responses of staff in them. In the popular press, one of the strongest and most emotional complaints about the rise in asylum seeking in the 1990s was that it was a drain on national revenues, through the benefits and services provided. The UK was claimed to be a 'soft touch', and its welfare state a 'magnet' for people from poorer countries, who were basically economic migrants. One of the reasons for the deterioration in the public services was, so it was claimed, the excessive demands made upon them by these foreigners.

In the more favourable interpretation of economic migration that began to be disseminated by government circles in 2000, this version started to be challenged.

> ... an initial analysis for the UK suggests that migrants contribute more in taxes and National Insurance than they consume in benefits and other public services. We estimate that the foreign-born population contributes around 10 per cent more to Government revenues than they receive in Government expenditure, ... if there were no foreign-born people in the UK, taxes (or borrowing) would have to rise, or expenditure would have to be cut, by £2.6 billion (the equivalent of about 1 pence on the basic rate of income tax), ... on average and overall, *migrants are not a burden on the public purse* (Glover *et al.*, 2001, p. 44).

However, this is a very aggregated and statistical view, which does little justice to the actual impacts of migrants on these services, or conversely of the responses of staff to migrants' needs. Above all, it takes no account of irregular migration as a factor, or whether public benefits and services attract irregular migrants to the country, and facilitate their stays.

In the literature on migration and welfare states in Europe, two themes dominate. One is the extent to which migration is a factor in the weakening of European nations' capacities to sustain characteristic systems for protecting wage levels and the standards of living of those citizens outside the labour market (Joppke, 1998). According to Freeman (1986, p. 61) immigration 'led to an Americanisation of European welfare politics' that threatened the whole social model. This view has been disputed as a general thesis (Rhodes and Van Appledoorn, 1998); the model has proved relatively resilient. The second theme is the extent to which immigrants and their descendants who have not gained citizenship of EU member states suffer social exclusion, partly because they are denied the rights to mobility within the Union (Geddes, 2000). Here the consensus is that Third Country nationals do suffer from damaging disadvantages.

The case of the UK can cast light on both of these debates, since it was an exception to the general run of EU member states in ways relevant to both dimensions of social policy. First, during the Conservative years the government embraced many reforms that deliberately took the public services in the direction of the US model, and further from the European one. Few of these have been reversed, and some have been consolidated, under New Labour. Second, a far greater proportion of postwar immigrants to the UK became citizens than in other EU member states, and especially more than in Germany. Hence, it is possible to examine how migration, and specifically irregular migration, affected standards in public services that were open to pressures from outsiders, and whether better access for migrants to UK citizenship reduced their risks of social exclusion.

To explore both these questions fully would be well beyond the scope of this chapter. However, our research findings are relevant for the central dilemmas. Turning its back on the principle of social protection through systems of entitlement, based on contributions to social insurance funds, the UK moved in the 1980s and 1990s towards targeted, selective provision for those who could demonstrate 'genuine need'. Under New Labour, the goals of the public infrastructure were redefined as the promotion of responsibility, inclusion and opportunity (Lister, 2000). Staff in services were required to be both accessible and 'user-friendly' in their practices, but also vigilant against fraud and abuse (DSS, 1998, ch. 9), and robust in enhancing independence (DoH, 1998). As we show, this set us a difficult tension between the attempt to respond without discrimination to the often desperate plight of migrants, and the pressure to turn away those who could not prove their destitution, or their proper immigration status. Under the weight of these contradictory expectations of accessibility and deterrence, staff were understandably often bewildered and besieged. Both the open-ended nature of the demand, and the requirement to carry out stringent tests of need, could contribute to falling standards.

In the midst of often chaotic and crisis-ridden organisational cultures, one of the principles most fiercely upheld was anti-racism, with its applications in anti-discriminatory practice. Staff were committed to defending the hard-won gains of the 1980s in this field, and hence to rejecting eligibility tests which – in filtering out irregular migrants – could put up barriers to access from ethnic minority citizens and entitled refugees and asylum seekers. Hence, this principle could become a more important totem than the quality of what was being provided. From our interviews, it was clear that irregular migrants from all three countries had little difficulty in gaining access to health care, and those with children were able to get them into schools.

Second, the research opened up puzzling questions about the extent to which other forms of public provision – residual housing, social assistance and welfare services generally – consolidated rather than offset their recipients' social exclusion. Of the three groups, those from Turkey were the ones with access to this provision, yet they were also quite clearly the most excluded in several dimensions. Whereas the Brazilians and Poles retained the advantages of mobility, including the option of returning to their countries (or of yo-yoing to and fro between the two, as many Polish migrants did), Turkish and Kurdish interviewees were trapped as much by their reliance on needs-related welfare systems as by the insecure, low-paid shadow employment in which they were engaged (Jordan, 1995, 1996). Thus, they took on many of the characteristics of the UK 'underclass', and resorted to many of its members' defensive strategies (see pp. 137–41).

This finding resonates depressingly with the evidence emerging from the minority ethnic communities in northern England, from the enquiries into the race riots in Bradford, Burnley and Oldham during the summer of 2001. Being poor, living in the worst appointed neighbourhoods and relying on a safety net of targeted public services, does not allow inclusion, even where minorities have access to the formal status of citizens. So it is not surprising that asylum seekers and other migrants who became part of these communities were included in their culture practices of resistance and survival, but not in the opportunities and facilities of mainstream UK society. Whether they came primarily for political or economic motives, absorption into the fabric of relationships on the margins, and thus into the host society's systems for managing its marginal members, made them into a special category of outsider, among other outsiders. Those who had a valid claim to refugee status often jeopardised it by taking shadow employment, turning themselves into irregulars. They justifiably accused the UK welfare state of criminalising them (see pp. 140–41).

What these findings again demonstrate is that it is dangerous to generalise about the outcomes of migration, without detailed analysis of the distortions caused by membership systems of all kinds in the host country. Migrants – and especially irregular migrants – do not enter simply as bearers of skills in search of their most productive allocation, nor do they enter a frictionless market economy. They come into an elaborate system of interlocking institutions, designed to enhance the interests of their members. In a very unequal society, with diverging life chances, irregular migrants may further damage the systems that are supposed to protect the least organised and most vulnerable citizens. And if these systems trap and exclude poor citizens, then they will trap and exclude migrants also.

ACCESS AND DISCRIMINATION

When the Blair government took office in 1997, it sought immediately to redefine the terms of membership of the UK polity. In line with the Third Way doctrines of Bill Clinton in the USA (Jordan, 1998), New Labour aimed to establish a 'new contract for welfare', in which responsibilities were emphasised as much as rights, work was promoted as the basis of all social provision and citizens were encouraged to be active in pursuit of their own needs and choices.

This version of social citizenship therefore promoted the idea that public services must derive their standards from the market, and supply them to 'the demanding, sceptical, citizen-consumer'.

> Society has become more demanding. Consumers expect ever higher levels of service and better value for money. ... Taxpayers want public agencies which meet their objects efficiently. The way in which a service is delivered can be as important as the service itself – as retailers know only too well, ... expectations of service quality and conscience have risen – as with the growth of 24–hour banking – but public services have failed to keep up with these developments; their duplication, inefficiency, and unnecessary complexity should not be tolerated (DSS, 1998, p. 16).

At the same time, government policy documents emphasised the requirement for public services to focus on 'genuine need', and encourage those able to do so to provide for themselves, as part of the new stress on responsibility. Public services should therefore make careful assessments of needs and eliminate fraud and abuse. Among the measures to do so were the tests of immigration status, first required by the Conservative government (Hansard, 1995, written answers, 18th July 1027–8), and reinforced subsequently (Immigration and Nationality Department, 1997).

The idea of immigration status checks cuts across strong traditions in the public services, and especially in the National Health Service. In the previous decade, and right up to the time of our research, considerable efforts had been made to improve access by minority ethnic communities, and promote equality of treatment. Among our interviewees in the health service one described the aims of such a project.

> ... when I first came to East London a few years ago, ... all the disadvantaged or excluded communities [were] having problems with access in terms of communication and information. I mean, this is, this has changed a lot, we have done a lot of good work, we have for example introduced the advocacy workers, we have produced some information, not only for the public, but also for service providers about the entitlement, ... and so on (equality manager, National Health Service, p. 2).

One of the advocates in this project explained:

> ... advocacy work on behalf of people who don't speak English, or speak little English, or just need somebody to go along with them when they visit doctors, GPs, opticians, dentists and so on. ... We interpret for the patient, give them advice about health, and challenge any racism if they face racism, discrimination ... (health advocate, p. 1).

This was in line with government policy on access to the public services, and especially the NHS.

> We are determined to improve access to health services – preventative and reactive – for those most in need. ... This principle of equal access is reflected in a new *NHS National Performance Framework*. For example, local services will be monitored to ensure that black and ethnic minority groups are not disadvantaged in terms of access to local health services (DSS, 1998, p. 47).

For these practitioners, the requirement to conduct checks of immigration status undermined this attempt to promote equal access. They insisted that it led to discrimination, as much against minority ethnic UK citizens as against foreign nationals seeking treatment.

> ... we don't ask anything, we don't mind if they are illegal, legal, students or *au pairs* as long as they need advocacy (health advocate, p. 4).

In local authority services, the emphasis was, if anything, more strong on resisting immigration status checks, with the trade unions also taking a stance on the issue.

> ... it is such a politically aware borough because we had so many problems with racism, ... by and large most people are UNISON members and actually have

taken the time and trouble to find out how not to discriminate ... but if they, if people want to ferret out illegals, they don't have anywhere to take it anyway, because they are not allowed to contact the Home Office, and they would get sacked if they did (resettlement officer, pp. 4, 12).

... we used to have a policy 'no passport service', it meant ... the housing officer was not allowed to ask for the passport of a person, or ask them about their immigration status, and to us you know everybody was treated equally, regardless of your sort of immigration status, that was our policy ... and we are, even with the changes in legislation, unless we have to ask about, you know, their status, we are not asking them, and we are not asking them about whether they are working or not working legally or illegally, we don't want to be involved in that sort of area (race equality worker, pp. 4, 11).

What is not acceptable is to ask for passports to be required, and this local authority has a policy for not requiring passports, because it is clearly discriminating if you're only asking one group of people for their passports. Last year the Department for Education and Employment issued a draft circular in a very worrying development, ... to local schools admission authorities, and in the circular they suggested that admissions officers should provide details to the Immigration and Nationality Department on families and children who were suspected to be illegal immigrants, who may not have credible documentation, and so on ... I mean, what was attempted to do was ... to introduce another level of internal control. But this would have been disastrous for refugees, because it would break that confidentiality in terms of the schools admission process, and would link (in refugees' and asylum seekers' minds) the schools with the rest of the state's apparatus, which it is in repressive countries. ... So it would have discouraged people from seeking school places, and would have undermined their trust ... (education centre worker, p. 7).

... we made it clear that we didn't think it was our job to check people's immigration status and that we weren't prepared to do that (teacher, p. 3).

From the interviews with undocumented migrants, it was clear that most did have access to medical services, even when they were in the country without any status, or as tourists. Among those from Brazil and Poland, several had received treatment, including operations; others had given birth in London.

Yes, I used it all the time. I am diabetic. Very easy assistance (Rico, p. 3)

I just filled a form, said that I was a student, and that was all. Very easy and accessible (Bete, p. 4).

I was pregnant and I miscarried the baby. I have been to the doctor about five times (Carmen, p. 2).

The NHS is very helpful. ... I had a small operation. I was in a panic because I didn't have money to pay. But I went in and out, had the treatment without paying anything (Farina, p. 12).

I have done five HIV tests since I've been here (Marcos, p. 2).

This is a very good thing. Legal, illegal but they help you out in the Health Service. They believe when you say you don't work, and give you tablets for free too. This has been very helpful here. I have never paid a doctor (Rosa, p. 5).

I had no problems registering and he saw me and prescribed some cream (Teresa, p. 6).

I never realised that I could see the doctor just like that, that they don't want to see your documents or anything like this (Olga, p. 6).

As soon as I went to the hospital I had an interpreter. You see, everything for free. Even when I went to the A and E department, when I had some problem with my pregnancy. And the medicines at the chemist, some expensive, everything free. I didn't pay anything. I just had to sign on the back of the prescriptions (Krystyna, p. 8).

Several Polish interviewees were very critical of the standard of treatment they received, or the waiting times in hospital receptions, but only one had experienced difficulties in registering or getting treatment.

The experiences of Turkish and Kurdish interviewees were slightly more mixed, but several had received a good deal of medical care, without problems.

We regularly went there during Fatima's pregnancy. There were no problems ... my wife was in hospital while expecting the baby (Osman, p. 8).

Then I went to the doctor, but used somebody else's name, and told them I was a student, and the doctor didn't ask about anything. I didn't know that the doctors, unlike the Home Office, don't need to see your documents (Metin, 2, p. 12).

I am registered with a GP. I was not registered in the beginning, but later I did register with my brother's GP (Emine, p. 7).

I am registered with a GP. I have received treatment from my GP and from the local hospital (Nermin, p. 3).

Others were afraid of going to doctors, either because they could not pay, or because their health needs related to irregular activities.

I did not have a GP because I did not know at that time about GPs. ... I did have many accidents in the work place. For example, once I fell down very badly on a slippery floor as I was mopping it and hurt my arm. But I did not seek any treatment, not even an x-ray, because I was afraid that they would ask me how it happened, and I could not tell them it happened at the workplace as I was working illegally (Emine, pp. 10–11).

Very few of the interviewees had children of school age, but those who did seemed to have no difficulties in getting them into education.

> ... at the moment my child is in primary school. I applied to two or three schools near where we lived. He was two and a half years old when I first applied for schools for him. I registered him both in the nursery and primary school sections, and I received responses from three schools, positive responses. And then I chose one of them. ... If anything, I had a very nice experience (Yasemin, p. 13).

Although the Turkish and Kurdish migrants in particular often needed help to access public services, usually because of their fears rather than because of checks on immigration status, it seems that they did get these essential services – albeit sometimes of a standard that did not impress them. It was this low standard of public provision, and the impact of irregular migrants' needs on already overloaded services, that was the next topic for our study.

STANDARDS IN PUBLIC SERVICES

At the time of our first and second research projects, rights to income support for those who applied for asylum after entering the UK had been removed by the Asylum and Immigration Act, 1996. However, after an appeal to the High Court, it was established that local authorities were obliged to provide shelter, under the National Assistance Act, 1948, for applicants who were homeless and without means. Many of the interviewees from Turkey had established claims to benefits dating from before the Act, or had applied for asylum on entering the country, and were therefore entitled to benefits. Others were not receiving benefits, either because their asylum claims had been refused, or because they had no immigration status. Finally, several who had arrived since 1996, and claimed asylum in the country, were not receiving either benefits or local authority accommodation and support, either because this had been refused, or because they had not sought it.

The High Court decision put local authorities in those boroughs with highest concentrations of asylum seekers in the front line, and several of those in our study area had set up specialised 'asylum teams' to deal with the heavy weight of applications for assistance. The restrictions on the amount and form of help they were mandated to provide meant that such teams were operating well below the standards seen as acceptable for UK citizens, or indeed those prevailing for asylum seekers in several other EU countries. We were able to interview four social workers and two managers from asylum teams in these boroughs about their work, and how they reconciled it with their professional values and standards.

These staff were operating an *ad hoc* system in response to a crisis situation. They were acutely aware of the shortcomings of the services they were providing, and found the work very stressful; yet they tried to account for their practices in terms of a professional code. In this sense, they had evolved a discursive strategy for occupational survival under conditions in which everyday realities caused dissonance with their expectations of their roles (Satyamurti, 1980). They recognised that they were acting under conditions of policy failure and reactive administrative response, and none claimed high or even adequate standards (Düvell and Jordan, 2001).

Three of the teams studied were in very provisional accommodation, in corners of larger offices, or in very cramped spaces. Their first task was to assess applicants eligibility for accommodation and food vouchers, and refer them on for any other needs. In this sense, their work was more like that of a prewar Poor Law relieving officer than any in the UK postwar welfare state. Three of them were working with families (and hence had responsibilities for assessing children's needs, including needs for protection); the other dealt with single adults only. One team was issuing food vouchers daily; another gave them on a fortnightly basis.

In assessing applicants' eligibility, the social workers used a mixture of income-related, housing-related and immigration status-related criteria, along with other criteria. But there was little consistency in how these were applied, either between teams or within them. The key concept was *destitution*, and various characteristics – being a family, not speaking English, being at risk from their own communities, or being of unkempt appearance – were all taken as indicators.

> ... if they can find assistance elsewhere ... if they are helped by friends or relatives, ... if they start working ... they would not meet the destitution criteria (manager, team 3).

Staff had not been specially prepared or trained for their work. Work with refugees was not part of their professional education or previous experience, and there was little in the way of policy interpretation from central or local government, so they 'gradually worked out what worked best for us'. Many of them were temporary staff, provided by agencies, or on short-term contracts. They developed defences against the unease experienced in the work, based on limiting their focus to the provision of immediate 'solutions' to the most desperate emergencies.

Part of this consisted in characterising applicants as being not as needy as they claimed to be. A social worker in team 4 said that asylum seekers 'had very high expectations' and 'tend to think that we could provide more than we can offer'; adding that there were 'a few families who are forever coming in, I want this, I want that, I need clothing, and we have got to go out of our way to provide it. ... When they don't have the service they expect to [get] they get very angry and frustrated'. Others said that 'initially we have had a lot of quite aggressive people, and a high level of complaints', or that they 'use emotional threats, saying "if you don't give me ... I will sleep in your office, do you want me to sleep outside in the street?".' They explained this in terms of the backgrounds of asylum seekers – 'many of them are actually graduates from their country, they have high aspirations, they want to improve themselves' – but explained that their service was for emergencies only; 'we are just responding to the crises as they occur' (social worker, team 2).

These staff acknowledged that they were assessors and rationers rather than helpers or counsellors, and that their work bore little relation to the exemplars in the professional textbooks.

> Given the staffing level, ... we can't spend a great deal of time sitting and talking to people. ... Although you may be dealing with one family who is very distraught and very difficult, ... you have got another family waiting equally distraught and equally in difficulty (team 1).

> ... you don't want to hear, ... you tend not to listen to the problems. All you want to see is the documents (team 2).

> I try to do a bit of counselling, but I can't actually spend too long going into that because there is a queue (team 4).

They also argued that, in making eligibility checks and rationing services, they had 'a duty to be responsible to those [who provide] money' (team 3).

> ... if you are giving the money to someone who is not entitled to a service it restricts the amount of money that goes elsewhere (team 4).

In addition to facing large numbers of applicants with pressing needs, these staff were also dealing with representatives from support groups and refugee organisations (see Chapter 6). These relationships were complicated, because – from the standpoint of the local authority workers – they saw these agencies as potential providers for the material and emotional needs of asylum seekers, especially when they were being funded by their own boroughs. The social workers hoped and expected that they – like other voluntary sector organisations – would provide services that complemented and supplemented the meagre allowance they supplied. For one manager, these groups

> ... have an interest in helping and supporting asylum seekers, ... we see them as the best people to help in situations. ... They are often very helpful, because their funding is dependent on the local authority (team 3).

By contrast, most of the representatives of these organisations that we interviewed saw their relationship with asylum teams as adversarial, 'fighting hard' to represent the interests of their members and clients – 'the best thing we can do is put pressure' (advice worker). They were very critical of the conditions endured by applicants who 'have to queue for hours and hours', 'they never have an interpreter there', and also of the consequences.

> [It is] absurd ... it destroys the family unit ... making the child more vulnerable (advice worker).

The social workers were put on the defensive by these responses. They accused these representatives and advocates of being biased and blinkered, lacking a wider vision of the issues at stake. They were

> ... actually misfocusing their advocacy towards us, in that it should be directed elsewhere [i.e., central government] ... they tend ... to have small caseloads, they are very specialised to specific groups, ... they only see themselves as the big picture ... they could be doing a lot more (team 3).

> I could not call them encounters, I call them conflicts ... extremely angry people on the phone pressurising you (team 2).

> Unhelpful most of the time, ... not aware of the criteria regarding their clients (team 4).

It was clear that these staff were not satisfied with the work they were doing, or the standards of service offered to asylum seekers, even though they needed to justify it to themselves in order to survive within this setting. Team 1's manager described it as 'a very basic minimal service ... at the lowest cost to the council'. Team 2's social worker remarked that 'you don't need social workers to do the job we are doing'. Team 3's said that although services for asylum seekers were 'a complete and utter mess', this team took some pride in making space 'to be involved with home visits and actually do some social work'. All sought some opportunity to practise according to professional standards.

> ... in the afternoons, when we do reviews, ... to talk about the other problems they have ... that is the moment I feel I am really doing social work. ... This is the first time I am seeing the client as a person, as a human being (social worker, team 1).

They themselves were directly affected by these tensions between rationing and deterrence on the one hand, and their aspirations to standards more consistent with professional values. Staff turnover was high.

... you just do it like factory work. ... We have a period of I would say 6 to 9 months, and then you would be burnt out (team 2).

From the perspective of the interviewees who were asylum seekers, these services were seen as of low quality, and to be avoided if possible.

I heard that they give you some £20–30 breakfast money. Then they have some sleeping rooms which are like a stable. I'd rather sleep with my friends than go to a place like that. That's why it's better for me to work illegally to earn my living (Mustafa, p. 6).

In many ways, these asylum teams were absorbing pressures that would otherwise have been made on other services of the local authorities, especially housing and social services departments. But they were also reflecting central dilemmas of the strategy adopted by the UK government in relation to immigration and the public services. It is simply impossible to combine accessibility, deterrence of ineligible applicants and extremely scarce resources with high-quality standards. These boroughs used asylum teams to do much of the 'dirty work' – checks on immigration status, rationing and turning away hard-pressed claimants – that the other services were resisting doing (see previous section, pp. 202–3). Staff working in the front line reflected these contradictions in their accounts of their practice.

Soon after this piece of research was completed, the government announced that it had decided not only to abolish income support benefit for all asylum seekers arriving in the UK, but also that they would be dispersed to other regions of the country, in order to avoid excessive pressures on the London boroughs.

Accommodation, in such circumstances, will be provided on a no choice basis, with no cash payment for this purpose being made to the asylum seeker. ... The nationwide approach will help to relieve the burden on provision in London, where the majority of asylum seekers are currently concentrated (Home Office, 1998, paras 8.21–2).

By the time of writing, this scheme of dispersal and food vouchers, through the National Asylum Support Service (NASS) of the Home Office, was already under review – an implicit acknowledgement that it had proved expensive and inefficient, as well as bringing suffering and hardship to asylum applicants. The new strategy had aimed to protect services for citizens, by putting the deterrent and rationing elements in the services for asylum seekers into an entirely separate system, using newly recruited staff, without the kinds of professional backgrounds of the social workers interviewed in our research. In an assessment of the new scheme, one researcher concluded:

In principle, the UK dispersal system should help reduce the pressures created by the concentrations of asylum-seekers in the South East. Under the right conditions, dispersal to cluster areas could also allow asylum-seekers to have better access to accommodation and services. However, problems with the new NASS arrangements mean that many asylum-seekers are not receiving adequate support in dispersal areas, and dispersal has not yet significantly reduced pressure on the South East. Some of these deficiencies may be transitional. ... However other problems – for instance pressure on emergency accommodation and dispersal to unsuitable accommodation – are linked to the structure of NASS and dispersal procedures. In particular, the centralised procedure for applications for NASS support creates substantial delays, NASS contracts with private suppliers have also proved to be problematic, leading to difficulties with the standard and location of accommodation. ... Finally, the low participation rate in the scheme has meant that over half of all asylum applicants opt to stay in London (Boswell, 2001, p. 39).

Our research indicates how they get by without benefits, and with the support of friends and organisations. However, this does not shift the whole burden from the public services in London.

ENFORCEMENT ETHOS AND INTER-AGENCY CONflICT

As we saw in the last chapter, one of the New Labour government's aims has been to tighten up the enforcement of rules in the public services, both for the sake of 'fairness', and in order to promote 'responsibility' (see p. 174). One strategy under which they have pursued this aim has been to bypass the mainstream services, which are suspected of harbouring Old Labour values and cultures, and entrust tasks to new agencies, with a more reliable enforcement ethos, such as the NASS (Jordan and Jordan, 2000). Another has been to reform and restructure existing organisations, such as the Benefit Agency, so as to give more priority to these aims.

Our research suggests that there are many limits to the potential success of these policy initiatives. The greatest of these is the sheer chaotic pressures on the public services (especially in London), the extent to which they have been run down and cultures of crisis management have prevailed. In this sense, things had already gone too far to be readily rescued by the setting of new targets, or the imposition of new management systems. In relation to immigration issues, moreover, the specific problems of the IND during this period were a major contributory factor, since public service staff, already ambivalent about co-operation in imposing restrictions, found that their attempts at communication were often balked by the administrative chaos at the IND end.

For example, staff in the asylum teams discussed in the last section were required to carry out checks of immigration status, and did so rather reluctantly – 'we are not an investigative branch', and 'we have to take things at face value' (team 2). But those whose teams' policies required them to verify immigration status with the Home Office experienced considerable frustration.

> ... our initial problem is checking to see whether they are actually asylum seekers, which tends to take some time; if we need to contact the Home Office their response is variable, it can be six weeks, sometimes you can actually get a verbal confirmation of their status, then you fax a request over and that response takes two to three weeks, up to six weeks, so ... (social worker, team 4).

Others made the general point that central government had been unable to resolve or rationalise the whole asylum issue, and had left it to the local authorities to pick up the pieces. Furthermore, among the many agencies and jurisdictions with some responsibility for the needs of asylum seekers, all had incentives to try to limit costs, to pass these on to others, and they often blamed each other for the plight of the most desperate applicants. While insisting that his borough had strong anti-racist policies, one racial equality officer of a local authority alleged that 'it is different to the Benefits Agency, they play it as a sport'.

It is quite difficult to do full justice to the content of the interviews with public service staff, simply because – when invited to speak about their work, and the issues affecting immigrants and asylum seekers – they described such complexity of rules, responsibilities and restrictions, and such detailed examples of inter-agency wrangling over these. Each service claimed to be coping with the failings and inequities of the other.

> ... the benefit system is getting worse; even if you can have benefits, there's a gap between what the landlord is charging you and the rent, what the housing benefit rent officer will say the house is worth. So there are often problems with people paying all of their rent ... and so come here for advice about that. The other problem is of the Benefits Agency, with such a mass and mushrooming of people being cut off wrongly, waiting maybe three months between applying for income support and getting a National Insurance number, and having their money in between. They are just needing representation to sort of point out that it's not really fair, and forcing them through the systems ... (refugee resettlement officer, p. 2).

Some staff saw the problems as stemming from a lack of strategic vision and organisational stability within the local authorities themselves.

> ... there are a number of issues which cut across a number of departments in the council, particularly across housing and social services, and there is a lack of coordination in the way which approaches have been taken. ... at the moment [borough] council's very much in a state of flux, within the housing department ...

nearly every member of the senior management is either applying for their jobs or has lost their jobs since complete major organisational change taking place there, and there is organisational change taking place within social services department ... [it] will be two separate organisations ... (social worker, p. 20).

Yet it was also clear that, on the other hand, irregular migrants did break the rules and circumvent the regulations, partly in order to cut through all this complexity, or resist what they saw as injustices within these systems. Public services staff recognised that, as well as being very inadequate for many of the needs of their most desperate users, they were also open to abuse by unscrupulous ones.

> We have cases where people are presenting children who aren't their own, aren't their children, who may well be the children of another family getting assistance in another local authority (manager, asylum team, p. 15).

In an interview in 2000, staff in the Benefits Agency responsible for issuing National Insurance numbers emphasised their attempts to be accessible and responsive to the needs of asylum seekers, but acknowledged that

> ... if someone is absolutely determined to get a National Insurance number through forged means they will do so (Benefits Agency, p. 10).

As we have seen in Chapter 5, several of the interviewees from Turkey readily acknowledged that they were breaking the benefits rules by doing undocumented work for cash while claiming. They justified this in terms of benefits being too low to cover living costs – much as many UK claimants of the same benefits do (Jordan *et al.*, 1992).

> It is prohibited and not right. You feel guilty. ... It is not legal and it might have consequences on the [Leave to Remain] or the income support. I heard of many people who were caught through their illegal work, and their benefit was taken away (Hasan, p. 4).

> When a family lives together, man, wife and child, they have to pay £150 per week for a flat, and a full-time job pays £200 at the most. ... On benefits you get around £115, £120, ... so that's why it's better to work illegally, because then you get £250, through the illegal wage. A lot of English people work illegally (Ahmet, p. 5).

In a system of such complexity, with so many conflicts of interest between the public services themselves, and all of them operating in an overstretched state, the idea that rules could be enforced fairly, without damaging consequences for those entitled or in need, was quite unrealistic. What happened was inevitably that rules were deployed in fairly arbitrary ways, to disqualify and exclude some individuals from benefits and services, and select others. Asylum seekers were among those most vulnerable to exclusions of various kinds. As with the indigenous population, some reacted by presenting their problems elsewhere, to another statutory or a voluntary agency, as a still more pressing and desperate problem. Halide, a Turkish woman aged 61, gave an example of such a situation when she was homeless.

> The council closes down at 3.30 p.m. – really they should close at 5.00 p.m., but they don't, they close at 3.30 p.m. They left everybody's [claims] unfinished, and they were asking me to leave and go out. But then she, the other lady, shouted at them and said, 'Either you house this lady here and now or I'll take you to the High Court'. When she did this, everybody started phoning around, and they found me a place at [name of hotel]. I went to stay there for two months. After two months they wanted me to leave. ... They wanted to throw me out, but, thank God, a solicitor I knew, a lady solicitor, rang again and said, 'You cannot put this lady into a hole like that. You have to put her somewhere comfortable, and somewhere she likes'. So I stayed on' (Halide, p. 8).

Alternatively, as we have seen, migrants seek their own solutions outside the rules, and justify their actions by pointing to the shortcomings and inequalities of the system. In imposing dispersal on the new applicants for asylum after 1999, the Labour government sought to cut through this whole mess, and create an entirely separate scheme for asylum seekers, to relieve the burdens on these services. In practice, not only did this create enormous problems over those who opted for dispersal; there still remained around half the applicants for asylum who preferred to stay outside the scheme, and take their chances without state support in London. In this they were often choosing to try to earn enough in the shadow labour market to support themselves, with the help of other members of their communities.

Overall, the greater emphasis on rationing and enforcement in all these services increased delays and frustrations. Critics argued that these were particularly felt by UK citizens from ethnic minorities, because some checks were applied to them in discriminatory ways.

> People from abroad needing to go through incredible hurdles in order to establish their entitlement to basic support, but long-term residents from ethnic minorities are again, you know, being seen as immigrants, and meeting the same kinds of intensive interrogation and suspicion and denial of benefits, there are serious delays in getting something which there is absolutely no doubt that they're entitled to (national NGO, 2000, p. 10).

CONCLUSIONS

Public services enter the economic analysis of the dynamics and the out-comes of migration in several ways. First, if migrants are entitled to certain benefits and services on entering the receiving country, this may give them an incentive that distorts the potential advantages of their arrival for the host economy. Second, even if they are not attracted by the inducement of such services, they may in fact end up by consuming more of them than they are able to contribute through taxation, because of their low earning power. Third, they may cause congestion and competition for certain facilities and services, because they concentrate in a particular area, and crowd out citi-zens. All these potential problems of immigration may apply particularly to irregular entry. Programmes that enable irregular migrants to claim on entry may encourage those with limited economic prospects to come; they may, in turn, become burdens upon the public purse; and they may also, through poverty, congregate in the districts where the public infrastructure is weakest and most overstretched.

Our research provides very mixed evidence about these issues. On the one hand, interviewees from Brazil and Poland were able to get access to the NHS, and the few who gained a settlement did also get housing benefit and (in one or two cases) income support (see pp. 143–6). Almost all of them lived in private rented accommodation, dispersed over a fairly wide area. Although rather few of them paid UK income tax when they lacked proper immigration status, it seems unlikely overall that they made claims on the public services which were burdensome for taxpayers. It was only after they regularised (for instance by marrying an EU or a UK citizen) that any claimed housing benefit or income support – but by then they were usually also paying income tax. In this sense, those who were 'pure' irregular economic migrants neither ensnared themselves in complex UK welfare systems, nor drew heavily upon the public purse. From a strictly economic point of view, their impact on the country's revenues and expenditures seems to have been broadly neutral, while their contribution in terms of productive work appears – on their own account at least – to have been rather positive.

As might be expected, a very different picture emerges from the analysis of the interviewees from Turkey. They were far more involved with social ben-efits, local authority housing and social welfare services of all kinds. At first sight their accounts, taken in conjunction with the interviews with public service staff, seem to provide examples of exactly the kinds of costs associ-ated with immigration, and particularly with asylum systems.

However, this impression is somewhat misleading. In the first place, al-though 18 of the interviewees had been asylum applicants at some time during their stays, only four had applied for asylum on entry – most had become asylum seekers after entering in another status, and often after quite prolonged stays. This indicated both that the benefits and services available for asylum seekers had not been what attracted them in the first place, and that asylum was often the only way of avoiding return to Turkey, and consequent loss of political freedoms.

Interviewees such as Osman and Baran made it plain that, although their reasons for coming to London were closely linked to political oppression in Turkey, they were originally living (in the late 1980s) as irregular migrants, and not as asylum seekers. Baran argued that many in their position applied only reluctantly and belatedly for asylum. He had come to London in 1988 as a student, having been a member of a political organisation in Turkey, and had lived in the UK as an illegal overstayer, working in a textile factory, before applying for asylum.

> Before 1989, 90 per cent of Turkish people lived here illegally. In those days, all that was required for entry … was a tourist visa or a student visa, and if one had that, one could stay and work as long as there was work. If you wanted to, you could return; no-one applied for asylum. No one, perhaps a very few … applied (Baran, p. 4).

He argued that an 'asylum movement' started among populations from Turkey, partly because of increased restrictions by the UK authorities (including raids on factories), and partly because of the deteriorating situation in Turkey. The migration narratives of other interviewees bore this out – that it was not the attractions of the benefits system that brought them to the UK. By the same token a further four interviewees from Turkey had stayed on without status – and hence without any entitlement to benefits or services – after their claims of asylum had failed. Taken together with the eight who had never claimed asylum, this indicates that benefits were at most a limited incentive.

What our research showed was that access to collective provision as asylum seekers did involve these migrants with the authorities in numerous ways, as well as requiring heavy inputs of time and resources from the benefits agencies and the public services. The interviewees' accounts argued that this whole process pauperised them, criminalised them and trapped them. Instead of contrasting it with their time as being without status, as a period of relative comfort and security, they insisted that it reinforced their economic exploitation, and their position on the margins of the UK society.

Seen from the perspective of the staff of public services, it is not difficult to understand why this was so. Asylum seekers formed a fringe group among an enormous marginal and needy population in London, who at any time might present themselves as in crisis – homeless, destitute, with serious health or social care problems, and so on. In this sense, migrants of all kinds were contributing to potential congestion, and a further deterioration of already overstretched services. This was not something intrinsic to irregular migration, or to asylum seeking. It was intrinsic to the UK systems (and especially those in London), under which such needs were met on the basis of giving attention to the most pressing emergencies, and with budgets that were not adequate to their tasks.

Furthermore, the boroughs where both irregular migrants and asylum seekers concentrated were among those in which public services were most hard-pressed, under-resourced and understaffed. Hence, they did contribute to the special pressures in these districts, which, in turn, caused further distortions, as the authorities adopted rationing systems and self-protective practices to cope with these.

Finally, a further irony was that, as conditions in these services deteriorated, and staff sought better opportunities and rewards in other occupations, or in the private sector, statutory agencies began to rely more and more on staff recruited from abroad. Public services professionals were the largest group of labour-market recruits from outside the EU, and they were mainly concentrated in London (Salt and Clarke, 2001). A typical scenario in these boroughs came to be a foreign recruit offering service to an asylum seeker or an irregular migrant. It is to the causes and consequences of this that we turn to in the next chapter.

9. Recruitment of labour from abroad

In this chapter we return to some of the earlier themes of the book – how labour mobility relates to capital mobility and trade, how globalisation is facilitated by managed migration regimes and how recruitment from abroad is used by national governments to address issues of mobility in their labour markets. Once again, we use the UK as a case study, and focus on how the agency most directly involved in the recruitment of overseas labour, Work Permits (UK) (formerly the Overseas Labour Service of the Department for Education and Employment) has adapted its practices to recent changes in policy. We also use interviews with recruits who have come to the UK (conducted in 2001), to illustrate how the perspectives of those who came to the UK under the work permit scheme compared with those of the irregular migrants' accounts analysed in the previous chapters.

The relevance of this comparative material is that it allows us to analyse the mobility of those who enter legally as foreign recruits to the UK labour market with the transnational movement of irregular migrants. As we show in this chapter, work permit holders are able to treat border crossing for the sake of work as economic mobility rather than migration (see Chapter 1), as long as they can find suitable channels between their country and the one to which they are being recruited. Business visa holders from Poland, by contrast, used this as a way of establishing a regular status after a period as irregular migrants in the UK.

In all, 11 work permit holders and three managers and human resources staff from India were interviewed, and four work permit holders and three business visa holders from Poland. These interviews were carried out in 2001–2, as part of the EC-funded research project; the work permit holders were contacted with the assistance of Work Permits (UK) and their employers. All but three of the Polish interviewees were conducted in their native language by the same interviewer who recruited the irregular migrants. These respondents enabled us to compare accounts given by labour-market recruits with spontaneous immigrants, and legal entrants from Poland with irregular workers.

Transnational mobility of labour under government-approved schemes now includes the following elements:

(a) *Intra-firm transfers of staff, and international partnership arrangements*
Because so many corporations now have branches in several countries, spending time abroad is part of the career expectation of managers, technicians and
highly skilled workers in a range of industries and services. The interviews
illustrate how this enables such people to develop life plans that include
transnational mobility, and to explore options for long-term migration.

Such employee strategies can be understood within the framework of the
strategic actions of firms, seeking to optimise their returns on capital investment in a range of developing and developed economies, by moving staff and
products between their branches in different countries. The existence of
forms of 'trade' within corporations, and of internal labour markets among
their branches, has been analysed in the economic literature (Salt, 1988).
Findlay (1990) argued that internal transfer policies within an international
company are as important for understanding flows of highly qualified staff as
states' migration policies. Companies offer inducements, including career
advantages, to staff willing to move abroad. In addition to this, both companies with international contracts and international recruitment agencies offer
channels for highly skilled workers to migrate, for particular projects or
posts. All these three kinds of recruitment were evident from our interviews.

(b) *Privatisation of public services*　In the First World countries, and especially in the USA and the UK, the most recent and fastest expansion of new
international companies involve services for health, education and social
care. Under the General Agreement on Trade in Services (GATS), the USA
was able to facilitate a global market in these services, which had previously
been provided by the public sector in most countries. US capital has flowed
into private sector development under the sponsorship in many cases of the
World Bank (Wade, 2001).

The strategies of both First World states and international corporations favour the development of a core of expertise in private services in their own
countries. From governments' point of view, this can supply the basis for a new
specialist export sector in the post-industrial 'knowledge-based economy', and
a replacement for declining industries and more traditional services. Hence,
governments in the USA and the UK back corporations to promote the privatisation of schools, hospitals, prisons and care facilities, in Europe and the
developing world (Hatcher, 2001; Monbiot, 2002). In relation to education:

> The government is incubating the emerging British edubusiness sector as a viable
> national and international money-earner capable of competing in the global mar-
> ket, before it is exposed to the full force of competition from the US edubusiness
> industry as a result of the free trade in services under a revised GATS (Hatcher,
> 2001, p. 52).

However, one of the problems of this growing sector is to attract suitable staff. Firms have to compete with the public sector services, and with private companies in higher-paying industries and services. In order to develop home-based private services, corporations have to recruit abroad. Some of our interviews were with Indian managers and staff, recruited by UK private sector nursing and social care homes.

(c) *Public service professionals* Partly as a result of competition for staff from private employers, but also because of problems of mobility for low-paid public sector staff in cities and neighbourhoods with high housing costs, there has been a mounting crisis of staffing in the health service, schools and social services departments in the UK, peaking in 2001. At the same time, recruitment in these occupations is the highest category for work permits granted to overseas citizens.

Of those granted work permits in 2000, almost 20 000 were 'health professionals' (1049), 'teaching professionals' (4368) or 'health associate professionals' (14477) (Salt and Clarke, 2001, p. 481). This was out of a total of almost 65 000 work permits and first permissions granted in that year – up from 24 000 in 1995 (ibid., p. 480). Altogether, by that year over a quarter of health professionals and 13 per cent of health associate professionals working in the UK were foreign-born (ibid., p. 479).

In addition to these three elements in the UK's global and domestic economic strategy (all of which are reflected in the accounts given by these interviewees), there is also the question of 'demographic balance'. In EU policy documents, this refers mainly to the falling birth rates in many EU states, and the ageing of their populations. In the UK, net migration has recently come to contribute equally to total population change with natural increase, each at about 100 000 per year, with the vast majority of non-British inward migrants in the age range 15–34 (Dobson, McLaughlan and Salt, 2001, p. 67). But another feature of inward migration has been the recruitment of foreign professional and managerial workers to replace outflows of UK citizens in these occupations (a net loss of 65 000 in the years 1994–9) (Salt and Clarke, 2001, p. 476). Finally, two-thirds of all foreign workers were in the south-east of England, with nearly half in London (ibid., p. 473), reflecting problems of mobility in UK labour markets, and the consequences of residential polarisation on housing costs (see pp. 30–33).

All this helps explain the more positive stance on economic migration taken by the UK government since 2000, including signs of a willingness to reconsider its approach to irregular migration. The impetus for change was, if anything, accelerated by the events of 11 September 2001. Speaking in the context of increased security measures, curbs on human rights protection and the possible introduction of identity cards, the new Home Secretary, David

Blunkett, put forward a series of new measures to enable economic migration by selected groups, and to 'improve the lives' of the 'hundreds of thousands of people working clandestinely in the UK in appalling conditions' (*The Guardian*, 3 October 2001). The White Paper published in February 2002 set out the details of new schemes to 'ease recruitment difficulties and skills shortages and also help to deal with illegal working' (Home Office, 2002, sect. 3.5). These included a 'Highly Skilled Migrant Programme', using a points system for skills, qualification and experience to select for entry without an employment offer (ibid., sects. 3.15–20); allowing students to switch to employment on graduation, or on qualification as nurses or doctors (ibid., sects. 3.22–4); admitting short-term casual workers for sectors other than seasonal agricultural labour (ibid., sect. 3.25); and expanding the Working Holidaymakers' Scheme to include all Commonwealth countries, to provide 'an additional, temporary, flexible workforce' (ibid., sects. 3.26–9). It also proposed 'extending the principles behind the [Working Holidaymakers'] scheme and its operation to a wider range of countries, including to the EU candidate countries' (sect. 3.28).

These proposals broke new ground in two ways. First, the new approach implicitly recognised irregular migrants, doing undocumented work in the UK, as a potentially valuable source of labour supply. They had, after all, proved their adaptability and will to work by undertaking the enterprise of migration. In particular, the proposed scheme for allowing temporary work by people from the former communist countries was significant. Second, by mentioning overseas recruitment, economic migration and the exploitation of undocumented immigrant workers in the same set of policy proposals (rather than emphasising the separation of legal migration channels from irregular 'illegal immigration', which was to be combated), he broadened the whole scope for policy debate. David Blunkett's speech (to the Labour Party Conference) was certainly the first time that a UK Home Secretary had spoken of 'improving the lives' of people who had flouted the immigration rules; and the first time for a long time that a UK minister had talked openly about ways of channelling informal and irregular employment into formal employment (rather than simply clamping down on 'fraud'). As he was the former Secretary of State for Education and Employment, this was significant, and the White Paper developed these themes further.

The UK therefore provides an instructive case study, both of the rapid pace of change in policies over the recruitment of non-EU workers, and of the relationship between this and undocumented work by immigrants. Work Permits (UK) is by no means typical of the EU – it is a very British institution. But even this prototypically New Labour agency is now in the throes of reform and restructuring, because it is about to be absorbed into the Home Office. The reasons why this may not prove straightforward for either side of this new partnership are clarified in this chapter, which explores the grey areas between immigration control and the facilitation of foreign recruitment from the per-spectives of both public service staff and the migrants themselves.

IMMIGRATION CONTROL AND THE WORK PERMIT SCHEME

Foreigners who enter the UK do so in a specific immigration status; some of these categories, such as foreign government staff or ministers of religion, are allowed to work without specific permission. The schemes under review in the new White Paper have hitherto accepted fairly modest numbers. The Seasonal Agricultural Workers Scheme, which takes a quota (9760 in 1999) from Central and Eastern Europe; the Working Holidaymakers' Scheme (mainly for Old Commonwealth countries, comprising 45 800 entrants in 1999); Overseas Domestic Workers (14 900) and *au pairs* (14 600) (Dobson, McLaughlan and Salt, 2001, p. 69). In addition, students are allowed to work, in ways that are consistent with their courses of study. Asylum seekers are granted permission to work by the Home Office, nominally after six months in the country, but in fact usually after a longer time, due to administrative delay.

Although the work permit scheme is supposed to be the main one under which overseas labour is recruited for the UK economy, the numbers holding work permits were until recently extremely small, and much fewer than in the early 1970s (Böhning, 1973). By 2000 there was growing evidence that the government wanted to speed up the process of granting work permits, ease restrictions and expand the number of foreign recruits. In September 2000 key workers were merged with other categories, and (as a pilot scheme) 'multi-national employers ... can now issue their own work permits for employees transferring from the company abroad' (Hodge, 2000). These represented about a quarter of all permits granted. At the same time, the period covered by a permit was extended from four to five years, a relevant extension because most legal immigrants who do not have recourse to public funds after four years are entitled to get indefinite leave to remain. That would allow them to change employer or profession, and switch the purpose of their stay, for example, to study or set up a business, as well as to claim benefits or student grants. Another pilot scheme added the category of 'inno-vators', aimed at attracting 'outstanding entrepreneurs' in 'science and technology, including ... e-commerce', and based on business plans rather than personal funds (IND, 2000).

The fact that this was a period of transition was also signalled in the interviews we conducted with Home Office IND and Work Permits (UK) staff in 2000–1. Quite different views were expressed about the purpose of the work permit scheme by the senior representatives of the two agencies. The former, echoing similar concerns by one Immigration Inspector of ISED, saw the scheme as protecting the UK worker from competition from abroad, and substitution or undercutting by foreign staff.

> ... the work permit system exists primarily to safeguard the interests of the UK workforce, so it's, they're subject to labour-market tests ...' (Home Office IND Policy Unit, p. 6).

However, a manager of Work Permits (UK) defined the purpose of his organisation quite differently.

> ... the basic aim of WP (UK) is to process work-permit applications, er, in the fastest possible time, to ensure that business and commerce, ehm, can operate fluently and smoothly (WP (UK) manager, p. 30).

This definition of their task was largely endorsed by the business confederations interviewed.

> We have a very good working relation with WP(UK), they feel easy to come and consult with us, ... they came along and listened to our members' concerns and some ... ideas and concerns have turned up in their final recommendations (Confederation of British Industries, p. 8).

This emphasis on being 'business-friendly' was more tentatively acknowledged by the Home Office Policy Unit spokesperson, who said that his own department recognised that

> ... perhaps we should look at the work-permit system to make sure it's not acting as a barrier to UK plc (Home Office IND Policy Unit, p. 4).

The managers of Work Permits (UK) explained that they had consulted widely about how to improve their service, and increase flexibility.

> There was some pressure there for us to re-look at and re-evaluate the existing criteria. ... My colleagues ... consulted a very wide range of people, including trade unions, ... all our major customers, ... immigration lawyers, ... other government departments. ... Putting categories on our skill shortage list, ... the process there is basically one of dialogue (Work Permits (UK) Manager, p. 14).

The 'pressure' mentioned came partly from the press, and especially *The Daily Telegraph*, which ran a number of articles in the summer of 2000, all aimed at highlighting the problems of expanding businesses – 'shortage of IT skills knocks companies' (19 June 2000); 'more than half of British businesses suffer from a shortage of skilled employees' (14 July 2000). An employer was quoted as saying: '... there are not enough people in this country coming into the road haulage industry, and we have struggled to find drivers. I just thought Gurkhas would be right for the job. They have all got British driving licences, we know their working history, they have all been security cleared, and British taxpayers have paid for their training. ... Veterans of transport units in the Nepalese-based infantry brigade have had applications for two-year work permits turned down by the Department for Education and Employment because officials say that the posts should only go to European Union residents' (*The Daily Telegraph*, 3 September 2000).

The managers and staff of Work Permits (UK) presented their agency's work to the researcher with some pride, as a model of a public service, under New Labour's criteria for a reformed and modernised system of immigration control. The government had set out this model in its White Paper.

> The control must operate in a way which provides them [passengers and applicants] with a fast and efficient service and so helps promote travel and business which contributes substantially to our economy (Home Office, 1998, sect. 2.2).

This was echoed by staff, who spoke of an environment 'driven by the ongoing and ceaseless globalisation ... the world has changed, the world has moved ... nation states are competing against each other' (Work Permits (UK) manager). Their aim was therefore to ensure 'that business and commerce can operate fluently and smoothly' (ibid.). One of the obstacles to this had proved to be the Home Office IND.

> ... the Home Office had attracted unfortunately quite a lot of criticism from the commercial sector, and the immigration lawyers' practice association wrote to the *Financial Times* because we were getting big delays when people were waiting to change their immigration status, and what we have done is, ehm, we have taken over questions and answers on the new passport endorsement arrangements (Work Permits (UK) manager, p. 5).

The difficulties were arising because those who entered as a student and wished to change to work permit holder, or who wanted to extend their work permit, had to undergo checks by the Home Office.

> The Home Office, ehm, had certain problems themselves in the time they took to do this ... what we've done is ... we stepped in and had a system whereby ... we stamp them on behalf of the Home Office. It may sound a bit subtle, but ... (Work Permits (UK) manager, p. 6).

The IND policy unit spokesman saw it quite differently.

... it's an operational process, it's just an administrative process, and it just saves documents travelling from Sheffield to, so the documents stay in Sheffield, but there's an agreed administrative process that the decision, the decision is taken on behalf of the Secretary of State for the Home Department. So that the decision is still taken here, but the actual stamping of the passports and implementing the decision for administrative convenience takes place in Sheffield, so there's a much more efficient, joined-up, one-stop shop operation, but it hasn't changed ministerial responsibility, department responsibility. No. (Home Office IND Policy Unit, p. 14).

GETTING A WORK PERMIT

Work permits are issued to employers in respect of foreign workers they are seeking to recruit; they then allow the latter to enter the country for immigration purposes. Work Permits (UK) deals exclusively with employers, and has no contact with potential employees; if a foreign worker or an immigrant contacts them, they are referred to the Home Office or elsewhere. In this section we analyse managers' and staff's accounts of how they make decisions during this period of transition, and how policy is shifting through the process of implementation itself.

However, our current research project also gave us the chance to interview some people (from India) who had been recruited through the work permit scheme, and their employers. This was a valuable complement to the interviews with staff of Work Permits (UK) that we did in 2000. It also made a very interesting comparison, both with the interviews with undocumented workers done in 1998 and 2000, and with the interviews with applicants for business visas (from Poland) done in those years. As we show in a later section, business visa applicants' accounts are almost indistinguishable from undocumented workers' narratives; but work permit holders accounts have very little in common with either of these two.

The managers and staff of Work Permits (UK) emphasised the *speed* with which *large numbers* of applications were processed, and the *flexibility* of their decision-making. With only 190 staff they had doubled the number of work permits granted between 1996 and 1999, and the scheme was still growing, in response to changes in government policy and the representation of employers and solicitors. They had defended their discretionary powers against the scepticism of a new minister, who wanted clearer criteria, on the grounds that these allowed them to act more speedily and efficiently.

Our current minister ... had the feeling that she was unhappy, or she was uncomfortable with the perception that she had because we had large grey areas ... where it was left to the discretion of officials to make decisions one way or the other. ... So you had a scenario where either the application met the criteria or didn't, ... and there was no area of interpretability that was left to officials, because the minister was unhappy with officials having that sort of power (Work Permits (UK) manager).

However, they had been able to convince her; 'even she has got to understand a lot better, quite quickly ... to actually come up to speed with how the work permit scheme operates'. As the agency's training document states, 'staff need to ... use discretion and flexibility as appropriate to meet employers' needs' (Work Permits (UK) 2000, p. 29).

... cases which maybe don't quite meet the criteria, however on an exceptional basis are allowed through ... we have always been a fairly flexible organisation ... even allowing some form of flexibility ... in cases where employers ask us to waive advertising ... or the overseas national is a few months short of senior-level expertise, we can be flexible on this (Work Permits (UK) manager).

Front-line staff explained how this worked out in practice. In general terms, known, familiar employers could expect to have applications processed *inside a week*. Most of the work done by practitioners was of this nature – approving applications, coming mainly from large firms or public services, who recruited regularly from abroad. This view was more or less borne out by the employers interviewed in 2001. A manager of a nursing home said that she had heard the process was slow in the past:

But now, they are perfect, it's all by Internet and e-mail, you get all the information and the form from the Internet, you type your details in. It's so quick, I get a permit within three weeks (manager, nursing home, p. 2).

A human resources manager, from a large information technology firm in India, working in partnership with a UK corporation, said that the process used to take six weeks, but that now she received an acknowledgement of her application for a permit the following day, and a permit after 10 days – 'very efficient'. This contrasted with dealings with the Home Office – 'they are so slow'. She also mentioned that the DfEE had required her to advertise posts in the UK, because she was recruiting so many staff (in internal transfers) from India. But recently Work Permits (UK) had lifted the requirement to advertise, and they could bring all the staff they needed.

New or occasional applicants could expect the process to take longer, as they were required to submit company accounts. However, even this requirement might be waived, for instance for a newly established firm.

In the guidance notes it does say, we do need to see accounts, but if they phone us and say we can't provide accounts ... what we will say then is that you can send us evidence ... usually in the form of invoices ... we will actually restrict the approval ... to 18 months (Work Permits (UK) caseworker, p. 7).

Similarly, in non-shortage occupations, the requirement to advertise in the UK and EU was not always enforced – 'if they can put in a good case as to why they haven't advertised ... we will ... consider waiving the criteria' (caseworker, pp. 5–6). In general terms, front-line workers were encouraged to use their initiative in these decisions.

It could be two or three times a day you may need to ask for advice on a case ... it probably sounds very vague but it just depends on the type of case, ... and obviously, the more experienced you become in casework, the better your judgement is going to be in that you are still more confident to make that decision and maybe not necessarily always go to the supervisor (Work Permits (UK) caseworker, p. 8).

The manager confirmed that in his 'own personal opinion, the balance ... is certainly ensuring that big companies get the people that they want, and that they get their work permits'. The spokesman for the Confederation of British Industries said:

... we want to promote a flexible and mobile workforce, we want employers within the UK to have the right and the ability to within reason employ the best people from wherever they are in the world (CBI, 2000).

That this was increasingly possible was confirmed by a solicitor who represents such companies.

Where a solicitor comes in is ... on the fringes. So the rules don't tell you everything, and therefore an experienced practitioner has to find out what's on the edge. ... You can get work permits for anything provided the person meets the requirements of the scheme (Solicitor, 2000).

Overall, the managers of Work Permits (UK) saw the direction of policy change as towards allowing more recruitment.

... if I was being totally honest with you I'd say that if anything we err on the side of ensuring that companies get their people ... we have actually dropped the hurdles a little bit, and that's inevitably going to let more people in (manager, pp.16, 29).

WORK PERMIT HOLDERS

Our interviews with Indian recruits to the UK labour market provided a comparison with the ones with irregular migrants. The first group of these interviewees were experts in information technology, and had either been transferred by their employers to branches or projects in the UK, or employed by UK companies. A human resources manager from one of these companies explained his activities as follows:

> We have a corporate head office in Bangalore, India, and we are part of a bigger company called [name], and ... we have established our offices in the UK about seven years back, and ever since we have been catering for the IT industry in the UK and in Europe. ... So we have branches in the USA, Japan, the UK. ... I would say about 60 people are here in the UK ... some of them are, er, on, er, what is called permanent residents, ... unlimited leave to remain' (human resources manager, pp. 1–2).

The work permit holders that we interviewed were in their 20s and 30s, graduates of Indian universities, and saw the experience of working in the UK as part of a career trajectory of their occupation, which included stays in a number of other countries.

> I'm an MSc, it's Master of Science in physics, and then I have done a Microsoft certificate. ... I applied through the Internet actually. ... As long as my employer is happy. I think two and a half years is this project. ... Actually, they give me £29,000 right now ... in the UK I don't know whether that is right or not. But I'm happy (Sanjay, pp. 1–3).

> I was supposed to go to the US in 2000. ... So there are many possibilities of going to any other countries where my company has offices. ... Interesting to visit another country and to study the working environment there, how people, culture, working culture, working environment, so usually that curiosity was there ... (Ravi, p. 2).

> Once you're 40, 45 you can't go, fly around like this ... it becomes difficult. You are more flexible when you are less than 30, 35. You can adapt to situations, you're more imaginative. These are some of the reasons. ... And then obviously I can also save some money, ... it's not just money that I'm here, it's this is the best years of my life ...' (Vijay, pp. 4–5).

Such workers – and the others who were recruited by academic institutions as scientists – lived in middle-class districts, rather than ones where minority ethnic groups were concentrated.

> It's an English, a small English residential area. I live within that. And I think that's a better idea to live than to live [there] in a community, where you tend to

become more, er, you tend to – what do you say? – become more inward (Vijay, p. 16).

When we first moved there in January 2001, ... there were very few Indians, Asians, people of Asian origin, and they've increased. ... Even the church I worshipped in there was just, you know, one or two people of Asian origin (Patrick [a Catholic], p. 11).

... last May, my wife and I purchased a three-bedroomed house. It is in [suburban residential district] (Anil, p. 8).

They also participated in English activities, and were members of English clubs and organisations.

I played in the company's cricket team, and ... Yeah, I'm a cricketer. I'm a little bit popular in terms of that, so a lot of people know me now. And I have a lot of other friends as well within the office (Vijay, p. 14).

Some people at work, people I play badminton with, ... I've taken part in a couple of programmes, Christian programmes, and people have been very welcoming there (Patrick, p. 12).

None of these recruits had encountered any difficulties or delays over their work permits, though the process of getting the necessary immigration documents from the UK consulates in India had been rather slow for some of them. Their main preoccupation was their families – both those left in India, and those who accompanied them.

I will go back, because the only problem I have is missing my parents. ... I will go to India in the months of January, February, because I have already got some 20 days' leave (Ravi, p. 9).

... everything revolves round whole families, it's not just one individual, and anything we do is like, gets spread across a whole chain of families. So if it's me and my wife it's my complete family and her complete family formed into one chain. ... That's the way we are tradition, tradition-wise we have grown up like that (Vijay, p. 15).

Some interviewees had had visits or longer stays from their parents, and some were considering bringing them to live in the UK.

... since they have grown old, they want more medical attention, and they are extremely happy with the NHS here, ... and now they are asking me if there is any possibility to come over here and stay with me (Anil, p. 11).

Children's education was seen as an important advantage of coming to the UK.

That's good for my son as well, he will get a good education, and … (Vijay, p. 5).

But when I got the job and the work permit, and I wanted to bring my son, they told me that I cannot bring my son – my husband, yes, but not my son. … In the end my son got a student visa, but now his course is finished, and he should go … (human resources manager, p. 4).

The other group of interviewees were managers and work permit holders in nursing homes and care homes. These were private companies, part of the commercial sector of the health and social services that has been expanding rapidly in the UK (see pp. 218–9). An Indian manager, who ran one company, said that 'finding staff is a nightmare'. She complained that UK staff came and left after a week, didn't turn up at the weekend and preferred to work in big shops, because it was easy work. She had to recruit qualified nurses, and Indian nurses were all graduates, but unused to having to do low-skilled practical tasks, such as the ones that were part of their duties in her homes.

In England, the first thing is that we need to teach them all the tasks nurses don't have to do in India. That's why we put them on six months trial and training. I also tell them to watch telly to improve their English (manager, p. 1).

One of the nurses in this group of homes explained the differences in her previous experience in India.

I worked for five years. I worked in two different hospitals, big hospitals, with 1,500 and with 2,500 patients, everything is big in India. … [I came] only for money, I came for the money. The wages are very low in India, you can't live on that. Here I earn good money. … Basically the same conditions. But here we have less patients … 40 patients and 15 nurses. But in India we have far more patients, many beds, we always rush from one bed to another. But there we do more doctor's type of work, we never wash patients, here we also do this (Usha, p. 1).

A male psychiatric nurse in another group saw his profession as a kind of passport for migration:

Well, in India nurses are not paid much, and in our place most of the population, … they all work in foreign lands, … my aunt is in America, one of my aunts is in South Africa, my brothers are in Saudi Arabia, they're outside the country. … I took up nursing because my aunt was a nurse, she works in America, so I wanted to go to America, so that's why I did nursing (Ajit, p. 4).

Although their salaries were more modest, it was clear that they, like the information technology specialists, saw their options for career development in global terms.

> I also applied for a visa to the US, and I have even been shortlisted, but they gave me a one year waiting time, and in the meanwhile I got this job and the work permit; and also my friends are here, so I came her (Usha, p. 4).

Her accommodation was provided by her employer, which she paid for out of her wages.

> I live here in the nursing home, next door, in a separate house, there are 13 girls, all from India except one, who is Japanese. We pay for that £50 per week. We have a kitchen there, a dining room and living room, with a TV ... We go to the beaches. At some time, when I have a day or two holiday, I'll go to London (Usha, p. 6).

Acceptance of this style of living both allowed the recruits a wider choice of career development pathways, and the possibility of access to other opportunities. A manager of another group of 12 homes for people with mental illnesses said:

> One of our Indian nurses recently 'disappeared' to Birmingham, but the contract is very strict, you cannot just take up another job, they can't change the employer, it is illegal (manager, p. 1).

BUSINESS VISAS

It was instructive to compare these accounts of recruitment through the work permit scheme with the narratives of Polish migrants who had applied for business visas. Unlike the recruits from India, those interviewees were already in the UK, and working in the shadow economy of undocumented work; they openly acknowledged to the interviewer that their motive for trying to get a business visa was purely strategic (see pp. 145–6). The goal was to establish a more advantageous immigration status that would allow them to pursue their informal economic activities in relatively greater security.

One of these respondents, Pawel, explained how he came to be an undocumented worker, and his motives for coming to the UK:

> To earn money, some money. First of all to bring some change to my life. ... Because I don't belong in Poland any more. My visa to the United States expired. I had been in the States; I wanted to stay there legally but my time passed and that's it. That's why I came here. ... Three times; six months each time ... I don't see any future for me in Poland. I also had a building firm in Poland. But contracting parties wouldn't pay; lots of cheating, lots of lies, and that ... there are no chances for normal co-operation there. I have been all over the world really (Pawel, p. 1).

Pawel had completed his studies (training to be a pilot), but 'there was too little money in it', and he had an opportunity to visit a friend in the USA, and to work in the building trade. He was already running a textile business in Poland, selling garments in Russia, but economic conditions changed, and he started his building firm, employing 30 people. He went bankrupt in 2000, because of not being paid by customers, and not paying taxes. Coming to London with an invitation from a friend, he did the kind of work other Polish undocumented workers take, as a waiter and on a building site. On this occasion, he had come by plane, without an address, and simply bluffed his way in as a tourist. He gave an address supplied by an air hostess, and said it was his uncle's. There were no checks.

> No, none, absolutely nothing; probably because of so many stamps in my pass-port. But I was lucky, I found a job the same day. It was a job on a building site. I came here on Friday and he asked me to come and start on Monday, so I went on Monday, and I still work there, and I have had enough (Pawel, pp. 4–5).

It was his employer who suggested he should try to legalise by getting a business visa, which he incorrectly thought led to a work permit (in fact, a permission to work from the Home Office).

> My boss suggested I should do it to be here legally, to be able to go back to Poland any time I like, to have some rights. I will pay taxes; I'll have some rights. I got the impression that he wanted me to apply for a business visa for his own good because he realises that he employs people illegally and he may face conse-quences. Whereas if I pay for getting a business visa myself, he will be safe as well. ... So the whole thing costs you around £800; which is not little when you consider how much you earn (Pawel, pp. 7–8).

Two other interviewees in 2001 gave the same kind of account of doing undocumented work for some time before applying successfully for business visas. This involved showing a sum of money in a bank account, and getting a National Insurance number; one woman had visited the DSS office five times to achieve this. It also required a valid tourist visa. Another building worker, Jarek, had been in the UK for five years without proper status.

> But I couldn't tell them I had stayed here without a visa for so long. I went to France for a day and came back to England with a brand new visa. That's what you have to do to legalise your stay here; everybody does it (Jarek, p. 3).

Both Pawel and Jarek commented on the embellishment of the business plans submitted on their behalf to the Home Office (see pp. 145–6).

> It's all fiction. I have never seen my business plan myself. I don't even know what's written there. They [accountants] just ask you how much money you

spend, how much you earn, how much you need more or less, on the basis of that they create your business plan. It's all just fiction. ... When I'm here I'm embarrassed to show my degree, I don't tell them, on the building site that I'm a pilot engineer (Pawel, p. 10).

... an accountant does it for you. He listens to what you want to include and then adds his own ideas, so in the end it's more his business plan than yours (Jarek, p. 7).

CONCLUSIONS

The UK work permit scheme allows highly skilled graduates and others to be recruited for the benefit of international businesses and UK public service organisations. There were some similarities in the accounts of young Indian recruits and those of undocumented workers in London. They saw the trip as a way of escaping from some of the constraints of life in their own country, of gaining new work and personal experiences, and exploring the possibility of longer-term migration. The business visa scheme seems to allow some Poles who are irregular migrants to regularise, and perhaps eventually to make the transition to the formal labour market.

The human resources strategies of international corporations, the development of private services in health, education and social care and the recent shortages of professionals in public services in the UK, all provided opportunities for these individuals to gain access to positions of advantage – jobs, pay, working conditions, experience and living arrangements. Interviewees from India all gained financially from their chance to move to the UK; they also commented on the better organised work environments, more rational planning of work processes and good co-operation with colleagues. They were able to live within easier travelling distance of their workplaces than in India, in most cases to work shorter hours, and hence to spend more time with partners and children. They could live in pleasant residential districts, and several became members of middle-class English clubs and organisations.

This illustrates how globalisation, and the actions of mobile capital in pursuit of profit, can benefit those individuals (including citizens of developing countries) with certain skills and abilities. The policies of the UK government, developed through its cutting-edge agency in this field, Work Permits (UK), facilitated these opportunities, both for firms transferring staff or recruiting from abroad, and for the staff and recruits themselves. Such policies and practices demonstrated that recruitment is non-discriminatory in terms of 'race', and allows the advancement of a professional élite from a developing country. Interviewees from India with good educational qualifications spoke of the barriers to the development of their careers in their own country, much as some of the interviewees from Brazil, Poland and Turkey did. The work permit scheme allowed them to find legal ways of making their skills available where they were needed, and the opportunities for mobility in UK society enabled them to choose pleasant communities in which to live, and to avail themselves of convivial and congenial recreational and cultural facilities.

These were all ways in which their regular status gave them important advantages over those working in the shadow economy. David Blunkett's speech to the Labour Party conference in 2001 acknowledged this discrepancy between the access to advantages for labour-market recruits from abroad, and the living and working conditions of undocumented workers in the shadow economy. This was at least a first step towards measures for re-examining immigration control systems, with a view to providing other legal channels into the labour market for people from abroad.

From an administrative standpoint, a major obstacle to these policies is the IND's notorious inefficiency in processing applications, as has been evident from the asylum debacle. When Work Permits (UK) did a survey of their 'customers' – businesses recruiting overseas workers – the replies were vitriolic about their colleagues in the Home Office. Respondents described it as 'quite desperate', 'a nightmare', 'incredibly frustrating' and 'a national disgrace' (Work Permits (UK), 1999, Appendix C). The incorporation of WP (UK) into the Home Office may as easily damage the former's reputation as improve the latter's.

One obvious difficulty in implementing the Home Secretary's new measures is that it involves the IND. Perhaps because of the awareness among migrants of the enforcement difficulties, and also because of the belated recognition that it is the unregulated labour market, and not social provision, that attracts irregular migrants to the UK, the government has announced a crackdown on both employers and undocumented foreign workers in the shadow economy. Under the headline 'Immigration hit squads to target 500,000 illegal workers', a lead story in *The Independent* on 21 January 2002, threatened a great increase in removal of such workers, and high-profile prosecutions of firms employing them. This is not necessarily inconsistent with the Home Secretary's earlier announcement, but it is certainly well beyond the IND's capabilities, and sounds like a noisy attempt to deter would-be migrants rather than a realistic policy thrust. Much the same could be said about the section of the White Paper about 'Illegal Working' which announced new measures to improve enforcement and tackle workplace offences, but acknowledged that it was a 'complex issue' (Home Office, 2002, sects. 5.5–21).

Instead of following this line, it would (at least in the longer term) make more sense to look for other ways of opening channels for legal migration. Why should not some entrants, who are able to produce evidence that they can support themselves, not be allowed to come as job seekers, perhaps for a limited period, of say six months? Why should there not be a more general amnesty for irregular migrants already here and supporting themselves? More generally, which immigration controls (if any) are compatible with global distributive justice? It is this last question that is the starting point of the final chapter.

10. In search of global justice

Irregular migration occurs because states make rules about who can legally cross their borders. Under conditions of globalisation, these rules promote transnational economic activity, but limit who can work and stay. In this final chapter, we turn to the justification of these restrictions, and ask which migration controls are consistent with principles of justice.

Political philosophy has not been much concerned with issues of migration; theories of distributive justice have been mainly about relationships among members of political societies, or sometimes between societies. Exceptions to this rule are Barry and Goodin (1992) and Cole (2000). Our research study of irregular migrants in the UK raised a number of questions about the justice of migration rules. Polish interviewees argued that the only fair principle was open borders, or at least an extension of the EU rules of free movement to include themselves. Migrants from Turkey said that the controls on their migration were part of a transnational system of economic and political oppression that could be countered only by transnational trade unions and political movements. Both views implied that issues of justice were at stake, and that irregular migration challenged unjust rules.

In the first chapter of this book, we identified a paradox of the kind of economic analysis we were undertaking. From the perspective of welfare economics, questions about distributions concerned the members of a polity. Thus, for instance, using either the Pareto or Kaldor–Hicks criteria of distributive optimality, decisions about whether to allow inward migration to a country should be made on the basis of their impact on the well-being of its citizens, and should not take account of their effects on the immigrants (Hadfield, 1995, p. 204). Conversely, from the perspective of global economic efficiency, and the allocation of resources to their most productive uses, considerations of the relative benefits to members of different states of a particular allocation were irrelevant (see pp. 25–6).

There is a parallel to this in theory about distributive justice. One approach seeks principles of justice that are concerned with the distribution of goods between members of a political community, and assumes that political authority derives from the capacity to create and sustain such goods, and distribute them justly within such a community. Another starts from the assumption that the task of political justice is to derive both rules for distribution and institutions of governance for populations (with natural endowments) and territories (with natural resources), prior to any political boundaries or borders. Hence, one standpoint starts with membership already established, and the other seeks general rules by creating membership systems. Neither can readily prescribe rules for individuals moving between political communities (Coleman and Harding, 1995, pp. 135–7).

Yet this is strange, because real-world polities are very much concerned with exactly such questions, both in terms of their internal governance, and in relation to other states. Within political borders, the right to decide in which community to live is a very important element in liberal democracy, and one that distinguishes such states from all kinds of totalitarianism. It is from the perspective of this right that unjust practices such as ethnic cleansing, forced migration and the Iron Curtain have all been condemned as violations of natural justice.

This freedom of choice over where to live is quite complex, as we show. Liberal democratic theory is strong on rights to leave communities, and rights not to be evicted once settled, but ambiguous over rights to enter and stay. Asylum law illustrates this, giving no entitlement to refuge in any particular country. Hence, issues over free movement must address conditions for entry as well as those for exit.

The freedom of individuals to choose where to live within a state does not remove the duty of the political authority to protect its members, and especially the most vulnerable members of its population, and to seek just distribution of the goods of membership between them. Even those public choice theorists who advocate a priority for 'voting with the feet' in decisions about the allocation of collective goods (see pp. 26–9) acknowledge that there is an overarching duty for the superior jurisdiction to make decisions about the welfare of citizens. Indeed, the whole debate about 'fiscal federalism' concerns the relative duties of the central and the local authorities in the provision of a collective infrastructure, not whether such authorities should concern themselves with justice over the welfare of their members (Oates, 1999).

In Chapter 2, we saw how the creation of the European Union (EU), with the Treaty of Maastricht in 1991, involved the establishment of new rights for freedom of movement between member states, by identifying a new species of member of a new kind of political community, the citizen of the EU. As part of the institutional structure of a single market, rights to free movement across national borders became 'constitutionalised', in 'a body of case law and associated institutional competencies' (Geddes, 2000, p. 3). But before these rights had been put in place, the member states and the Commission were careful to establish mechanisms for redistribution, for the sake of 'social cohesion'. The result is claimed to be an 'area of freedom, security and justice', as much as a space for the unimpeded mobility of members.

All this suggests that issues of justice are at stake when individuals wish to choose which community to live and work in, and when political authorities decide on which foreigners to allow to cross their borders, and on what terms. In this chapter we first consider the general arguments for and against controls on the movement of people across borders. Then we examine the problem of balancing 'exit rights', associated with greater mobility and the hegemony of market relations, with those connected to political participation and solidarity - membership rights of 'voice' and 'loyalty' (Hirschman, 1970). Finally, we briefly analyse what kinds of transnational regimes and institutions might address the issues of justice that we have identified, and try to implement the principles that emerge from this investigation.

THE JUSTIFICATION OF BORDER CONTROLS

If we consider that the right to decide where to live and work (which community to join) is fundamental to political justice under liberal democracy, this suggests that it is border control, not free movement, that needs to be justified. It may well be that there are certain circumstances in which controls are necessary, but the onus is on those who wish to give legitimate reasons for controls to define these circumstances. In a liberal democratic state, or in a supranational grouping such as the EU, it would only be in an emergency that the authorities would introduce restrictions on these rights. Normally, the overall flows of the labour market and residential mobility would be managed through policies to encourage movements of population towards certain cities and regions, or out of others. Since it is, at least in principle, possible to imagine a global regime for managing world population movements through such measures, in the same ways that national and EU regimes seek to promote well-functioning labour markets and balanced residential patterns, controls (in the forms of rules against entry) should be seen as exceptional. This is especially the case, since most people do not move from their home areas, even if they are quite free to do so (see pp. 28–9).

When it came to listing the 'primary social goods' to be distributed equally among members as the 'basic structure of society', John Rawls named 'freedom of movement and free choice of occupation against a background of diverse opportunities' as the second of these, after 'basic rights and liberties' (Rawls, 1996, p. 181). Carens (1987) argues that in Rawls' liberal theory of justice, the veil of ignorance behind which members make their contract about this structure should exclude knowledge of all the specific contingencies that would constitute citizenship of a particular country, and hence that the 'original position' is about a world without borders. In the work of libertarians like Nozick (1974), sovereign individuals with exclusive rights to their persons and property should be free to enter into contracts with all others; the role of just governments is to uphold such rights, not to create barriers (such as national borders) that infringe them unnecessarily. On the other hand, libertarians might endorse the collective rights of landowners with 'morally unimpaired' ownership titles to choose those they would allow to enter what would in effect be their 'private community', on the grounds that others would be 'trespassers' (Steiner, 1992, pp. 88, 91–2).

Only utilitarianism among modern liberal traditions seems readily to accommodate border controls, on the basis of a calculation of the costs and benefits of immigration to a state's citizens. But even here, the fundamental consideration is the utility of individuals, and since there is a strong presumption that migration is welfare-enhancing for the world as a whole (Sykes, 1995, pp. 164–81; Straubhaar, 2000), the global aggregate of individual utilities might be taken as a more relevant measure.

This therefore shifts the burden of justification onto states, as the guardians of borders, and the arbiters of 'communities of fate', in which individuals' membership is largely an accident of birth. States are required to justify themselves as closed systems, which use force to keep out would-be members, which claim the right to select applicants, and lay down the terms on which they may enter. The possible elements in some such justification include the following:

(a) *As providers of public goods*   The obvious reason why the predecessors of states came into existence was to create the order necessary for economic and social development by monopolising violence, and defending territories and their populations from external threat. The capacity to mobilise citizens in self-defence might still represent an argument for maintaining border controls. Both Serbia (in Kosovo) and Macedonia have recently alleged that inward migration by Albanians intentionally destabilised their societies.

It might further be argued that the evolution of states (by economic competition and military conflict) has enabled viable units to emerge, roughly corresponding to the most efficient size for guaranteeing property rights, promoting trade and minimising transaction costs (Spruyt, 1995). These, in turn, have been able to establish markets, providing local efficiency and equity where larger or global regimes would have been more expensive or less effective (Coleman and Harding, 1995, p. 38). Although such arguments fail to explain away the worst excesses of colonialism, imperialism and racism, their protagonists might maintain that no viable alternative to states emerged, at least until recently.

As part of such a claim, political units could, in theory, be seen as potential parties in a counterfactual deliberation on distributive justice, such as those between individuals in Rawls (1971) and Dworkin (1981). Suppose that the earth's resources and populations had been divided up between states in some such process (Coleman and Harding, 1995, p. 37), as in an auction or a lottery, and then each allowed to develop them in a distinctive way. This might have been an agreed just outcome of their deliberations.

From the point of view of global welfare, what has historically proved to be of greatest value has been the diversity of societies; initial allocations were not decisive. After all, wealthy and populous civilisations first emerged in North Africa and the Middle East. Until the Renaissance period, Western European societies were rather backward, compared with these and others, in the Far East and parts of Central and South America. Right up to the early 19th century, it was not clear that technological innovation and trade were to give Western Europe and the USA such key advantages.

In this way, a liberal democratic justification for restrictions on free movement might be developed. But this would have to go beyond the simple argument for an international system of states, each with its own jurisdiction over individual liberties and property rights. Such a system could take the form of a global federation of these states, or a global free market regime that included entitlement to free movement. Border controls require the additional justification that restricting immigration is necessary in order to provide the public goods characteristic of liberal democracy, and specifically that the public goods provided are requirements of social justice (Woodward, 1992). As we have seen in Chapter 8, the fact that immigrants do add to congestion and inequity in the provision of public services may be a consequence of the particular form of collective provision in a country, rather than evidence that immigration necessarily causes such violations of justice.

(b) *As providers of the resources of community*   Closely linked to such arguments is the claim that communities provide the resources (social capital) in which individuals form identities, projects and life plans, and set goals based on reasonable and fair expectations of other members (Kymlicka, 1991, pp. 162–81) Membership of political communities is relevant for distributive justice, but as a framework for individual choices, rather than what is to be distributed. Border controls allow such communities to develop, and it is within them that conceptions of the most efficient and equitable relationships between members are generated. The idea of political justice was a product of a particular kind of community (the Greek city state); modern ideas of distributive justice have been made possible by the development of welfare states in Western European and Australasian regimes.

In order to justify border controls, this line of argument would be required to show that membership is a key resource for the cultural practices of liberal democracies, that such regimes are most conducive to distributive justice and that control of entry to membership is necessary for protecting that kind of political community. This gives liberals a far harder task than the one set themselves by communitarians, or by those who, like Walzer, argue that it is part of states' sovereignty to determine who enters, in order to uphold their political values, including openness and free movement of citizens between internal communities (Walzer, 1983, pp. 61–2). What matters is stability, and mutual commitment to their common life; states' primary duties are to their members in such versions of justice.

Historically, success in establishing liberal democratic regimes does not seem to correlate closely with restrictive policies on immigration. Although the USA, Canada, Australia and New Zealand have all at various times made racist and restrictive immigration rules, they have been among the more successful political communities of this kind, and all are countries largely made up of immigrants.

It is perfectly possible to grant that territories and populations should be divided up into administratively and economically viable units, and that membership of communities is an important resource both for identities and for the distinctive practices of political justice within liberal democratic systems, without conceding the need for future border controls. The EU is an example of a region of the world in which internal borders between countries were opened, where previously they had been seen as essential for both these purposes. In the next section, we consider whether the principles under which border controls were taken down within the EU could be applied in a much wider context.

EXIT, VOICE AND LOYALTY

So far we have argued that the right to live and work in the community of one's choice is regarded as a very important principle of justice (as well as economic efficiency) in liberal democratic thought. Within systems for distributive justice, institutions are devised to reconcile freedom of movement of this kind with other principles, such as the protection of society's most vulnerable members. But this does not imply that all such institutions and systems *promote* mobility, and encourage members to shift about between communities. The two sets of arguments developed in the previous section make a convincing case for encouraging distinctive ways of life in particular localities, and the development of a diversity of relatively stable political communities, where members are committed to common interests. What they do not show is that border controls are the best way to achieve these aims. In this section, we argue that a combination of open borders and other measures would be more likely to achieve those goals.

In Hirschman's famous formulation of the issue, the task of all human institutions – commercial and political – is to find the 'optimum mix' between exit and voice, since 'the presence of the exit option can sharply reduce the probability that the voice option will be taken up widely and effectively' (Hirschman, 1970, p. 76). Individuals are more likely to remain loyal to an organisation if they believe they can influence it, and that it will improve what it offers them in return for loyalty (ibid., p. 77).

In political theory of justice, the problem has tended to be stated in the form of finding a balance between liberty and equality. Markets and capitalism promote a particular type of liberty – the freedom to leave relatively disadvantageous situations and enter more advantageous ones (an exit strategy). This may take the form of ceasing to buy a particular product, or to use a particular factor of production, or quitting a particular location, but it involves disengagement. Conversely, the politics of democracy and equality among citizens requires individuals and groups to negotiate about the terms of their engagement with each other, and to reach collective solutions that are advantageous for all (a voice strategy). But in liberal democratic theory, these have not been so distinct, since political activity clearly involves exit options (changing one's party allegiance or switching one's vote), while exit strategies often involve collective action for equal access to advantage (Cohen, 1993), including membership and voice in political and economic units.

The recognition that mobility is a central feature of the freedom that is intrinsic to liberal forms of justice has been a distinctive feature of modern political thought. Before the Renaissance period, ideas of justice were associated with the dispensations of rulers, concerned with harmony, stability and order. Machiavelli was the first modern political theorist because he recognised that conflict and movement were inescapable elements in a dynamic, prosperous society, and that politics must deal in them rather than suppress them. Hobbes claimed that the originality of his political theory lay in his design of rules for free beings in constant motion; in *Leviathan*, all life was motion, and being alive was moving from a desire to its satisfaction, and then on to the next (Hobbes, 1651, XI, p. 64). From Hobbes onwards, political theory was required to cater for agents who were competitive and commercial, and who sought 'power after power'.

Liberty and equality were the twin claims associated with the new economic relations. Markets promoted freedom of exchange and movement that gave rise to revolutionary ideas about autonomous individuals, living together in democratically governed communities. Starting with the English Civil War and the US and French Revolutions, bids for liberty and equality made on behalf of specific groups have inexorably been extended to others (women, slaves, black people), and eventually to humanity in general. But these claims were blocked by actual relationships of exploitation and dominance in the structures of economic and political systems (Callinicos, 2000, pp. 24–5). Marx explained this contradiction between the apparent freedom of the labour contract and the experiences of inequality and exploitation in the hidden relations of production. Socialism has attempted, through control of productive processes, to redistribute freedom and material resources in favour of the masses.

But, at the root of all egalitarian theories of justice there has always been a puzzle about mobility, and how to counter the advantages held by capitalists in this respect, without undermining the freedoms bestowed by markets. Adam Smith was the first to point out that:

> The capital ... that is acquired to any country by commerce and manufactures, is all a very precarious and uncertain possession, till some part of it has been secured and realised in the cultivation and improvement of its lands. A merchant, it has been said very properly, is not necessarily the citizen of any particular country. It is in a great measure indifferent to him from what place he carries on his trade; and a very trifling disgust will make him remove his capital, and together with it all the industry which it supports, from one country to another. No part of it can be said to belong to any particular country, either in buildings, or in the lasting improvement of lands (Smith, 1776, III.iv.24).

The state socialism of the Soviet Union solved this problem by taking all productive resources into public ownership; social democracy nationalised a few key industries, and tried to deal with inequalities by redistributing income, and providing universal social services. State socialism collapsed in the face of competition from other systems under global economic integration; social democracy has been forced to moderate its redistributive aims once capital burst its national shackles.

GLOBALISATION, CONFLICT AND JUSTICE

Globalisation has linked the fates of the world's populations without providing political institutions for just distributions between them. The technology that enables financial élites to move money around the world in immensely profitable ways is irrelevant to the living standards of the vast majority of people (Bauman, 1998). The world's richest 200 individuals more than doubled their wealth between 1994 and 1998, to a sum equal to the income of 41 per cent of the world's population (UN, 1999, p. 37). Three of these super-rich were worth the combined national incomes of the 36 poorest countries.

While 1.3 billion people live on less than US$1 a day, the disparity between the incomes of the richest and the poorest fifth of the world's population grew from ratios of 60:1 in 1990 to 74:1 in 1997 (UN, 1999, p. 3). Migration represents a claim to be included in systems for distributive justice (Bommes, 1999).

Hence, the conflict at the borders of First World countries arises because they are the barriers behind which the advantaged defend themselves against these demands from the world's mass of underprivileged people. Whether as free individuals or as collective actors, migrants have historically been a force for dynamism and change (Bach and Schraml, 1982). As Zolberg argues, although 'in appearance apolitical, exit constitutes one of the most effective weapons the weak can wield' (Zolberg, 1989, p. 422) against oppression or exploitation. In that perspective, both individual decisions and mass exodus are driven by similar aspirations and expectations; but these put migrants in potential conflict with the authorities in receiving countries.

> It appears that human history is a history of tug-of-war between institutional policies to mould people's behaviour to achieve certain economic and political goals and individuals' attempts to free themselves from institutional constraints ... . One area in which such conflicting tendencies between institutional goals and individual needs and desires are most apparent is migration (Shrestha, 1987, p. 329).

The threat posed by migrants has evoked images of war to the death. Zolberg quotes a US historian and policy adviser writing that 'the rich will have to fight and the poor will have to die if mass migration is not to overwhelm us all' (Zolberg and Benda, 2000, p. 3). This takes a Malthusian view of migrants, as dangerous to prosperity by their sheer numbers; it is the poor rather than poverty that must be eliminated. The events of 11 September 2001 have reminded the world of the perils of allowing the plight of huge populations to become the focus for armed conflict, instead of for the search for global justice. They have also emphasised how the pathways of globalisation make the rich countries more vulnerable if such conflict occurs.

Reviewing the history of the twentieth century, Hobsbawm has made a parallel between the present indifference of the West towards the poverty of many nations and the genocidal policies towards groups within states under fascist regimes (Hobsbawm, 1994, pp. 705–10). The political challenge of the new century is to include the poor in systems for justice, rather than allow their plight to become the issue around which the sides in a new global conflict are mobilised.

All this gives strong indications of the need for new institutions for global justice, but not the means by which they might be created, or the form that they should take. From the analysis so far, it seems that they must be consistent with a world of sovereign political communities, but enable justice within and between them. The present combination of trade and aid has failed, both because it consolidates and reinforces inequalities, and because it destabilises redistributive regimes.

Freedom of exit from oppression and exploitation has been readily accepted in liberal political theory, but not the means to make such rights effective. Three aspects of the limitations on attempts to implement equal liberty are important for the issues of border control and free movement, and for the attempt to balance exit, voice and loyalty.

(a) *The asymmetry of exit and entry rights*   Being free to leave oppressive or exploitative communities does not imply freedom to enter more liberal and equal ones. This affects every level of social interaction, as we have seen throughout this book. Although there are many opportunities for migrants who leave their countries to find channels for entry to First World societies, few of these give entitlement to long-term residence or citizenship. Asylum seekers who are forced to flee cannot choose where to stay, and no state has a duty to accept them. But this is paralleled in the social relations of liberal democratic polities, where citizens are free to leave deprived and lawless neighbourhoods, but usually lack the means to gain access to prosperous and peaceful ones.

In this respect 'liberal egalitarian' thought is closer to libertarianism than its proponents choose to recognise. Our research study in the UK showed that work permit holders, admitted as temporary residents but able to command quite high salaries, had much the same access to the privileges of good collective facilities and clubs as better-off UK citizens, whereas asylum seekers, even when given refugee status, tended to be trapped in excluded and impoverished communities. In other words, money and property holding are effective passports to the advantages of membership, and the dynamics of exclusion apply to poor citizens as well as poor immigrants.

Like well-off citizens, foreigners can buy their way into the best facilities in liberal states, if not into citizenship itself (see the example of Mohammad Fayed in the UK). This largely invalidates the argument that political communities are 'voluntary associations', and hence (by analogy) have the moral authority to refuse entry to those they prefer not to select. Restricting entry violates *equal* liberty if the criteria for restriction are arbitrary or discriminatory. In other words, the grounds for granting or refusing membership have to be relevant to the type of community or association, and non-relevant features (such as gender or skin colour) should not be employed. Ability to purchase houses or business assets might be regarded as relevant for some kinds of community, but not for a political association, whose membership should surely consist in some broader contribution to the common good.

The rights to enter and stay in a country are increasingly more significant than the rights to settle permanently or take citizenship. Most businesspeople, and many academics and highly skilled technicians (such as the Indian IT workers interviewed in Chapter 9) take for granted that their lifestyle is transnational, and that they work and stay in other countries for protracted periods, but are unlikely to emigrate permanently. In the same way, the research on transnationalism and 'globalisation from below' (Basch, Glick Schiller and Blanc-Szanton, 1994; Portes, 1998; Vertovec, 2001) suggests the spontaneous development of strong cross-border links between people who live 'neither here nor there'. Hence, it is important that any asymmetry between the rights to exit and those to entry is closely scrutinised, to see whether it is morally justifiable, on relevant criteria.

(b) *National and local inequalities of resources and power in political communities*   The aim of balancing exit and voice rights implies that political institutions should not encourage the use of exit options and strategies over voice ones. Indeed, the notion of democratic membership implies that individuals seek first to achieve justice through participation, negotiation and compromise. The 'victory of democracy' in the former communist countries of the Soviet Bloc would have been undermined, not strengthened, if their populations had all streamed across their borders into Western Europe. Yet the democratic victors of the EU had such little faith in the immediate attractions of the new political order that they at once erected all the barriers of Fortress Europe described in Chapter 3. Closed borders were intended to force those populations to learn the ways of democracy, and to work out systems of competition and co-operation for the common good among themselves.

Globalisation, by fostering inequality, encourages exit strategies and weakens voice ones, because it gives higher payoffs to the former than the latter. It undermines redistributive systems, and discourages the least advantaged from political participation. But it does all these things within countries as well as between them, so this is an issue for liberal egalitarians that cannot be addressed simply by relying on border controls. The strengthening of voice options, the improvement in incentives for participation, and the discovery of new redistributive institutions more suited to current economic conditions, are all challenges for political communities that can neither be escaped by emigration, nor solved by restrictions on entry.

For the post-communist countries 'in transition', transnational activity (including a quota of irregular migration) provides a temporary safety valve. Faced with a ratio of 11:1 between average incomes in Germany and Poland (Stalker, 2000), it is little wonder that so many young Poles opt for occasional short- or medium-term trips abroad, to earn for specific targets. Our data on irregular migrants from Poland in London suggests that this does relatively little damage to the host society, where there is a demand for their labour. This might be contrasted with asylum seeking by the Roma minorities in the Czech and Slovak Republics, which is clearly a protest against their oppression and exclusion, and indicates the lack of incentives for political participation in those countries since 1989 (Castle-Kanerova and Jordan, 2001). Their plight urgently requires measures to improve their membership rights, voice opportunities and economic situation within those polities.

(c) *Inequality of exit options among members of national and local communities* If the goal is to encourage democratic membership and participation, then any institutions that promote equality should also seek to redistribute exit options within that community in such a way as to give greater incentives for members to engage and co-operate on fair terms, rather than to seek advantage through mobility.

At present, options for exit of all kinds are unequally distributed, and hence individuals and groups have unequal access to advantage (Cohen, 1995). Not only capitalists, but also skilled workers, can insist on differentials in their rewards, as their price for co-operation. The incentives of higher pay, as well as profits, are based on the threat of exit if their demands are not met; the 'very trifling disgust' of which Adam Smith wrote, is enough to undermine loyalty or solidarity. This kind of claim is compared by Cohen to a kind of blackmail or kidnap demand, based on threats not to contribute unless specially rewarded, and hence rejected as inappropriate for relations among members of a community concerned with justice (Cohen, 1992, pp. 269–70).

The distribution of exit options is closely linked to the distribution of resources and responsibilities. For example, women are now formally free to leave relationships with men in most countries, but in fact it is much more often men who leave women. This is because men usually have more income, and women usually have more responsibility for caring for children and other relatives, and feel bound to such relationships by bonds of love and duty. Women could not have the same exit options as men unless both income and caring activities were distributed equally between them. This was made clear by John Roemer's thought experiment on exploitation and class, in which the relevant assets for a system of production (feudalism, capitalism and state socialism) were redistributed equally between the groups participating in that economic order, and then all had the opportunity to withdraw (Roemer, 1982). Exploitation was revealed when a group that previously had no exit options exercised this choice, and refused to co-operate any further under that particular productive system.

What all this indicates is that the moves towards equality and justice that occurred within First World welfare states in the period after the Second

World War went only part of the way towards achieving those goals. Social insurance benefits were steps towards the 'decommodification of labour power' (Esping-Andersen, 1990), but they did not give workers the unconditional income to withdraw from unchosen contracts. They were surrounded by conditions tying them to employment, since greatly tightened under workfare and welfare-to-work regimes (Cox, 1999). Child benefits and child care services allowed women to become secondary household earners, but not to choose freedom as heads of separate households. Anti-discrimination measures opened up opportunities for education and professional careers for black élites, but this enabled them to leave the inner city ghettos, and move to leafy suburbs. It actually left the populations of those districts more disadvantaged and deprived than they were before (Wilson, 1989; 1997).

NEW INSTITUTIONS FOR REDISTRIBUTION UNDER GLOBALISATION

A principle for redistribution of resources, under which the right for all to withdraw from unfair contracts, damaging relationships and disadvantaging communities could be established, has been discussed in political philosophy for many years. It is the system for providing each individual with an income (or assets producing an income) that would allow each unconditional autonomy, because each could subsist without dependence on co-operation with another. This would, in turn, guarantee the possibility of withdrawal from unchosen, unjust and exploitative relationships and systems of production. It would redistribute and equalise exit rights and opportunities and should, in turn, make those who are at present holders of power or assets that allow unilateral exit more willing to negotiate over fair terms of co-operation.

The basic income proposal is one variant of this principle (Jordan, 1985, 1989, 1998, Parker, 1989; Van Parijs, 1995; Barry, 1997; Fitzpatrick, 1999). The other is the social dividend or demogrant (Ackerman and Alstott, 1999; Le Grand and Nissan, 2000). Under the first approach, the state would redistribute a weekly or monthly sum to every citizen, sufficient for subsistence, and without distinctions based on labour-market role or household status. Under the second, it would give a capital sum (or land, in an agricultural economy) to produce such an income.

If this system was introduced in a single country or group of countries, and made available to all who entered, it would be an incentive to inward migration, or a justification for closed borders. However, if all countries in the world introduced some such scheme, at the level that their national economies could afford, this would have the opposite effect, of discouraging migration. In such a situation, someone who chose to enter another country might be allowed to keep his or her entitlement from the sending country, but not qualify for the entitlement of citizens of the receiving one. Hence, the basic income or demogrant would promote stability and the sense of membership of a political community while still allowing those who chose to move to do so.

Some advocates of basic income argue that its introduction as a new principle for redistribution within states should be combined with the strengthening of border controls. For example, Philippe Van Parijs insists that because capital mobility should in theory equalise profits and wages as effectively as migration, and is a 'less painful process', it would be better to combine such redistributive measures with restrictions on entry during a transitional period (Van Parijs, 1992, p. 164). However, we have argued that the evidence of the effects of accelerated movement of capital points strongly to increased inequalities worldwide (both within and between countries). The only sense in which incomes in First, Second and Third World countries are coming closer is that earnings of certain sections of workers have fallen – relatively small groups of unskilled people in Western Europe, but very large proportions of the working class in the USA and the former communist countries (Luttwak, 1999). It might also be suggested that the system of basic incomes related to the GNPs of different countries would not discourage migration. For citizens of poorer countries, the incentives of higher earnings in richer ones would still remain. Even if the basic income in their own country reduced poverty-driven emigration, it would not necessarily affect opportunity-driven movement to wealthier societies. But opportunity-driven migration (the 'pull' factors associated with higher earning possibilities) are considered to be fundamental to the dynamism and growth potential of national economies, and to the processes that allow internal mobility and development. It is the migrants who would respond to such incentives – more skilled and better educated – who would be most favoured by the receiving country, and likely to be targeted for recruitment by the selective systems analysed in Chapter 9. The shift towards a more favourable view of economic migration focuses exactly on this group, but continues to try to prevent or restrict poverty-driven migration, in the guise of asylum seeking and clandestine entry. Hence, the main issue would become one of tackling 'brain drain' effects on sending countries.

Another possible objection is that the international basic income scheme would favour migrants over unskilled citizens in labour markets. Even the very small part of their subsistence costs met by the basic income from a poor country would help them to compete against citizens for low-paid work. However, the basic income scheme for citizens, with its more generous rate of unconditional payment, would do something to even out the advantages enjoyed by migrants, with their better education and work experience. Furthermore, as we have shown in Chapters 5 and 9, some such issues are already present in disguised forms in First World countries like the UK, where irregular migrants are a more attractive workforce than indigenous claimants. Furthermore, official systems like the business visa scheme allow irregular migrants to find legal channels into the labour market that further advantage them over excluded citizens (pp. 230–32).

From an entirely different standpoint, some might argue that the presence in a wealthy country, with a high level of basic income for its citizen population, of migrants with much lower basic incomes from their countries of origin, would undermine attempts to include all legal residents in social welfare provision. If the goal of equal provision for non-citizen residents were considered to have priority over free movement, this would certainly be a valid objection to the proposal. That policy goal, however, both favours emigrants from poor countries over their fellow citizens who stay at home, and gives an incentive for immigration, including irregular immigration. From a global perspective, it seems better to sacrifice this aim, as long as all migrants are included in aspects such as health and social care, safety and physical security.

Finally, there would be important and contentious issues around the acquisition of citizenship, at which point migrants would qualify for the basic income of the new country of residence. This would give incentives for migrants to seek naturalisation for purely economic reasons, rather as some undocumented workers from Brazil and Poland undertook marriages for the sake of their immigration status, and thereby qualified for social benefits (see pp. 144–6). It might transfer some of the contentious issues at present focused on border crossings to the naturalisation process. Liberal theorists are generally agreed that legal immigrants have a moral right to be given citizenship after a certain period of residence, and most states apply versions of some such rule. But in many there are also already economic incentives, including those arising from eligibility for benefits, either for prolonging stays to get permanent resident status, or for becoming citizens. It seems unlikely that these problems can ever be entirely eliminated, or that the basic income scheme would significantly exacerbate them.

UNEVEN DEVELOPMENT AND MIGRATION

In the philosophical literature of justice, the basic income and social dividend were much discussed in the 1990s, but almost always in the context of redistributions between the members of a hypothetical affluent society. At the same time as these theoretical debates were raging, in the real world, actual income transfers in such countries were being made more conditional, and more closely tied to work and household roles. Under measures for 'activation' of claimants of all kinds of benefits, regimes of workfare and welfare-to-work tried to test eligibility more strictly, reducing the scope for citizens to claim benefits as alternatives to low-paid, dirty or dangerous jobs, or violent, unreliable relationships.

One of the reasons why welfare state regimes shifted in these directions was that globalisation increased the exit options for capital, by opening up the possibilities for developing new regions for industrial (and eventually electronically equipped service) production. Activation and workfare systems were part of the response by First World states to the competition for investment enforced by capital's increased mobility. From this perspective, proposals such as basic income and social dividend became more and more utopian, since they ran against the grain of economic development. Capital is the dominant economic interest within the new order, and its advantages rest on maintaining a system of very diverse national economies, each of which allows slightly different version of exploitation, and all of which versions are reinforced by state welfare regimes. Keeping the producers of raw materials backward and poor, relying on plentiful supplies of unskilled and semi-skilled labour in the newly industrialising and post-communist countries, and supplying labour-intensive private services to the ageing populations of the rich nations, are all complementary elements in this global strategy of capital. Often the government of the USA, the richest country in the world, has lent its support to the pursuit of this strategy (Wade, 2001, 2002).

It is easy to see how new migration regimes fit into this picture. Since the costs of maintaining non-active populations fall on the workers of particular states more than on capital, flexibility in the short-term supply of skilled and unskilled labour where it is needed is a more important goal than retraining or activating any particular workforce, from capital's perspective. Recruitment of highly skilled or highly mobile workers for immediate vacancies within an international labour market is therefore a useful instrument. Let nation states worry about considerations such as congestion of public services or demographic balances, and about the cost of transfers; capital is concerned only with migration systems that guarantee its supplies of suitable workers (see pp. 221–3 for evidence of this from the UK).

This dominance of capital has been reinforced by the operation of international organisations. The International Monetary Fund (IMF) and the World Bank are controlled by the rich creditor nations of the First World, and work to ensure that poor debtor states honour their commitments to repay. To this end, they impose conditions on loans to developing countries that often reinforce their disadvantages, and impede their development. The World Trade Organisation (WTO) has – at least until recently – worked to agendas set by the richest four participants in trade negotiations (the USA, EU, Canada and

Japan) which largely excluded such topics as tariffs on or subsidies to agricultural products and textiles, the main concerns of the developing world. It has been estimated that the poor countries could export $700 billion more each year if the rich countries had not succeeded in imposing continued import protections for their markets (United Nations Conference on Trade and Development, 2000). Hence, the benefits of trade liberalisation have hitherto largely accrued to the First World, and specifically to capital in the rich states. It was only after the shock to the world economy through the events of 11 September 2001 that the negotiations of the WTO at Doha, Qatar the following November produced some promised gains for the poorer countries, notably on overriding patent rules in the interests of health, and hence bringing down the costs of importing medicines, and on reducing the EU's farm support system (Denny, 2001).

Globalisation has therefore consisted in the development of the world economy under conditions most favourable for capital and the First World countries, and under terms that discriminate against the developing countries in the liberalisation of trade. International organisations have hitherto contributed little to global justice in these processes.

For these reasons, it is doubtful whether an international regime for managing migration, such as the General Agreement on the Movement of People proposed by Straubhaar (2000), would be a step towards international justice. Straubhaar argues that the main goal of such a regime should be to deal with the problem that rich countries want to recruit highly skilled workers, whereas poor ones want to send their surplus of less skilled people; the outcome risks a brain drain in the sending countries, which consolidates processes of uneven development. His main proposed solution – following Bhagwati (1976) – is to impose migration tax on those choosing to move abroad, and to allow sending countries to continue to tax the incomes of high-earning emigrants, thus exposing them to double taxation of their salaries. 'Citizens would become *taxable world-wide* by their home country, as long as they would like to keep their old citizenship.... That means that they pay an extra fee as compared to the citizens of the destination country' (Straubhaar, 2000, p. 31).

This regime would represent a kind of economic border control, and would certainly encourage irregular migration in the form of tax evasion. The idea of a global system of basic incomes or social dividends would be a subsidy for stability and solidarity, instead of a tax on mobility, as in this proposal. It would not penalise migration by choice, but instead seek to improve the lot of less mobile populations; and it would not require an international organisation for its implementation. Migration can be a source of dynamism and development, not least in First World countries (see pp. 51–2).

The obvious problem that lays the project for a global basic income scheme open to the charge of utopianism is therefore the whole range of economic and political interest that could be expected to oppose it. Let us first address the problems in the post-communist and developing worlds, where notoriously corruption among élites, lack of respect for minority and human rights, and the absence of democratic traditions are all seen as insuperable barriers to the politics of equality, justice and good governance, on which such a scheme would rely. Here international organisations of a rather different kind might contribute to more hopeful prospects. Pogge (2001) advocates a standing Democracy Panel of developing countries, able to issue rulings when the exercise of political power no longer matches constitutional rules (for instance, after a military coup or a fraudulent election). If the Panel declared a regime not to be legitimate, this would mean that lending to it could not give rise to legal claims, or purchase of resources create legal ownership rights. Countries could qualify to join this scheme after a period of democratic governance, and membership would create strong disincentives for reversion to undemocratic systems, or breaches of constitutional protections for individual and minority rights.

Clearly this would not, on its own, provide resources for the proposed basic income or social dividend schemes. Here a possible source might be the proposed Tobin Tax (on speculative trading in currencies) or – if that turned out to be too easily evaded – a levy on the extraction of natural resources, or on the discharge of pollutants. The proceeds from such funds would be distributed to poorer countries to enhance basic income or social dividend schemes, under which they supplied basic security to their citizens. First World countries are already making some such conditions about benefiting their poorest inhabitants in the provision of aid to these countries.

It might be objected to that there would be little justice in poor countries giving basic incomes to their citizens, which could be used to subsidise emigration to richer states, where migrants would pay taxes to the receiving government on their higher earnings. However, evidence on remittances to families in the home countries by migrants suggests that poor sending countries could benefit overall from such payments (Keely and Tran, 1989).

In the aftermath of the events of 11 September 2001, First World leaders such as Tony Blair made high-minded speeches about the responsibility of the richest and most powerful states towards the solution of problems of political instability, civil war and terrorism in the developing world. So far this has mainly consisted of bombing Afghanistan, and threatening to bomb other countries. Support for systematic efforts to promote democracy and reduce abuses of human rights, along with improvements in economic welfare, would greatly reduce the need for special measures of humanitarian protection.

Throughout this book, one of our arguments has been that open borders would reduce the need for programmes to allow asylum seeking, and reduce the costs associated with these. At present, there are some 12 million refugees in the world, mostly in poor countries adjacent to the ones from which they have fled, and only 3 million in the First World countries. Wars and other emergencies would still cause flows of this kind, and refugees would still need special measures for resettlement, because of the trauma associated with forced migration. However, many of the distortions noted in our research study (see pp. 214–16) would be greatly reduced under these proposals.

Without accompanying measures to deal directly with poverty and political oppression, open borders would not be certain to benefit those who are today's refugees. Better opportunities for economic migrants with education and skills in First World labour markets might crowd out the poorest and most oppressed, who could therefore have the least chance of improving their position through exit. This is why redistribution of resources and democratisation processes would be integral to achieving justice with freedom of movement.

Turning now to the prospects for the basic income scheme in developed countries, there are some reasons for suggesting that this might evolve as a response to the unresolved issues reviewed in Chapter 3. There we argued that the activation principle, trying to draw women and claimants from informal economic activity into formal employment, had certain natural limits. 'Almost full part-time employment' (Hemerijck, 2001, p. 169) still has a built-in inequity between those insiders (mostly prime age men) in full-time, decently paid jobs, and those outsiders (mostly women, younger and older workers, and members of ethnic minorities) in peripheral, secondary employment. It also requires the subsidisation of low wages – whether by social insurance contribution rebates in the European states (Scharpf, 1995, 1997), or by tax credits of the US–UK model. Both of these create anomalies within their respective income maintenance systems; for instance in the UK the amount given in tax credits to such workers will quite quickly overhaul the level of support for those 'in genuine need' of social assistance, because of age or physical frailties (Jordan *et al.*, 2000, ch. 2). Further recruitment from informal activities will leave a shortage of unpaid carers, volunteers and community activity to provide the cement for society. Many of those tasks are more efficiently done on an informal basis, even from a narrowly economic perspective, quite apart from spillover effects in social capital (Putnam, 2000). Hence, it may become necessary to improve incentives for unpaid activities, by something like a 'participation income' (Atkinson, 1995). Eventually it would be more administratively simple and efficient to convert this into a basic income (Jordan *et al.*, 2000, ch. 3); even though the new model income maintenance system started from increased conditionality, it could end up by giving everyone an unconditional basic income.

A main stumbling block to the evolution of such a policy dynamic would be the costs of accommodation. If one aim of a new approach was to give all citizens more autonomy in deciding on what hours of paid work to offer, and on what terms, as well as how to co-operate together outside the labour market, then a great obstacle would be the enormous variation in such costs in different regions of the same country. This is especially the case in the UK, with its high proportion of home ownership. Salt and Clarke (2001) have pointed out that the vast bulk of labour migration into the UK is to the south-east region, and to London in particular (40 per cent of all legal labour migration to the UK). Our research leads us to believe that the proportion of irregular migration could be even higher. As Salt and Clarke show, this has been relatively stable for the past 25 years, and reflects the barriers to migration from other regions represented by the costs of moving to London from areas of unemployment to ones of high demand for workers. Hence a new approach to income maintenance would be required to address housing costs quite separately as an issue, rather than try to avoid it by relying on legal and irregular migration as a way of achieving equilibrium.

Each First World country would face specific obstacles of this kind to the development of a tax and benefit system that would be consistent with open borders, yet strive towards justice between members of its political community. Yet the important point that we are attempting to establish in this chapter is that such goals are not only feasible aims of policy (as in the EU), but also logical extensions of long-standing, established institutions, still largely preserved in welfare states. Open borders are not necessarily – as Freeman (1986) suggested – a means of subverting these systems, and substituting a US version, more friendly to the interests of global capital. Open borders could be part of a combined thrust towards more dynamism in economic growth and greater justice between world populations.

CONCLUSIONS

The policy background to this book about irregular migration has been a shift towards greater awareness of the potential economic benefits of lifting some of the restrictions on movements into First World countries, and hence some specific policies for labour-market recruitment from the developing world. However, these changes are quite marginal, and do not address the central issues relevant for migration from the poorer countries of the world, or the questions of global justice that lie behind them.

In this chapter we have tried to set out the background against which steps towards opening borders might be taken – the general principles that could inform the direction of more detailed measures. At least the political culture in the EU is now rather more favourable towards inward migration and open to the idea that it is welfare-enhancing. The challenge now is to find ways in which more openness for highly skilled recruitment of a few chosen recruits is not matched by more restrictive policies for others, trying to enter by different channels. In this respect there is some encouragement in the UK in more active engagement between the government and the immigrant support organisations, and in tentative moves towards amnesties, and recruitment from the irregular migrant population.

Irregular migration is the thorniest issue in the very complex question of justice in migration management. But we have argued that globalisation makes it inescapable as a topic for policy. Irregular migrants provide us with important clues about the larger forces at work in the global economy, and how governments might best deal with them for the sake of justice between members of the world community.

Bibliography

Abella, M. (1995), *Policies and Institutions for the Orderly Movement of Labour Abroad*, Geneva: International Labour Office.

Ackerman, B. and A. Alstott (1999), *The Stakeholding Society*, New Haven, CT: Yale University Press.

Ad Hoc Group on Immigration (1992), *Setting up a Centre for Information, Discussion and Exchange on the Crossing of Borders and Immigration (CIREFI)*, adopted at the meeting of Ministers, London, 30 November–1 December, SN 4816/92, WGI, confidential.

Alt, J. and R. Fodor (2001), *Rechtlos? Menschen ohne Papiere*, Karlsruhe: Van Loeper Literaturverlag.

Altonji, J. and D. Card (1991), 'The effects of immigration on the labour market outcomes of less skilled natives', in Abowd, J.M. and R.B. Freeman (eds.), *Immigration, Trade and the Labour Market*, Chicago: University of Chicago Press, 201–234.

Amjad, R. (1996), 'Philippines and Indonesia: on the way to a migration transition', *Asian and Pacific Migration Journal*, **5**(2/3), 339–66.

Anderson, B. (2000), *Doing the Dirty Work: The Global Politics of Domestic Labour*, London: Zed Books.

Anderson, P. (1999), 'From the wailing wall to the "dignified juggler": making a living as an undocumented migrant in the United Kingdom', in Eichenhofer, E. (ed.), *Migration and Illegalität*, Osnabrück: Universitätsverlag Rasch, 157–76.

Ardill, N. and N. Cross (1987), *Undocumented Lives: Britain's Unauthorised Migrant Workers*, London: Runnymede Trust.

Asian Regional Programme on International Labour Migration (1990), *Statistical Report 1990: International Labour Migration from Asian Labour-sending Countries*, Bangkok: UNDP-ILO Asian Regional Programme.

Asylum Aid (1997), *Annual Report, 1996/7*, London: Asylum Aid.

Atkinson, A.B. (1995), *Public Economics in Action: The Basic Income/Flat Tax Proposal*, Oxford: Oxford University Press.

Bach, R.L. and L.A. Schraml (1982), 'Migration, crisis and theoretical conflict', *International Migration Review*, **16**(2), 320–41.

Badescu, G. (2001), 'Trust and Democracy in the Former Communist Countries', Cluj, Romania: Department of Political Science, Babes Bolyai University.

Baldwin, M. (2000), *Care Management and Community Care: Social Work Discretion and the Construction of Policy*, Aldershot: Ashgate.

Banerjee, B. (1983), 'Social networks in the migration process: empirical evidence on chain migration in India', *Journal of Developing Areas*, **17**(2), 185–96.

Barry, B. (1997), 'The attractions of basic income', in J. Franklin (ed.), *Equality*, London: Institute for Public Policy Research, 157–71.

Barry, B. and R.E. Goodin (eds.) (1992), *Free Movement: Ethical Issues in the Transnational Migration of People and of Money*, University Park, PA: Pennsylvania State University Press.

Basch, L.G., N. Glick Schiller and C. Blanc-Szanton (1994), *Nations Unbound: Transnational Projects, Post-colonial Predicaments, and De-territorialised Nation States*, Langhome, PA: Gordon and Breach.

Bauböck, R. (1994), *Transnational Citizenship: Membership and Rights in International Migration*, Aldershot: Edward Elgar.

Bauer, T. and K. Zimmerman (1997), 'Network migration of ethnic Germans', *International Migration Review*, **31**, 143–9.

Bauman, Z. (1998), *Globalization: The Human Consequences*, Cambridge: Polity.

Beck, U., (1992), *Risk Society: Towards a New Modernity*, London: Sage.

Becker, B.K. and C.A.G. Egler (1992), *Brazil: A New Regional Power in the World Economy*, Cambridge: Cambridge University Press.

Begg, D., S. Fischer and R. Dornbusch (1991), *Economics* (Third Edition), London: McGraw-Hill.

Bhaba, J. and S. Shutter (1994), *Women's Movement: Women under Immigration, Nationality and Refugee Law*, London: Trenthouse.

Bhagwati, J.N. (1976), *The Brain Drain and Taxation: Theory and Empirical Analysis*, Volume 2, Amsterdam: North-Holland.

Bhagwati, J.N. and J.D. Wilson (1989), *Income Taxation and International Mobility*, Cambridge, Mass: MIT Press.

Bhagwati, J.N. and T.N. Srinivasan (1983), *Lectures on International Trade*, Cambridge, Mass: MIT Press.

Biernacki, P. and D. Waldorf (1981), 'Snowball sampling: problems and techniques of chain referral sampling', *Sociological Methods and Research*, **10**(2), 134–57.

Bischoff, J. (1999), 'Herrschaft der Finanzmärkte: Kern der Globalisierung', *Widerspruch*, **38**, 25–37.

Bittner, E. (1965), 'The police on skid row: a study in peace keeping', *Sociological Review*, **32**, 699–715.

Blair, T. (1998), Preface to DSS, *A New Contract for Welfare*, Cm 3805, London: Stationery Office, i–iv.

Blaschke, J. and B. Amman (1988), 'Kurden in der Bundsrepublik: ihr soziale und kulturelle Situation', in Mönch-Bucak, Y. (Ed.), *Kurden: Alltag und Widerstand*, Bremen: Eigenverlag, 90–99.

Bloch, A. (1994), *Refugees and Migrants in Newham: Access to Services*, London: London Borough of Newham.

Bloch, A. (1996), 'Refugees in Newham', in Butler, T. and M. Rustin (eds.), *Rising in the East: The Regeneration of East London*, London: Lawrence and Wishart.

Bloeme, L. and R.C. van Geuns (1987), *Ongeregelt Ondernemen: een Onderzoek naar Informele Bedrijvigheid*, The Hague: RWV.

Blundell, R., A. Duncan, G. McCrae and C. Meghir (1999), *The Labour-market Impact of the Working Families Tax Credit*, London: Institute for Fiscal Studies.

Böcker, A. (1994), 'Chain migration over legally closed borders: settled migrants as bridgeheads and gatekeepers', *Netherlands Journal of Sociology*, **30**(2), 87–106.

Böhning, W.R. (1972), *The Migration of Workers in the United Kingdom and the European Community*, Oxford: Oxford University Press.

Bommes, M. (1999), *Migration und nationaler Wohlfahrtsstaat: Ein differenzsierungstheoretischer Entwurf*, Opladen: Westdeutscher Verlag.

Borjas, G. (1987), 'Immigrants, minorities and labour market competition', *Industrial and Labour Relations Review*, **40**, 382–92.

Borjas, G. (1990), *Friends or Strangers?: The Impact of Immigrants on the US Economy*, New York: Basic Books.

Boswell, C. (2001), *Spreading the Costs of Asylum Seekers: A Critical Assessment of Dispersal Policies in Germany and the UK*, London: Anglo-German Foundation for the Study of Industrial Society.

Bourdieu, P. (1999), 'No change without movement', *Le Monde Diplomatique*, 5 June, 1–3.

Bovenkerk, F. (1982), 'Op eigem Kracht om hoog. Etnisch ondernemerschap en de oogkleppen van het minderhedencircuit', *Intermediair*, **18**(8).

Boyd, M. (1989), 'Family and personal networks in international migration: recent developments and new agendas', *International Migration Review*, **23**, 638–70.

Boyle, M. (1996), 'World cities and the limits of global control', *International Journal of Urban and Regional Research*, **20**, 498–517.

Bratsberg, B. (1995), 'Legal versus illegal US immigration and source country characteristics', *Journal of International Economics*, 715–26.

Brenner, R. (1998), 'Uneven development and the long downturn', *New Left Review*, **229**, 191–2.

Breuer, M., T. Faist and B. Jordan (1996), 'Collective action, migration and welfare states', *International Sociology*, **10**(4), 369–86.

Brown, G. (1997), 'Why Labour is still loyal to the poor', *The Guardian*, 2 August.

Brueckner, J.K. (2000), 'Welfare reform and the race to the bottom: theory and evidence', *Southern Economic Journal*, **66**(3), 505–25.

Buchanan, J.M. (1965), 'An economic theory of clubs', *Economica*, **32**, 1–14.

Buchanan, J.M. (1968), *The Demand and Supply of Public Goods*, New York: Rand MacNally.

Bunyan, T. (ed.) (1993), *Statewatching the New Europe: A Handbook on the European State*, London: Statewatch.

Callinicos, A. (2000), *Equality*, Cambridge: Polity.

Carens, J.H. (1987), 'Aliens and citizens: the case for open borders', *Review of Politics*, **49**(2), 251–73.

Carey-Wood, J., K. Duke, V. Karn and T. Marshall (1995), *The Settlement of Refugees in Britain*, Home Office Research and Planning Unit Report, London: HMSO.

Castle-Kanerova, M. and B. Jordan (2001), *Local Strategies for Civic Inclusion in a European Context: The Roma in the Czech Republic*, ESRC 'One Europe or Several?' Programme, Working Paper W34/01, Brighton: University of Sussex.

Castles, S. with M.J. Miller (1993), *The Age of Migration: International Population Movements in the Modern World*, Basingstoke: Macmillan.

Centre for Economics and Business Research (2001), Annual Report on London's Economy, quoted in the *Evening Standard*, 11 July, 11.

China Statistical Publishing House (1998), *China Statistical Abstract, 1997*, Beijing: Government of China.

Chiswick, B.R. (1999), 'The economics of illegal migration for the host economy', paper presented at an International Expert Meeting on Irregular Migration: Dynamics, Impact and Policy Options, Jerusalem, 29 August–2 September.

Cohen, G.A. (1992), 'Incentives, inequality and community', in Peterson, G.B. (ed.), *The Tanner Lectures on Human Values*, XIII, Salt Lake City: University of Utah Press, 135–57.

Cohen, G.A. (1993), 'Equality of what? On welfare, goods and capabilities', in Nussbaum, M. and A. Sen (eds.), *The Quality of Life*, Oxford: Oxford University Press, 23–41.

Cohen, G.A. (1995), *Self Ownership, Freedom and Equality*, Cambridge: Cambridge University Press.

Cole, P. (2000), *Philosophies of Exclusion: Liberal Political Theory and Immigration*, Edinburgh: Edinburgh University Press.

Coleman, J.L. and S.K. Harding (1995), 'Citizenship, the demands of justice, and the moral relevance of political borders', in Schwartz, W.F. (ed.), *Justice in Immigration*, Cambridge: Cambridge University Press, 18–64.

Collinson, S. (1994), *Europe and International Migration*, London: Pinter/ Royal Institution of International Affairs.

Corry, D. (1996), *Economics and European Union Migration Policy*, London: Institute for Public Policy Research.

Cox, R.H. (1998), 'From safety nets to trampolines: labour market activation in the Netherlands and Denmark', *Governance: An International Journal of Politics and Administration*, **11**(4), 397–414.

Cox, R.H. (1999), *The Consequences of Welfare Reform: How Conceptions of Social Rights are Changing*, Norman, OK: Department of Political Science, University of Oklahoma.

Cross the Border (1999), *Kein Mensch ist illegal: Handbook zur Kampagne*, Berlin: ID-Verlag.

Cuff, E.C. (1980), 'Some issues in studying the problem of versions in everyday situations', Occasional Paper 3, Manchester: University of Manchester, Department of Sociology.

Cullis, J. and P. Jones (1994), *Public Finance and Public Choice: Analytical Perspectives*, London: McGraw-Hill.

Cyrus, N. (1996), 'Some aspects of a multi-sited ethnography of undocumented Polish labour migration in Berlin', Frankfurt (Oder): Department of Cultural Anthropology, European University 'Viadrina'.

Cyrus, N. and D. Vogel (2000) *Immigration as a Side-Effect of Other Policies: Principles and Consequences of German Non-Immigration Policy*, report prepared for the project 'Does Implementation Matter?' Oldenburg: University of Oldenburg.

Cyrus, N. and D. Vogel (2001), 'Immigration control in the labour market in Germany: patterns, practices and perceptions of success', paper presented at a seminar at Exeter University, 3–5 March.

Day, S. and J. Shaw (2001), 'European Union electoral rights and the political participation of migrants in host polities', Manchester: School of Law, University of Manchester.

Dahya, B. (1973), 'Pakistanis in Britain: transients or settlers?' *Race*, **14**(3), 241–77.

Denny, C. (2001), 'A free market – for some', *The Guardian*, 2 October, 17.

Department for Education and Employment (DfEE) (2001), *Labour Force Survey*, London: Stationery Office.

Department of Health (1998), *Modernising Social Services: Promoting Independence, Improving Protection, Raising Standards*, Cm 4169, London: Stationery Office.

Department of Social Security (DSS) (1998), *A New Contract for Welfare*, Cm 3805, London: Stationery Office.

Department of Social Security (2001), *Social Security Statistics*, London: Stationery Office.

Devillanova, C. (2001), 'Regional insurance and migration', *Scandinavian Journal of Economics*, **103**(2), 333–49.

Dinsmoor, J. (1990), *Brazil: Responses to the Debt Crisis: Impact on Savings, Investment and Growth*, Washington, DC: Inter-American Development Bank.

Dobson, J., G. McLaughlan and J. Salt (2001), 'International migration and the United Kingdom: recent patterns and trends', in Home Office, *Bridging the Information Gaps: A Conference of Research on Asylum and Immigration*, 1 Whitehall Place, London, 21 March, 66–70.

Dummett, M. (2001), *On Immigration and Refugees*, London: Routledge.

Durkheim, E. (1933), *The Division of Labour in Society*, New York: Free Press.

Düvell, F. (1996), 'Fluchtlingslager heute', *Zeitschrift fur Sozialgeschichte des 20 und 21 Jahrhunderts*, **9**(1), 47–58.

Düvell, F. (2002), 'Globalisierung, Modernisierung des Migrationsregimes und Krisenangriff', *Materialien*, Berlin: Association A.

Düvell, F. and B. Jordan (1999), 'Immigration, asylum and citizenship: social justice in a global context', *Imprints: A Journal of Analytical Socialism*, **4**(1), 15–36.

Düvell, F. and B. Jordan (2001), '"How low can you go?" Dilemmas of social work with asylum seekers in London', *Journal of Social Work Research and Evaluation*, **2**(2), 189–205.

Düvell, F. and B. Jordan (2001), 'Asylum and economic migration: biographical evidence', Exeter: Exeter University, Department of Social Work.

Dworkin, R. (1981), 'What is equality? Part II: equality of resources', *Philosophy and Public Affairs*, **10**, 283–345.

Eade, J. (1989), *The Politics of Community: The Bangladeshi Community in East London*, Aldershot: Avebury.

Eichenhofer, E. (1999), *Migration und Illegalität*, Osnabrück: Universitätsverlag Rasch.

Entorf, H. (2000), *Rational Migration Policy Should Tolerate Non-zero Illegal Migration Flows: Lessons from Modelling the Market for Illegal Migration*, Discussion Paper 1999, IZA (Institute for the Study of Labour), Bonn: IZA.

Escribano, J. (1997), *A Directory of Services for Refugees and Asylum Seekers in Hackney*, London: Hackney Churches Refugee Network.

Espenshade, T.J. (1995), 'Unauthorized immigration to the United States', *Annual Review of Sociology*, **21**, 195–216.

Esping-Andersen, G. (1990), *The Three Worlds of Welfare Capitalism*, Cambridge: Polity.

Esping-Andersen, G. (1996), 'Welfare states without work: the impasse of labour-shedding and familialism in Continental European social policy', in Esping-Andersen, G. (ed.), *Welfare States in Transition: National Adaptations in Global Economies*, London: Sage, ch. 3.

Esping-Andersen, G. (1999), 'The jobs-equality trade-off', paper presented at a summer school on Welfare States in Transition, European University Institute, Florence, 8 July.

Espinosa, K. and D. Massey (1997), 'Undocumented migration and the quantity and quality of social capital', in Pries, L. (ed.), *Transnationale Migration, Soziale Welt*, Sonderband 12, Baden Baden: Nomos (2001), 141–62.

European Commission (1990), *Policies on Immigration and the Social Integration of Migrants in the European Community*, Experts' Report, Brussels (sec. 90, 1813 final), European Commission.

European Commission (1991), *Communication from the Commission to the Council and the European Parliament on Immigration*, SEC(91) 1855 final, Brussels: European Commission.

European Commission (1997), *Proposal to the Council for a Joint Action Based on Article K3(2)(b) of the Treaty of the European Union Concerning Temporary Protection for Displaced Persons*, Com (97) 93 final.

European Commission (1999), 'Communication on a Concerted Strategy for Modernising Social Protection', *European Social Policy*, Supplement 100, Brussels: European Commission.

European Commission (2000), *Communication from the Commission to the Council and the European Parliament on a Concerted Strategy for Immigration and Asylum* (Mr Vitorino and Mrs Diamantopoulous), Brussels: European Commission, Com (2000) 757 final.

European Commission (2001a), *Communication from the Commission to the Council and the European Parliament on a Common Policy on Illegal Immigration*, Com (2001) 672 final, Brussels: European Commission.

European Commission (2001b), *Compilation of Replies to the Questionnaire on Illegal Migratory Flows from the Balkans*, note from the General Secretariat to CIREFI, 6437/01, CIREFI 10, Comix 139, 7 March, Brussels: European Commission.

European Commission (2001c), *Liaison Officers: Common Use of Liaison Officers of EU Member States*, note from the Presidency to Police Co-operation Working Party, 5406/1, Enfopol 6, 17 January, Brussels: European Commission.

European Council (1999), *Conceptual Framework to be Used in Exchange of Data on Illegal Entry in International Co-operation*, from Presidency to CIREFI, 9738/99, CIREFI 37 Brussels: European Council.

European Council (2000), *Note from the Presidency to Article 36 Committee and Strategic Committee on Immigration, Frontiers and Asylum*, Subject:

programme for External Relations in the Field of Justice and Home Affairs, 5229/00 (Limité) Enfopol 4, 11 January, Brussels: European Council.

European Foundation for the Improvement of Living and Working Conditions (1990), *Mobility and Social Cohesion in the European Community: A Forward Look*, Dublin: European Foundation.

European Race Bulletin (2000), 'The dispersal of xenophobia', *Bulletin 33/ 34*, London: Institute for Race Relations.

Evason, E. and R. Woods (1995), 'Poverty, deregulation of labour markets and benefit fraud', *Social Policy and Administration*, **29**(1), 40–54.

Faist, T. (1997), 'Immigration, citizenship and nationalism: internal internationalization in Germany and Europe', in Roche, M. and R. Van Berkel (eds.), *European Citizenship and Social Exclusion*, Aldershot: Ashgate, 213–26.

Faist, T. (1999), *Transnationalization in International Migration: Implications for the Study of Citizenship and Culture*, ESRC Transnational Communities Programme, WPTC 99–08, Oxford: Oxford University.

Faist, T., K. Sieveking, U. Reim and S. Sandbrink (1998), *Ausland in Inland: Die Beschäftigung von Werkvertragsarbeitnehemern in der Bundesrepublik Deutschland*, Baden-Baden: Nomos.

Fan, C.C. (1995), 'Of belts and ladders: state policy and uneven regional development in post-Mao China', *Annals of the Association of American Geographers*, **82**(4), 421–49.

Fan, C.C. and Y.Q. Huang (1998), 'Waves of rural brides: female marriage migration in China', *Annals of the Association of American Geographers*, **85**(2), 227–51.

Fawcett, J.T. (1989), 'Networks, linkages and migration systems', *International Migration Review*, **23**, 671–80.

Fekete, L. (2000), 'The emergence of xeno-racism', *European Race Bulletin*, **37**, 3–7.

Fernandes, L.F. (1999), 'Re-regulation in the European Union', paper presented at an ESRC Network Meeting, University of Braga, Portugal, 17 November.

Findlay, A. (1990), 'A migration channels approach to the study of high-level manpower movements: a theoretical perspective', *International Migration*, **28** (1), 15–22.

Findlay, A. (1996), 'Skilled international migration and the global city', *Transactions, Institute of British Geographers*, **21**, 54–65.

Findlay, A., H. Jones and G.M. Davidson (1998), 'Migration transition or migration transformation in the Asian dragon economies?', *International Journal of Urban and Regional Research*, **22**(4), 643–64.

Fischer, P.A., E. Holm, G. Malmberg and T. Straubhaar (2000), *Why Do*

People Stay? Insider Advantages and Immobility, HWW Discussion Paper 112, Hamburg Institute of International Economics.

Fitzpatrick, T. (1999), *Freedom and Security: An Introduction to the Basic Income Debate*, London: Macmillan.

Foldvary, F. (1994), *Public Goods and Private Communities: The Market Provision of Social Services*, Aldershot: Edward Elgar.

Forschungsgesellschaft Flucht und Migration (FFM) (1997), *Ukraine: Von der Toren der Festung Europa*, Berlin: Verlag der Buchläden.

Freeman, G.P. (1986), 'Migration and the political economy of the welfare state', *Annals of the American Academy of Social and Political Sciences*, **485**(1), 51–63.

Garson, J.-P. (2000), 'Where do illegal migrants work?', *OECD Observer*, 8 March, *http://www.oecdobserver.org*

Geddes, A. (2000), *Immigration and European Integration: Towards Fortress Europe*, Manchester: Manchester University Press.

George, S. and Gould, E. (2000), 'Liberalisation comes on tiptoe', *Le Monde Diplomatique*, 2 July.

Gershuny, J.I. (1983), *Social Innovation and the Division of Labour*, Oxford: Oxford University Press.

Glick-Schiller, N., L. Basch and C. Blanc-Szanton (1992), *Towards a Transnational Perspective on Migration: Race, Class, Ethnicity and Nationalism Reconsidered*, New York: New York Academy of Science.

Glover, S., C. Gott, A. Loizillon, J. Portes, R. Price, S. Spencer, V. Srinivasan and C. Willis (2001), *Migration: An Economic and Social Analysis*, RDS Occasional Paper 67 (Home Office), London: Stationery Office.

Goffman, E. (1969), *Interaction Ritual: Essays in Face-to-face Behaviour*, London: Penguin.

Goza, F. (1994), 'Brazilian immigration to North America', *International Migration Review*, **28**(1), 136–52.

Griffith-Jones, S. and O. Sunkel (1989), *Debt and Development Crises in Latin America: The End of an Illusion*, Oxford: Clarendon Press.

Grimwade, N. (1989), *International Trade: New Patterns of Trade, Production and Investment*, London: Routledge.

Group of Co-ordinators (1989), *The Palma Document: Free Movement of Persons – A Report to the European Council*, Madrid: Group of Co-ordinators.

Hackney Community Law Centre (1998), *Annual Report, 1997/8*, London: HCLC.

Hadfield, G.K. (1995), 'Just borders: normative economics and immigration law', in Schwartz, W.F. (ed.), *Justice in Immigration*, Cambridge: Cambridge University Press, 201–11.

Hall, J. (1995), *Civil Society: Theory, History, Comparison*, Cambridge: Polity Press.

Hampton, J. (1995), 'Immigration, identity and justice', in Schwartz, W.F. (ed.), *Justice in Immigration*, Cambridge: Cambridge University Press, 67–93.

Haringey Strategic Planning (1997), *Refugees in Haringey: Research and Development Project*, London: Haringey Borough Council.

Harris, C. (1987), 'British capitalism, migration and relative surplus-population', *Migration*, **1**, 47–90.

Hatcher, R. (2001), 'Getting down to business: schooling in the globalised economy', *Education and Social Justice*, **3**(2), 45–59.

Häussermann, H. (1997), *Zuwanderung und Stadtentwicklung*, Leviathan: sonderheft 17, Wiesbaden: Westdeutscher Verlag.

Held, D. and A. McGrew (1994), 'Globalization and the liberal democratic state', *Government and Opposition*, **28**(2), 261–85.

Hemerijck, A. (2001), 'Prospects for effective social citizenship in an age of structural inactivity', in Crouch, C., K. Eder and D. Tambini (eds.), *Citizenship, Markets and the State*, Oxford: Oxford University Press, 134–70.

Herbert, U. (1986), *Die Geschichte der Auslanderbeschäftigung in Deutschland, 1880–1986: Saisonarbeiter, Zwangsarbeiter, Gastarbeiter*, Berlin: J.H.W. Dietz Nachf.

Hilbert, R.A. (1992), *The Classical Roots of Ethnomethodology: Durkheim, Weber and Garfinkel*, Chapel Hill, NC: University of North Carolina Press.

Hirsch, F. (1977), *Social Limits to Growth*, London: Routledge and Kegan Paul.

Hirsch, J. (2001), 'Das neue Gesicht des Imperialisimus', *IZSW*, **251**, 33–35.

Hirschman, A.O. (1970), *Exit, Voice and Loyalty: Responses to Decline in Firms, Organizations and States*, Cambridge, Mass: Harvard University Press.

HM Treasury (2000), *Pre-Budget Report*, London: Stationery Office.

Hobbes, T. (1651), *Leviathan*, ed. M. Oakeshott (1966), Oxford: Blackwell.

Hobsbawm, E. (1994), *The Age of Extremes*, London: Michael Joseph.

Hodge, M. (2000), 'Work permit system will make it easier for firms', DfEE press release 416/00.

Hoerder, D. (ed.) (1985), *Labour Migration in the Atlantic Economies: The European and North American Working Class during the Period of Industrialisation*, Westport, CT: Greenwood Press.

Hollifield, J.F. (1998), 'Migration, trade and the nation state: the myth of globalisation', paper presented at a conference on Managing Migration in the 21 Century, Bundeswehrhochschule, Hamburg, 21–23 June.

Home Office (1998), *Fairer, Faster and Firmer: A Modern Approach to Immigration and Asylum*, Cm 4018, London: Stationery Office.

Home Office (2002), *Secure Borders, Safe Haven: Integration with Diversity in Modern Britain* (White Paper), London: Stationery Office.

Huffschmid, J. (1999), *Politische Ökonomie der Finanzmärkte*, Hamburg: VSA.

Hughes, G. (1987), 'Fiscal federalism in the UK', *Oxford Review of Economic Policy*, **3**(2), 1–23.

IM Media (1997), *Sans Papiers – Chronique d'un Mouvement*, Condé-sur-Noireau: Corlet.

Immigration and Nationality Directorate (IND) (1997), *Annual Report*, London: Home Office.

Immigration and Nationality Directorate (IND) (2000), *Information about Innovators*, London: Home Office.

Inman, R.P. and P.L. Rubinfeld (1997), 'The political economy of federalism', in Mueller, D.C. (ed.), *Perspectives on Public Choice: A Handbook*, Cambridge: Cambridge University Press, 73–105.

Institute of Race Relations (2000), *European Race Bulletin*, Special Report on Xeno-racism, Bulletin 37.

Iversen, T. and A. Wren (1998), 'Equality, employment and budgetary restraint: the trilemma of the service economy', *World Politics*, **50**, 507–46.

Jahn, A. and T. Straubhaar (1998), 'A survey of the economics of illegal immigration', *South European Politics and Society*, **3**, 16–42.

Jones, H. and A. Findlay (1998), 'Regional economic integration and the emergence of the East Asian international migration system', *Geoforum*, **29**(4), 401–27.

Joppke, C. (1998), *Immigration and the Nation State*, Oxford: Oxford University Press.

Jordan, B. (1985), *The State: Authority and Autonomy*, Oxford: Blackwell.

Jordan, B. (1989), *The Common Good: Citizenship, Morality and Self-interest*, Oxford: Blackwell.

Jordan, B. (1995), 'Are New Right policies sustainable? "Back to Basics" and public choice', *Journal of Social Policy*, **24**(3), 363–84.

Jordan, B. (1996), *A Theory of Poverty and Social Exclusion*, Cambridge: Polity.

Jordan, B. (1998), *The New Politics of Welfare: Social Justice in a Global Context*, London: Sage.

Jordan, B. and A. Travers (1997), 'The informal economy: a case study in unrestrained competition', *Social Policy and Administration*, **32**(3), 292–306.

Jordan, B. and D. Vogel (1997a), *Which Policies Influence Migration Decisions? A Comparative Analysis of Qualitative Interviews with Undocumented Immigrants in London and Berlin*, Bremen: ZeS Arbeitspapier 14/97.

Jordan, B. and Vogel, D. (1997b), 'Leben und arbeiten ohne regulären

Aufenthaltsstatus: Brazilianische MigrantInnen in London und Berlin', in Häusserman, H. (ed.), *Zuwanderung und Stadtentwicklung*, Wiesbaden: Westdeutscher Verlag, 215–31.

Jordan, B. and J. Loftager (2001), 'Arbeitsmarktaktivierung in Grossbritannien und Dänemark', in Zilian, H.G. and J. Flecker (eds.), *Soziale Sicherheit und Strukturwandel der Arbeitslosigkeit*, München: Rainer Hamppverlag, 48–68.

Jordan, B. and C. Jordan (2000), *Social Work and the Third Way: Tough Love as Social Policy*, London: Sage.

Jordan, B., D. Vogel and K. Estrella (1996), 'Brazilian undocumented workers in London and Berlin', paper presented at a seminar on Irregular Migration, Centre for Social Policy Research, Bremen, 11 December.

Jordan, B., M. Redley and S. James (1994), *Putting the Family First: Identities, Decisions, Citizenship*, London: UCL Press.

Jordan, B., P. Agulnik, D. Burbidge and S. Duffin (2000), *Stumbling Towards Basic Income: The Prospects for Tax-benefit Integration*, London: Citizen's Income Study Centre.

Jordan, B., S. James, H. Kay and M. Redley (1992), *Trapped in Poverty? Labour-market Decisions in Low-income Households*, London: Routledge.

Juhn, C., K.M. Murphy and R.H. Topel (1991), *Unemployment, Non-employment and Wages: Why has the Natural Rate Increased with Time?*, Brookings Papers on Economic Activity, Washington: Brookings Institute.

Just, W.-D. (1993), *Asyl von Unten*, Reinbeck: Rowohlt.

Karmi, G. (1992), *Refugees and the National Health Service*, London: Northeast and North-west Thames Regional Health Authority.

Kasarda, J.D., J. Friedrichs and K. Ehlers (1992), 'Urban industrial restructuring and minority problems in the U.S. and West Germany', in Cross, M. (ed.), *Ethnic Minorities and Economic Change and North America*, Cambridge: Cambridge University Press, 250–75.

Keely, C.B. and Bao Nga Tran (1989), 'Remittances from labor migration: evaluations, performance and implications', *International Migration Review*, **23**(3), 500–25.

Kennedy, P. and V. Roudometof (2001), *Communities across Borders under Globalising Conditions: New Immigrants and Transnational Cultures*, ESRC Transnational Communities Programme, WPTC 01–17, Oxford: Oxford University.

Kindleberger, C. (1967), *Europe's Postwar Growth: The Role of Labour Supply*, Cambridge, Mass: Harvard University Press.

Kleff, H.J. (1985), *Vom Bauern zum Industriearbeiter: zur kollektieven Lebensgeschichter der Arbeitsmigranten aus der Türkei*, Mainz: Verlag Manfred Werkmeister.

Kloosterman, R.C., J. Van der Leun and J. Rath (1999), '"Mixed embeddedness":

(in)formal economic activities and immigrant businesses in the Netherlands', *International Journal of Urban and Regional Research*, **2**3(3), 252–65.

Krugman, P. (1991), *Geography and Trade*, Cambridge, Mass: MIT Press.

Kymlicka, W. (1991), *Liberalism, Community and Culture*, Oxford: Oxford University Press.

Lasch, S. (1994), 'The making of an underclass: neo-liberalism versus corporatism', in Brown, P. and R. Crompton (eds.), *Economic Restructuring and Social Exclusion*, London: UCL Press, 157–74.

Lavenex, S. (2001), *The Europeanisation of Refugee Policies: Between Human Rights and Internal Security*, Aldershot: Ashgate.

Layard, R. and S. Nickell (1994), 'Unemployment in the OECD Countries', in Tachibanaki, T. (ed.), *Labour Market and Economic Performance: Europe, Japan and the USA*, New York: St Martin's Press, 253–95.

Layton-Henry, Z. (1989), 'British immigration policy and politics', in LeMay, M.C. (ed.), *The Gatekeepers: Comparative Immigration Policy*, London: Praeger, 59–93.

Le Grand, J. and D. Nissan (2000), *A Capital Idea: Start-up Grants for Young People*, London: Fabian Society.

Lee, R.M. (1993), *Doing Research on Sensitive Topics*, London: Sage.

Levitas, R. (1998), *The Inclusive Society? Social Exclusion and New Labour*, Basingstoke: Macmillan.

Lewis, J. (1992), 'Gender and the development of welfare regimes', *Journal of European Social Policy*, **2**(3), 159–71.

Lewis, W.A. (1954), 'Development with unlimited supplies of labour', *Manchester School*, **22**, 139–91.

Lin, G.C.S. (1997), *Red Capitalism in South China: Growth and Development of the Pearl River Delta*, Vancouver: University of British Columbia Press.

Linder, S.B. (1961), *An Essay on Trade and Transformation*, New York: Wiley.

Lipsky, M. (1980), *Street-level Bureaucrats: Dilemmas of the Individual in Public Services*, New York: Russell Sage Foundation.

Lister, R. (2000), 'To Rio via the Third Way: New Labour's "welfare" reform agenda', *Renewal*, **4**(3), 9–20.

Lukes, S. (1974), *Power: A Radical View*, London: Macmillan.

Luttwak, E. (1999), *Turbo-capitalism: Winners and Losers in the Global Economy*, London: Weidenfeld and Nicholson.

MacDonald, R. (1994), 'Fiddly jobs, undeclared work and the something for nothing society', *Work, Employment and Society*, **8**(4), 507–30.

Madrick, J. (1997), *The End of Affluence*, New York: Simon and Schuster.

Mahler, S.J. (1995), *American Dreaming: Immigrant Life on the Margins*, Princeton, NJ: Princeton University Press.

Maldonado, C. (1982), 'The loneliness of the illegal migrant', *Morning Star*, 18th October.

Maldonado, C. and T. Esward (1983), 'Migrant workers in the UK', *Race Today*, **15**(1), 8–9.

Marcus, G. (1992), 'Past, present and emergent identities: requirements for ethnographies of late twentieth-century modernity', in Lasch, S. and J. Friedman (eds.), *Modernity and Identity*, Oxford: Blackwell, 309–30.

Markusen, J.R. (1988), 'Production, trade and migration with differentiated skilled workers', *Canadian Journal of Economics*, **21**(2), 231–59.

Marske, C.E. (1991), *Communities of Fate: Readings in the Social Organisation of Risk*, Lanham, VA: University Press of America.

Marterbauer, M. and E. Walterskirchen (1999), 'Bestimmungsgründe des Anstiegs der Arbeitslosigkeit in Österreich', *WIFO-Monatsberichte*, **72**(3), 353–74.

Martin, J. and C. Roberts (1984), *Women and Employment: A Lifetime Perspective*, London: Department of Employment and Office of Population Censuses and Surveys.

Martin, S. (1998), 'Politics and policy responses to illegal migration in the US', paper presented at a conference on Managing Migration in the 21st Century, Hamburg, 21–23 June.

Mead, L.M. (1986), *Beyond Entitlement: The Social Obligations of Citizenship*, New York: Free Press.

Medico International (1994), 'Innenansichten eines schmutzigen Krieges: die Situation der Kurden in der Westtürkei', *Kurdistan Aktuell*, extra Nr. 2, Frankfurt.

Meehan, E. (1993), *Citizenship and the European Community*, London: Sage.

Minford, P. (1991), *The Supply-Side Revolution in Britain*, Aldershot: Edward Elgar/IEA.

Monbiot, G. (2002), 'Schooling up for sale', *The Guardian*, 8 January, 15.

Mönch-Bucak, Y. (1988), 'Die Kurdische Sprache', in Mönch-Bucak, Y. (ed.), *Kurden: Alltag und Widerstand*, Bremen: Eigenverlag, 104–113.

Morrison, J. (1998), *Costs of Survival*, London: Refugee Council.

Negri, T. (1984), *Marx beyond Marx: Lessons from the Grundrisse*, South Hadley, Mass: Bergin and Garvey.

No-one Is Illegal (2000), *Without Papers in Europe*, Berlin: Schwarze Risse.

North, D.C. (1990), *Institutions, Institutional Change and Economic Performance*, Cambridge: Cambridge University Press.

Nozick, R. (1974), *Anarchy, State and Utopia*, Oxford: Blackwell.

Oates, W.E. (1972), *Fiscal Federalism*, New York: Harcourt Brace Jovanovich.

Oates, W.E. (1985), 'Searching for Leviathan: an empirical study', *American Economic Review*, **79**, 578–83.

Oates, W.E. (1999), 'An essay on fiscal federalism', *Journal of Economic Literature*, 37, 1120–49.

OECD (1992), *SOPEMI 1992: Trends in International Migration*, Paris: OECD.

OECD (1999), *Trends in International Migration*, Part III, Clandestine Immigration and Political Issues, Paris: OCED.

Okólski, M. (1996), 'Poland's population and population movements: an overview', in Jazwinska, E. and M. Okólski (eds.), *Causes and Consequences of Migration in Central and Eastern Europe*, Warsaw: Migration Research Centre, Institute for Social Studies, University of Warsaw, 19–50.

Olson, M. (1982), *The Rise and Decline of Nations: Economic Growth, Stagflation and Social Rigidities*, New Haven, CT: Yale University Press.

Overseas Labour Service (1999), *Overseas Labour Service Customer Satisfaction Survey, 1999*, Sheffield: Hallam University.

Pamuk, S. (1986), 'Die Industrialisierung der Türkei in der nachkriegsperiode', *Jahrbuch zur Geschichte und Gesellschaft des Vorderen und Mittleren Orients, 1985/6*, 47–56.

Parker, H. (1989), *Instead of the Dole: An Enquiry into the Integration of the Tax and Benefit Systems*, London: Routledge.

Pogge, T. (2001), 'Interview: globalising, with justice', *Imprints: Journal of Analytical Socialism*, **5**(3), 199–220.

Policy Studies Institute (1993), *Review of Advice Services in Leicester*, Leicester: PSI.

Portes, A. (ed.) (1995), *Economic Sociology of Immigration: Essays on Networks, Ethnicity and Entrepreneurship*, New York: Russell Sage Foundation.

Portes, A. (1996), 'Globalization from below: the rise of transnational communities', in Smith, W.P. and R.P. Korczenwicz (eds.), *Latin America in the World Economy*, Westport, CN: Greenwood Press, 157–68.

Portes, A. (1998), *Globalization from Below: The Rise of Transnational Communities*, ESRC Transnational Communities Programme, WPCT 98–01, Oxford: Oxford University.

Portes, A. and S. Sassen-Koob (1987), 'Making it underground: comparative material on the informal sector in Western market economies', *American Journal of Sociology*, **93**(1), 30–61.

Portes, A. and L.E.Guarnizo (1990), 'Tropical capitalists: US-bound immigration and small enterprise development in the Dominican Republic', in Diaz-Briquets, S. and S. Weintraub (eds.), *Migration, Remittances and Business Development, Mexico and the Caribbean Basin Countries*, Boulder, Colo: Westview Press, 101–31.

Power, A.E. (1997), *Estates on the Edge: The Social Consequences of Mass Housing in Europe*, London: Macmillan.

Pries, L. (1996), 'Internationale Arbeitsmigration und das Entstehen transnationaler soziale Raüme', in Faist, T., F. Hillman and K. Zühlke-Robinet (eds.), *Neue Migrationsprozesse: Politisch-Institutionelle Regulierung und Wechselbeziehungen zum Arbeitsmarkt*, Bremen: ZeS Arbeitspapier 6/97, University of Bremen, 21–31.

Putnam, R.D. (2000), *Bowling Alone: The Collapse and Revival of American Community*, New York: Simon and Schuster.

Putnam, R.D. (2001), 'Social Capital: Research Prospects', paper presented at a conference on Social Capital: Interdisciplinary Perspectives, Exeter University, 15–20 September.

Ramdin, R. (1987), *The Making of the Black Working Class in Britain*, Aldershot: Wildwood House.

Rath, J. (1999), 'The informal economy as bastard sphere of social integration: the case of Amsterdam', in Eichenhofer, E. (ed.), *Migration und Illegalität*, Osnabrück, Universitätsverlag Rasch, 117–36.

Rawls, A.W. (1989), 'Language, self and the social order: a reformulation of Goffman and Sacks', *Human Studies*, **12**, 142–72.

Rawls, J. (1971), *A Theory of Justice*, Oxford: Oxford University Press.

Rawls, J. (1996), *Political Liberalism*, New York: Columbia University Press.

Refugee Advice Centre (1996), *Annual Report, 1996*, London: RAC.

Refugee Council (1997a), *Just Existence*, London: Refugee Council.

Refugee Council (1997b), *Refugee Resources in the UK*, London: Refugee Council.

Refugee Council (1997c), *An Agenda for Action: Challenges for Refugee Settlement in the UK*, London: Refugee Council.

Rex, J., D. Joly and C. Wilpert (1992), *Immigrant Associations in Europe*, Aldershot: Gower.

Rhodes, M. and B. Van Appeldoorn (1998), 'Does migration from less developed countries erode the welfare state?', paper presented at a conference on Migration and the Welfare State in Contemporary Europe, European University Institute, Florence, 21–23 May.

Roche, B. (2000), 'UK migration in a global economy', speech to a conference on Migration in a Global Economy, Institute for Public Policy Research, 11 September.

Roche, B. (2001), Keynote address, Home Office Conference on 'Bridging the Information Gaps: A Conference of Research on Asylum and Immigration', 1 Whitehall Place, London, 21 March.

Roemer, J. (1982), *A General Theory of Exploitation and Class*, Cambridge, Mass: Harvard University Press.

Rothstein, B. and D. Stolle (2001), 'Social capital and street-level bureaucracy: an institutional theory of generalized trust', paper presented at a conference on Social Capital: Interdisciplinary Perspectives, Exeter University, 15–20 September.

Rowlingson, K., C. Whyley, T. Newburn and R. Berthoud (1997), *Social Security Fraud*, DSS Report No. 64, London: HMSO.

Russell, S. and M. Teitelbaum (1992), *International Migration and International Trade*, World Bank Discussion Paper 160, Washington: World Bank.

Salt, J. (1988), 'Highly-skilled international migrants, careers and internal labour markets', *Geoforum*, **19**, 387–99.

Salt, J. and J. Clarke (2001), 'Foreign labour in the United Kingdom: patterns and trends', *Labour Market Trends*, October, 473–83.

Sassen, S. (1988), *The Mobility of Labor and Capital: A Study in International Investment and Labor Flow*, Cambridge: Cambridge University Press.

Sassen, S. (1991), *The Global City: New York, London, Tokyo*, Princeton, NJ: Princeton University Press.

Sassen, S. (1996), *Migranten, Siedler, Flüchtlinge: Von der Massenauswanderung zur Festung Europa*, Frankfurt: Fischer.

Satyamurti, C. (1980), *Occupational Survival: The Case of the Local Authority Social Worker*, Oxford: Blackwell.

Scharpf, F.W. (1995), 'Subventionte Niedriglohn-Beschäftigung statt bezahlter Arbeitslosigkeit', *Zeitschrift für Sozialreform*, **41**, 65–82.

Scharpf, F.W. (1997), 'Economic integration, democracy and the welfare state', *Journal of European Public Policy*, **4**, 18–36.

Scharpf, F.W. (1999), *The Viability of Advanced Welfare States in the International Economy: Vulnerabilities and Options*, Working Paper 99–9, Cologne: Max-Planck Institute for the Study of Societies.

Scheffer, M.R. (1992), 'Trading places: fashion, retailers and the changing geography of clothing production', *Netherlands Geographical Studies*, 150, 230–57.

Schumpeter, J. (1942), *Capitalism, Socialism and Democracy*, London: Allen and Unwin (1947).

Scott, J.C. (1985), *Weapons of the Weak: Everyday Forms of Peasant Resistance*, New Haven, CT: Yale University Press.

Seiffarth, O. (1997), *Der Dritte Pfeiler der Europäischen Union und die Regierungskonferenz unter besonderer Berücksichtigung der Asyl und Einwanderungspolitik*, Vienna: International Centre for Migration Policy Development.

Seligman, A.B. (1992), *The Idea of Civil Society*, New York: Free Press.

Sever, O. (1984), *Türkei: zwischen Mititarherrschaft und Demokratie*, Hamburg: VSA Verlag.

Shrestha, N.R. (1987), 'International policies and migration behaviour: a selective review', *World Development*, **15**(3), 329–45.

Shue, V. (1995), 'State sprawl: the regulatory state and social life in a small

Chinese city', in Davis, D.S., R. Kraus, B. Naughton and E. Perry (eds.), *Urban Spaces in Contemporary China: The Potential for Autonomy and Community in Post-Mao China*, Cambridge: Cambridge University Press, 90–112.

Silverman, D. (1985), *Qualitative Methodology and Sociology*, Aldershot: Gower.

Sivanandan, A. (1982), 'Asian and Afro-Caribbean struggles', in A. Sivanandan (ed.), *A Different Hunger*, London: Pluto, 3–54.

Sivanandan, A. (2000), 'Refugees from globalism', *CARF*, **57** (8/9), 10–12.

Smith, A. (1776), *An Inquiry into the Nature and Causes of the Wealth of Nations*, eds. Campbell, R.H. and A.S. Skinner (1976), Oxford: Clarendon Press.

Smith, C.J. (2000), 'The transformative impact of capital and labor mobility on the Chinese city', *Urban Geography*, **21**(8), 670–700.

Smith, M.P. and L.E.Guarnizo (eds.) (1998), *Transnationalism from Below*, New Brunswick, NJ: Transaction.

Smith, R. (1994), 'The imagining, making and politics of a transnational community between Ticuani, Puebla, Mexico, and New York city', Doctoral thesis, New York: Columbia University.

Solomos, J. (1986), 'Riots, urban protest and social policy: the interplay of reform and social control', Policy Papers in Ethnic Relations, 7, Warwick: Centre for Ethnic Relations.

Solow, R.M. (1990), *The Labour Market as a Social Institution*, Oxford: Blackwell.

Spruyt, H. (1995), *The Nation State and Its Competitors*, Princeton, NJ: Princeton University Press.

Stalker, P. (2000), *Workers without Frontiers: The Impact of Globalization on International Migration*, Geneva: International Labour Office/Lynne Rienner.

Statewatch (1996), *Statewatch Bulletin*, **6**(1), 15.

Statewatch (1999), *Statewatch Bulletin*, **9**(5), 27.

Statewatch (2001), *Statewatch European Monitor*, **3**(1), 4.

Steiner, H. (1992), 'Libertarianism and the transnational migration of people', in Barry, B. and R.E.Goodin (eds.), *Free Movement*, University Park, PA: Pennsylvania State University Press, 87–94.

Stiglitz, J.E. (1986), *Economics of the Public Sector*, New York: W.W. Norton.

Straubhaar, T. (2000), *Why Do We Need a General Agreement on Movements of People (GAMP)?*, HWWA Discussion Paper 94, Hamburg: Hamburg Institute of International Economics.

Straw, J. (2001), 'Globalisation benefits us all', *The Guardian*, 10 September, 15.

Sykes, A.O. (1995), 'The welfare economics of immigration law: a theoretical survey with an analysis of US policy', in Schwartz, W.F. (ed.), *Justice in Immigration*, Cambridge: Cambridge University Press, 158–200.

Szreter, M. (2001), 'The symbiotic relationship between social capital and the state: how is social capital formed and how is it destroyed?', paper presented at a conference on Social Capital: Interdisciplinary Perspectives, Exeter University, 15–20 September.

Tap, R. (1993), 'Het Turkse bedrijfsleven in Amsterdam', Groningen: University of Groningen, Interfaculty Business Administration.

Tapinos, G. (2000), 'Illegal immigrants and the labour market', *OECD Observer*, 8 March, *http://www.oecdobserver.org*

Thomas, B. (1973), *Migration and Economic Growth: A Study of Great Britain and the Atlantic Community*, Cambridge: Cambridge University Press.

Tiebout, C. (1956), 'A pure theory of local expenditures', *Journal of Political Economy*, **64**, 416–24.

Topel, R.H. (1994), 'Wage inequality and regional labour market performance in the US', in Tachibanaki, T. (ed.), *Labour Market and Economic Performance*, New York: St. Martin's Press, 93–128.

Tronti, M. (1966), *Operorie e Capitale*, Torino: Giulio Einaudi.

United Nations (1999), *Human Development Report, 1999*, New York: United Nations.

United Nations Conference on Trade and Development (2000), *Report*, *www.unctad.org/en/press/pr2816en.htm*

US Commission on Immigration Reform (1996), *Report to Congress*, Washington: Government Printing Office.

Van de Bunt, A. (1992), 'Bijlmer bedrijvigheid: Haalbaarheidsonderzoek naar de ontwikkeling van het kleinbedrijf in de Bijlmermeer', Amsterdam: Stuurgroep Vernieuwing Bijlmermeer.

Van der Leun, J. (1999), 'Modes of incorporation: undocumented migrants in an advanced welfare state: the case of the Netherlands', paper presented at an International Export Meeting on Irregular Migration: Dynamics, Impact and Policy Options, Jerusalem, 29 August–2 September.

Van Parijs, P. (1992), 'Commentary: citizenship, exploitation, unequal exchange and the breakdown of popular sovereignty', in Barry, B. and R.E.Goodin (eds.), *Free Movement*, University Park, PA: Pennsylvania State University Press, 155–66.

Van Parijs, P. (1995), *Real Freedom for All: What (If Anything) Can Justify Capitalism*, Oxford: Clarendon Press.

Vertovec, S. (2001), *Transnational Social Formations: Towards Conceptual Cross-fertilization*, paper presented at a workshop on Transnational Migration: Comparative Perspectives, Princeton University, June 30–July 1.

Vertovec, S. and R. Cohen (eds.) (1999), *Migration, Diasporas and Trans-nationalism*, Cheltenham: Edward Elgar.

Vogel, D. (2000), 'Migration control in Germany and the United States', *International Migration Review*, **34**(2), 390–422.

Wade, R.H. (2001), *Governing the Market*, Princeton, NJ: Princeton University Press.

Wade, R.H. (2002), 'The American Empire', *The Guardian*, 5 January, 18.

Waltham Forest Immigration Aid Centre (1996), *Annual Report, 1995/6*, London: WFIAC.

Walzer, M. (1983), *Spheres of Justice*, Oxford: Blackwell.

Wegge, S. (1998), 'Chain migration and information networks: evidence from the nineteenth century', *Journal of Economic History*, **58**(4), 957–87.

Weiner, M. (1995), *The Global Migration Crisis: Challenges to States and to Human Rights*, New York: Harper Collins.

Wetherell, M. and J. Potter (1988), 'Discourse analysis and the identification of interpretative repertoires', in Antaki, C. (ed.), *Analysing Everyday Explanation*, London: Sage, 168–83.

White, J.B. (1994), *Money Makes Us Relatives: Woman's Labour in Urban Turkey*, Austin, Tex: University of Texas Press.

Wildasin, D.E. (1995), 'Factor mobility, risk and redistribution in the welfare state', *Scandinavian Journal of Economics*, **97**, 527–46.

Wilson, W.J. (1989), *The Truly Disadvantaged: The Underclass, the Ghetto and Public Policy*, Chicago, IL: Chicago University Press.

Wilson, W.J. (1997), *When Work Disappears: The World of the New Urban Poor*, London: Vintage.

Woodward, J. (1992), 'Commentary: liberalism and migration', in Barry, B. and R.E.Goodin (eds.), *Free Movement*, University Park, PA: Pennsylvania State University Press, 59–84.

World Bank (1990), *World Development Report, 1989/90*, Washington: World Bank.

World Bank (1995), *World Development Report, 1994/5*, Washington: World Bank.

World Bank (1999), *World Development Report, 1998/9*, Washington: World Bank.

Wrench, J., A. Rea and N. Ouali (eds.) (1999), *Migrants, Ethnic Minorities and the Labour Market: Integration and Exclusion in Europe*, Basingstoke: Macmillan/Centre for Research on Ethnic Relations, University of Warwick.

Zhang, W. (2001), 'Economic integration and its impacts on cross-strait relations', *Cambridge Review of International Affairs*, **14**(2), 201–21.

Zimmerman, K. (1994), 'Labour market impact of migration', in Spencer, S.

Immigration as an Economic Asset: The German Experience, London: Trentham/IPPR.

Zolberg, A.R. (1989), 'The next waves: migration theory for a changing world', *International Migration Review*, **23**(3), 403–30.

Zolberg, A., A. Suhrke and S. Aguayo (1989), *Escape from Violence: Conflict and the Refugee Crisis in the Developing World*, New York: Oxford University Press.

Zolberg, A.R. and P.M. Benda (eds.) (2000), *Global Migrants, Global Refugees*, New York: Berghahn.

6, P., D. Leat, K. Selzer and G. Stoker (1999), *Governing in the Round: Strategies for Holistic Government*, London: Demos.

Index

accommodation centres 44–5
accounts
  by interviewees 96, 127–32, 217
  learners' 99, 102, 128–30
  political 99, 138–42
  travellers' 100, 102, 106, 128–9
  workers' 99, 104, 127–8, 130
activation 16, 30, 55, 59, 69, 72–5, 201, 250, 253
Afghanistan 1, 252
Africa 18, 84, 154, 191, 195
  North 36, 49, 51, 239
  West 196
agriculture 4, 7, 19, 44, 47, 74, 247
  in Brazil 87
  irregular employment in 173, 187
  Polish workers in 88, 134–5
  recruitment for 44, 220–221
  subsidies for 251
Albania 238
America
  Central and South 239
amnesties 44, 155, 159, 234, 255
Amsterdam
  informal sector in 63, 138
  Treaty of 38, 49
Asia
  Development Bank 22
  East 20–25, 33, 239
  migration systems in 33–4, 83
  South-east 18–24, 33, 83, 87
Asians 11, 15, 44, 67, 84, 151, 171, 195, 228
  entrepreneurs 191
  Kenyan 40
  Ugandan 40
  in USA 61–2, 83
associations 4, 244
  Central and East European 153
  Turkish and Kurdish 91, 99, 106, 115, 136–7, 141, 153, 161–2, 180–181

asylum seekers 1–2, 4, 6–7, 11, 15–17, 32–3, 37–52, 68, 85, 91, 95, 113, 142, 150–167, 172–6, 190, 198, 221, 236, 244, 246, 248, 252–3
  access to services 200–215
  advisers to 152, 154–67, 177
  EU regulation of 38–9, 44–9
  from Poland 89, 103–4, 119, 142, 145–6
  policy in UK 79–80, 82, 195–7
  and social benefits 82–3, 205
  teams 205–9, 212
  training for 137
  from Turkey 91–2, 98, 105–11, 120–122, 136–9, 147–9, 162–3, 180, 194
au pairs 44, 67–8, 98, 106, 221
  from Turkey 121, 138, 141–2, 147–8
Australia 23, 31, 52, 56, 65, 69, 239–40
Austria 65–6

Balcerowicz Plan 89
banking 19, 21
Barcelona Declaration 51
basic income 247–54
Baylav, A. 97
Belgium 44
benefits 16, 31, 55, 165, 198–9, 211, 254
  access to 8, 95, 98, 109, 152, 155, 156, 160–161, 205, 209, 213–14, 221, 149–50
  fraud 58, 64, 94, 114, 165, 191, 212
  housing 143–4, 211, 214
Benefits Agency 11, 183, 210–212
Benefits Agency Benefits Fraud Investigation Service (BABFIS) 172–3, 183–4, 188–92
Berlin 68, 71, 101
  Brazilians in 101, 114–16, 148, 172, 179–80, 188